60p

RUSSIAN EDITION
PUBLISHED BY DECISION
OF THE CENTRAL COMMITTEE
OF THE COMMUNIST PARTY
OF THE SOVIET UNION
(BOLSHEVIKS)

Пролетарии всех стран, соединяйтесь!

ИНСТИТУТ МАРКСА—ЭНГЕЛЬСА—ЛЕНИНА при ЦК ВКП(б)

И.В. СТАЛИН

СОЧИНЕНИЯ

★

О Г И З

ГОСУДАРСТВЕННОЕ ИЗДАТЕЛЬСТВО ПОЛИТИЧЕСКОЙ ЛИТЕРАТУРЫ

Москва · 1946

J. V. STALIN

WORKS

VOLUME
2

1907—1913

FOREIGN LANGUAGES PUBLISHING HOUSE

Moscow · 1953

Published in Great Britain by
LAWRENCE AND WISHART LTD.
81 Chancery Lane, London, W.C.2
1953

CONTENTS

1913

PREFACE

Volume 2 of the *Works* of J. V. Stalin contains writings mainly of the period from the latter half of 1907 to 1913, prior to Comrade Stalin's exile to the Turukhansk region, where he remained until February 1917. These works cover mainly two periods of Comrade Stalin's revolutionary activities, the Baku period and the St. Petersburg period.

The writings of the first half of 1907 deal with the tactics of the Bolsheviks during the first Russian revolution ("Preface to the Georgian Edition of K. Kautsky's Pamphlet *The Driving Forces and Prospects of the Russian Revolution*," the article "The Election Campaign in St. Petersburg and the Mensheviks," and others). The articles of this period were published in the Georgian Bolshevik newspapers *Chveni Tskhovreba* and *Dro*. They appear in Russian for the first time.

The writings from June 1907 onwards—in the period of Comrade Stalin's revolutionary activities mainly in Baku—deal with the struggle the Bolsheviks waged against the Menshevik liquidators for the preservation and strengthening of the underground revolutionary Marxist Party ("The Party Crisis and Our Tasks," "Resolutions Adopted by the Baku Committee on January 22, 1910," "Letters From the Caucasus"). Questions concerning the leadership of the revolutionary labour movement and the trade unions are dealt with in the articles: "What Do Our Recent Strikes Tell Us?" "The Oil Owners on Economic Terrorism," "The Conference and the Workers," and others. An analysis of the Fifth Congress of the R.S.D.L.P. is presented in the article "The London Congress of the R.S.D.L.P. (Notes of a Delegate)." J. V. Stalin's articles of this period included in Volume 2 were published in the newspapers *Bakinsky Proletary*, *Gudok* and *Sotsial-Demokrat*.

The latter half of 1911 marked the beginning of the St. Petersburg period of Comrade Stalin's revolutionary activities (1911-1913). As the head of the Russian Bureau of the Central Committee, Comrade Stalin directed the work of the Party in Russia in carrying out the decisions of the Prague Conference of the Party. It was in this period that the works were written dealing mainly with the new revolutionary upsurge in the labour movement and with the tasks of the Bolshevik Party in connection with the elections to the Fourth State Duma. Among these are the leaflet "For the Party!", the articles "A New Stage," "They Are Working Well. . . .", "The Ice Has Broken! . . . ", "Mandate of the St. Petersburg Workers to Their Labour Deputy," "The Will of the Voters' Delegates," "The Elections in St. Petersburg," and others. These articles were published in the St. Petersburg newspapers *Zvezda* and *Pravda*.

This volume includes J. V. Stalin's well-known work *Marxism and the National Question* (1913), in which the Bolshevik theory and programme on the national question are developed.

The article "On Cultural-National Autonomy," which Comrade Stalin wrote during his exile in Turukhansk region, and a number of other works, have not yet been discovered.

Marx-Engels-Lenin Institute
of the C.C., C.P.S.U.(B.)

1907 – 1913

PREFACE TO THE GEORGIAN EDITION
OF K. KAUTSKY'S PAMPHLET
THE DRIVING FORCES AND PROSPECTS OF THE RUSSIAN REVOLUTION[1]

Karl Kautsky's name is not new to us. He has long been known as an outstanding theoretician of Social-Democracy. But Kautsky is known not only from that aspect; he is notable also as a thorough and thoughtful investigator of tactical problems. In this respect he has won great authority not only among the European comrades, but also among us. That is not surprising: today, when disagreements on tactics are splitting Russian Social-Democracy into two groups, when mutual criticism often aggravates the situation by passing into recrimination and it becomes extremely difficult to ascertain the truth, it is very interesting to hear what an unbiassed and experienced comrade like K. Kautsky has to say. That is why our comrades have set to work so zealously to study Kautsky's articles on tactics: "The State Duma," "The Moscow Insurrection," "The Agrarian Question," "The Russian Peasantry and the Revolution," "The Anti-Jewish Pogroms in Russia," and others. But the present pamphlet has engaged the attention of the comrades far more than those works, and that is because it touches upon all the main questions that divide Social-Democracy into two groups. It appears that Plekhanov, who recently sought

the advice of foreign comrades to clear up our burning
problems, submitted these problems also to Kautsky
with a request to answer them. As is evident from what
Kautsky says, the present pamphlet is an answer to that
request. After that, it was, of course, natural that the
comrades should pay greater attention to the pamphlet.
Obviously, that also enhances the importance of the
pamphlet for us.

It will be very useful, therefore, if we recall, if
only in general outline, the questions of our disagreements and, in passing, ascertain Kautsky's views on this
or that question.

On whose side is Kautsky, whom does he support,
the Bolsheviks or the Mensheviks?

The first question that is splitting Russian Social-
Democracy into two parts is the question of the general
character of our revolution. That our revolution is a
bourgeois-democratic and not a socialist revolution, that
it must end with the destruction of feudalism and not
of capitalism, is clear to everybody. The question is,
however, who will lead this revolution, and who will
unite around itself the discontented elements of the
people: the bourgeoisie or the proletariat? Will the
proletariat drag at the tail of the bourgeoisie as was
the case in France, or will the bourgeoisie follow the
proletariat? That is how the question stands.

The Mensheviks say through the mouth of *Martynov*
that our revolution is a bourgeois revolution, that it is
a repetition of the French revolution; and as the French
revolution, being a bourgeois revolution, was led by the
bourgeoisie, so our revolution must also be led by the
bourgeoisie. "The hegemony of the proletariat is a harm-

ful utopia. . . ." "The proletariat must follow the
extreme bourgeois opposition" (see Martynov's *Two Dictatorships*).

The Bolsheviks, however, say: True, our revolution
is a bourgeois revolution, but that does not mean in the
least that it is a repetition of the French revolution,
that it must necessarily be led by the bourgeoisie, as
was the case in France. In France, the proletariat was
an unorganized force with little class consciousness
and, as a consequence, the bourgeoisie retained the hegemony in the revolution. In our country, however, the
proletariat is a relatively more class conscious and organized force; as a consequence, it is no longer content
with the role of appendage to the bourgeoisie and, as
the most revolutionary class, is coming out at the head
of the present-day movement. The hegemony of the proletariat is not a utopia, it is a living fact; the proletariat is actually uniting the discontented elements
around itself. And whoever advises it "to follow the
bourgeois opposition" is depriving it of independence,
is converting the Russian proletariat into a tool of the
bourgeoisie (see Lenin's *Two Tactics*).

What is K. Kautsky's view on this question?

"The liberals often refer to the great French revolution and often do so without justification. Conditions
in present-day Russia are in many respects quite different
from what they were in France in 1789" (see Chapter III
of the pamphlet). . . . "Russian liberalism is quite different from the liberalism of Western Europe, and for
this reason alone it is a great mistake to take the great
French revolution simply as a model for the present Russian revolution. The leading class in the revolutionary

movements in Western Europe was the petty bourgeoisie, especially the petty bourgeoisie in the large cities" (see Chapter IV). . . . "The day of bourgeois revolutions, i.e., revolutions in which the bourgeoisie was the driving force, has passed away, and it has passed away also for Russia. There, too, the proletariat is no longer a mere appendage and tool of the bourgeoisie, as was the case during the bourgeois revolutions, but is an independent class, with independent revolutionary aims" (see Chapter V).

That is what K. Kautsky says about the general character of the Russian revolution; that is how Kautsky understands the role of the proletariat in the present Russian revolution. The bourgeoisie cannot lead the Russian revolution—hence, the proletariat must come out as the leader of the revolution.

The second question of our disagreements is: Can the liberal bourgeoisie be at least an ally of the proletariat in the present revolution?

The Bolsheviks say that it cannot. True, during the French revolution, the liberal bourgeoisie played a revolutionary role, but that was because the class struggle in that country was not so acute, the proletariat had little class consciousness and was content with the role of appendage to the liberals, whereas in our country, the class struggle is extremely acute, the proletariat is far more class conscious and cannot resign itself to the role of appendage to the liberals. Where the proletariat fights consciously, the liberal bourgeoisie ceases to be revolutionary. That is why the Cadet-liberals, frightened by the proletariat's struggle, are seeking protection under the wing of reaction. That is why they are fighting the revolution rather than the reaction. That is why the Cadets[2] would sooner conclude an alliance with the reaction against the revolution than with the revolution. Yes, our liberal bourgeoisie, and its champions the Cadets, are the allies of the reaction, they are the "enlightened" enemies of the revolution. It is altogether different with the poor peasants. The Bolsheviks say that only the poor peasants will extend a hand to the revolutionary proletariat, and only they can conclude a firm alliance with the proletariat for the whole period of the present revolution. And it is those peasants that the proletariat must support against the reaction and the Cadets. And if these two main forces conclude an alliance, if the workers and peasants support each other, the victory of the revolution will be assured. If they do not, the victory of the revolution is impossible. That is why the Bolsheviks are not supporting the Cadets, either in the Duma or outside the Duma, in the first stage of the elections. That is why the Bolsheviks, during the elections and in the Duma, support only the revolutionary representatives of the peasants against the reaction and the Cadets. That is why the Bolsheviks unite the broad masses of the people only around the revolutionary *part* of the Duma and not around the *entire* Duma. That is why the Bolsheviks do not support the demand for the appointment of a Cadet ministry (see Lenin's *Two Tactics* and "The Victory of the Cadets").

The Mensheviks argue quite differently. True, the liberal bourgeoisie is wavering between reaction and revolution, but in the end, in the opinion of the Mensheviks, it will join the revolution and, after all, play a revolutionary role. Why? Because the liberal bourgeoisie played

a revolutionary role in France, because it is opposed
to the old order and, consequently, will be obliged to
join the revolution. In the opinion of the Mensheviks,
the liberal bourgeoisie, and its champions the Cadets,
cannot be called traitors to the present revolution, they
are the allies of the revolution. That is why the Mensheviks support them during the elections and in the Duma.
The Mensheviks assert that the class struggle should never eclipse the general struggle. That is why they call upon
the masses of the people to rally around the *entire* Duma
and not merely around its revolutionary *part*; that is why
they, with all their might, support the demand for the appointment of a Cadet ministry; that is why the Mensheviks
are ready to consign the maximum programme to oblivion,
to cut down the minimum programme, and to repudiate the
democratic republic so as not to frighten away the Cadets.
Some readers may think that all that is libel against the
Mensheviks and will demand facts. Here are the facts.

The following is what the well-known Menshevik
writer *Malishevsky* wrote recently:

"Our bourgeoisie does not want a republic, consequently, we cannot have a republic . . . ,"and so ". . . as
a result of our revolution there must arise a constitutional system, but certainly not a democratic republic."
That is why Malishevsky advises "the comrades" to
abandon "republican illusions" (see *First Symposium*,[3]
pp. 288, 289).

That is the first fact.

On the eve of the elections the Menshevik leader *Cherevanin* wrote:

"It would be absurd and insane for the proletariat to
try, as some people propose, jointly with the peasantry,

to enter into a struggle against both the government and the bourgeoisie for a sovereign and popular Constituent Assembly." We, he says, are now trying to reach agreement with the Cadets and to get a Cadet ministry (see *Nashe Delo*,[4] No. 1).

That is the second fact.

But all that was only written words. Another Menshevik leader, *Plekhanov*, did not confine himself to that and wanted to put what was written into practice. At the time when a fierce debate was raging in the Party on the question of electoral tactics, when everybody was asking whether it was permissible to enter into an agreement with the Cadets during the first stage of the elections, Plekhanov held even an *agreement* with the Cadets inadequate, and began to advocate a direct bloc, a temporary *fusion*, with the Cadets. Recall the newspaper *Tovarishch*[5] of November 24 (1906) in which Plekhanov published his little article. One of the readers of *Tovarishch* asked Plekhanov: Is it possible for the Social-Democrats to have a common platform with the Cadets; if it is, "what could be the nature . . . of a common election platform?" Plekhanov answered that a common platform was *essential*, and that such a platform must be "a sovereign Duma.". . . "There is no other answer, nor can there be" (see *Tovarishch*, November 24, 1906). What do Plekhanov's words mean? They have only one meaning, namely, that during the elections the Party of the proletarians, i.e., Social-Democracy, should actually *join with* the party of the employers, i.e., the Cadets, should jointly with them publish agitational leaflets addressed to the workers, should in fact renounce the slogan of a popular Constituent Assembly and the Social-Democratic minimum programme and instead issue the Cadet slogan of a sovereign Duma. Actually, that means renouncing our minimum programme to please the Cadets and to enhance our reputation in their eyes.

That is the third fact.

But what Plekhanov said somewhat timidly was said with remarkable boldness by a third Menshevik leader, *Vasilyev*. Listen to this:

"First of all, let the whole of society, all citizens... establish constitutional government. Since this will be a people's government, the people, in conformity with their grouping according to class and interests . . . can proceed to settle all problems. Then the struggle of classes and groups will not only be appropriate, but also necessary. . . . Now, however, at the present moment, it would be *suicidal and criminal*. . . ." It is therefore necessary for the various classes and groups "*to abandon all 'the very best of programmes' for a time and merge in one constitutional party*. . . ." "My proposal is that there should be a common platform, the basis of which should be the laying of the elementary foundations for a *sovereign* society which alone can provide a corresponding Duma. . . ." "The contents of such a platform are . . . a ministry responsible to the people's representatives . . . free speech and press . . ." etc. (see *Tovarishch*, December 17, 1906). As regards the popular Constituent Assembly, and our minimum programme in general, all that must be "abandoned" according to Vasilyev. . . .

That is the fourth fact.

True, *Martov*, a fourth Menshevik leader, disagrees with the Menshevik Vasilyev and haughtily reproves him for having written the above-mentioned article (see

Otkliki,[6] No. 2). But Plekhanov speaks in high praise of Vasilyev, who, in Plekhanov's opinion, is a "tireless and popular Social-Democratic organizer of the Swiss workers" and who "will render numerous services to the Russian workers' cause" (see *Mir Bozhy*[7] for June 1906). Which of these two Mensheviks should be believed? Plekhanov or Martov? And besides, did not Martov himself write recently: "The strife between the bourgeoisie and the proletariat strengthens the position of the autocracy and thereby retards the success of the emancipation of the people"? (See Elmar, "The People and the State Duma," p. 20.) Who does not know that this non-Marxist view is the real basis of the liberal "proposal" advanced by Vasilyev?

As you see, the Mensheviks are so enchanted with the "revolutionariness" of the liberal bourgeoisie, they place so much hope on its "revolutionariness," that to please it they are even ready to consign the Social-Democratic programme to oblivion.

How does K. Kautsky regard our liberal bourgeoisie? Whom does he regard as the true ally of the proletariat? What does he say on this question?

"At the present time (i.e., in the present Russian revolution) the proletariat is no longer a mere appendage and tool of the bourgeoisie, as was the case during the bourgeois revolutions, but is an independent class, with independent revolutionary aims. But where the proletariat comes out in this manner *the bourgeoisie ceases to be a revolutionary class.* The Russian bourgeoisie, in so far as it is liberal at all and pursues an independent class policy, undoubtedly hates absolutism, but it hates revolution still more. . . . And in so far as it wants political freedom it does so mainly because it regards it as the only means of putting an end to revolution. Thus, *the bourgeoisie is not one of the driving forces of the present-day revolutionary movement in Russia*. ... *The proletariat and the peasantry alone* have a firm community of interests during the whole period of the revolutionary struggle. And this is what must serve as the basis of the entire revolutionary tactics of Russian Social-Democracy. ... Without the peasants we cannot today achieve victory in Russia " (see Chapter V).

That is what Kautsky says.

We think that comment is superfluous.

The third question of our disagreements is: What will be the class content of the victory of our revolution, or, in other words, which classes must achieve victory in our revolution, which classes must win power?

The Bolsheviks assert that as the proletariat and the peasantry are the main forces in the present revolution, and as their victory is impossible unless they support each other, it is they who will win power, and, therefore, the victory of the revolution will mean the establishment of the *dictatorship of the proletariat and peasantry* (see Lenin's *Two Tactics* and "The Victory of the Cadets").

The Mensheviks, on the other hand, reject the dictatorship of the proletariat and peasantry, they do not believe that power will be won by the proletariat and the peasantry. In their opinion power must come into the hands of a Cadet Duma. Consequently, they support with extraordinary zeal the Cadet slogan of a responsible ministry. Thus, instead of the dictatorship of the proletariat and peasantry, the Mensheviks offer us the dictatorship of the Cadets (see Martynov's *Two Dictator-ships*, and also the newspapers *Golos Truda*,[8] *Nashe Delo*, and others).

What is K. Kautsky's view on this question?

On this point Kautsky bluntly says that "the revolutionary strength of Russian Social-Democracy and the possibility of its victory lie in the community of interests of the industrial proletariat and the peasantry" (see Chapter V). That is to say, the revolution will be victorious only if the proletariat and the peasantry fight side by side for the common victory—the dictatorship of the Cadets is anti-revolutionary.

The fourth question of our disagreements is: During revolutionary storms a so-called provisional revolutionary government will, of course, automatically arise. Is it permissible for Social-Democracy to enter the revolutionary government?

The Bolsheviks say that to enter such a provisional government is not only permissible from the point of view of principle, but also necessary for practical reasons, in order that Social-Democracy may effectively protect the interests of the proletariat and of the revolution in the provisional revolutionary government. If in the street fighting the proletariat, jointly with the peasants, overthrows the old order, and if it sheds its blood together with them, it is only natural that it should also enter the provisional revolutionary government with them, in order to lead the revolution to the desired results (see Lenin's *Two Tactics*).

The Mensheviks, however, reject the idea of entering the provisional revolutionary government. They say that it is impermissible for Social-Democracy, that it is unseemly for a Social-Democrat, that it will be fatal for the proletariat (see Martynov's *Two Dictatorships*).

What does K. Kautsky say on this point?

"It is quite possible that with the further progress of the revolution victory will be achieved by the Social-Democratic Party. . . ." But it does not mean that "the revolution which Russia is passing through will at once lead to the introduction in Russia of the socialist mode of production, even if it *temporarily entrusted the helm of state to Social-Democracy*" (see Chapter V).

As you see, in Kautsky's opinion, not only is it permissible to enter a provisional revolutionary government, it may even happen that "the helm of state will temporarily" pass entirely and exclusively into the hands of Social-Democracy.

Such are Kautsky's views on the principal questions of our disagreements.

As you see, Kautsky, an outstanding theoretician of Social-Democracy, and the Bolsheviks are in complete agreement with each other.

This is not denied even by the Mensheviks, except, of course, for a few "official" Mensheviks who have probably not set eyes on Kautsky's pamphlet. Martov, for example, definitely says that "in his final deduction, Kautsky *agrees* with Comrade Lenin and his like-minded friends who have proclaimed the democratic dictatorship of the proletariat and peasantry" (see *Otkliki*, No. 2, p. 19).

And that means that the Mensheviks *do not agree* with K. Kautsky, or rather, that Kautsky *does not agree* with the Mensheviks.

And so, who agrees with the Mensheviks, and with whom, finally, do the Mensheviks agree?

Here is what history tells us about it. On December 27 (1906), a debate was held in Solyanoi Gorodok (in St. Petersburg). In the course of the debate the Cadet leader P. Struve said: "You will all be Cadets. . . . The Mensheviks are already being called semi-Cadets. Many people regard Plekhanov as a Cadet and, indeed, the Cadets can welcome much of what Plekhanov says now; it is a pity, however, that he did not say this when the Cadets stood alone" (see *Tovarishch* of December 28, 1906).

So you see who agrees with the Mensheviks.

Will it be surprising if the Mensheviks agree with them and take the path of liberalism? . . .

February 10, 1907

Reprinted from the pamphlet
Signed: *Koba*

Translated from the Georgian

THE ELECTION CAMPAIGN
IN ST. PETERSBURG
AND THE MENSHEVIKS

Nowhere was the election campaign fought with such intensity as it was in St. Petersburg. Nowhere were there such conflicts between the parties as in St. Petersburg. Social-Democrats, Narodniks, Cadets, Black Hundreds, Bolsheviks and Mensheviks in the Social-Democratic movement, Trudoviks,[9] Socialist-Revolutionaries and Popular Socialists among the Narodniks, Left and Right Cadets in the Cadet Party—all waged a fierce struggle. . . .

On the other hand, nowhere was the complexion of the various parties revealed so clearly as it was in St. Petersburg. It could not have been otherwise. An election campaign is real action—and the nature of parties can be ascertained only in action. It is obvious that the more fiercely the struggle was waged, the more distinctly was the complexion of the respective combatants bound to be revealed.

In this respect, the conduct of the Bolsheviks and the Mensheviks during the election campaign is extremely interesting.

You probably remember what the Mensheviks said. Even before the elections they had said that a Constituent Assembly and a democratic republic were an unnecessary burden, that what was needed first of all was a Duma and a Cadet ministry and, consequently, what was needed was an election agreement with the Cadets. If that were not achieved, they said, the Black Hundreds would win. Here is what the Menshevik leader *Cherevanin* wrote on the eve of the elections:

"It would be absurd and insane for the proletariat to try, as some people propose, jointly with the peasantry, to enter into a struggle against both the government and the bourgeoisie for a sovereign and popular Constituent Assembly" (see *Nashe Delo*, No. 1).

Plekhanov, another Menshevik leader, seconding Cherevanin, also rejected a popular Constituent Assembly and proposed instead a "sovereign Duma," which was to become a "common platform" for the Cadets and the Social-Democrats (see *Tovarishch*, November 24, 1906).

And the well-known Menshevik *Vasilyev* said more frankly that the class struggle "at the present moment would be suicidal and criminal . . . ," that the various classes and groups must "abandon all 'the very best of programmes' for a time and merge in one constitutional party . . ." (see *Tovarishch*, December 17, 1906).

That is what the Mensheviks said.

The Bolsheviks, from the very beginning, condemned that position of the Mensheviks. They said that it would be unseemly for Socialists to enter into an agreement with the Cadets, that the Socialists must come out independently in the election campaign. In the first stage of the election, agreements are permissible only in exceptional cases, and then only with parties whose slogans of the day are: a popular Constituent Assembly, confiscation of all the land, an eight-hour day, etc. The Cadets, however, reject all this. The "Black-Hundred danger" was invented by the liberals to frighten certain naive people. The Black Hundreds cannot "capture" the Duma. The Mensheviks only repeat the words of the liberals when they talk about the "Black-Hundred danger." But there is a "Cadet danger," and it is a real danger. It is our duty to rally all the revolutionary elements around ourselves and fight the Cadets, who are concluding an alliance with reaction against the revolution. We must fight simultaneously on two fronts: against the reaction and against the liberal bourgeoisie and its champions.

That is what the Bolsheviks said.

The opening day of the St. Petersburg Social-Democratic conference[10] drew near. Here, at this conference, two sets of tactics were to be presented to the proletariat: the tactics of agreement with the Cadets, and the tactics of fighting the Cadets. . . . Now, at this conference, the proletariat was to appraise everything the Bolsheviks and Mensheviks had said hitherto. But the Mensheviks had a presentiment that defeat awaited them, they had a foreboding that the conference would condemn their tactics, and they, therefore, resolved to leave the conference, to break with Social-Democracy. For the sake of an agreement with the Cadets the Mensheviks started a split. They wanted to get "their men" into the Duma by bargaining with the Cadets.

The Bolsheviks emphatically condemned that spineless behaviour. They proved by figures that there was no "Black-Hundred danger." They ruthlessly criticized the Socialist-Revolutionaries and Trudoviks and openly called upon them to rally around the proletariat against the counter-revolution and the Cadets.

While the Bolsheviks were uniting the revolutionary elements around the proletariat, while they were undeviatingly pursuing the uncompromising tactics of the proletariat, the Mensheviks were negotiating with the Cadets behind the backs of the workers.

Meanwhile, the Cadets were gradually inclining to the right. Stolypin invited the Cadet leader *Milyukov* to see him "for negotiations." The Cadets unanimously instructed Milyukov to negotiate with the reaction "on behalf of the Party." Obviously, the Cadets wanted to conclude an agreement with the reaction against the revolution. At the same time, another Cadet leader, *Struve*, openly stated that "the Cadets want an agreement with the monarch with the object of obtaining a constitution" (see *Rech*,[11] January 18, 1907). It was evident that the Cadets were entering into an alliance with the reaction.

Nevertheless, the Mensheviks entered into negotiations with the Cadets, they still sought an alliance with them. Poor fellows! They had no idea that by entering into an agreement with the Cadets they were entering into an agreement with the reaction!

Meanwhile, the discussion meetings, sanctioned by the authorities, commenced. Here, at these meetings, it became definitely clear that the "Black-Hundred danger" was a myth, that the fight was chiefly between the Cadets and the Social-Democrats, and that whoever entered into an agreement with the Cadets was betraying Social-Democracy. The Mensheviks were no longer to be seen at the meetings; they tried to intercede for the Cadets two or three times, but they glaringly disgraced themselves and kept away. The Mensheviks—the hangers-on of the Cadets—were already discredited. Only the Bolsheviks

and the Cadets remained in the discussion arena. The
meetings were taken up entirely with the struggle between them. The Socialist-Revolutionaries and the Trudoviks declined to negotiate with the Cadets. The Popular
Socialists wavered. The Bolsheviks became the leaders in
the election campaign.

Where were the Mensheviks in the meantime?

They were negotiating with the Cadets for three seats
in the Duma. It may sound incredible, but it is a fact;
and it is our duty openly to tell the truth.

The Bolsheviks declared: Down with the hegemony
of the Cadets!

The Mensheviks, however, *rejected this slogan*, and
thereby submitted to the hegemony of the Cadets and
dragged at their tail.

Meanwhile, elections took place in the workers' curia.
It turned out that *in the Menshevik districts the workers had
nearly everywhere elected Socialist-Revolutionaries as their
voters' delegates.* "We cannot vote for those who compromise
with the Cadets; after all the Socialist-Revolutionaries
are better than they are, "—that is what the workers said.
The workers called the Social-Democrats liberals, and
preferred to go with the bourgeois-democrats, with the
Socialist-Revolutionaries! That is what the opportunism
of the Mensheviks led to!

The Bolsheviks pursued their uncompromising tactics
and called upon all the revolutionary elements to unite
around the proletariat. The Socialist-Revolutionaries
and Trudoviks openly associated themselves with the
Bolshevik slogan: Down with the hegemony of the Cadets!
The Popular Socialists broke with the Cadets. It became
obvious to everybody that the agreement between the

Social-Democrats on the one hand and the Socialist-Revolutionaries and Trudoviks on the other would under no circumstances split the vote to such a degree as to let the Black Hundreds win. Either the Cadets or the extreme Left would win—the "Black-Hundred danger" was a myth.

Meanwhile, the Cadets broke off negotiations with the Mensheviks. Evidently an agreement failed to come off. The Bolsheviks, however, concluded an agreement with the Socialist-Revolutionaries, Trudoviks and Popular Socialists, isolated the Cadets, and launched a general offensive against the reaction and the Cadets. Three election lists were put up in St. Petersburg: the Black Hundreds, the Cadets and the extreme Left. Thus, the Bolsheviks' forecast that there would be three lists came true in spite of the Mensheviks.

Rejected by the proletariat, left empty-handed by the Cadets, made a laughingstock of by the Socialist-Revolutionaries and Trudoviks and disgraced by history, the Mensheviks laid down their arms and voted for the list of the extreme Left, *against the Cadets*. The Vyborg District Committee of the Mensheviks openly stated that the Mensheviks would vote for the extreme Left, against the Cadets.

And that meant that the Mensheviks repudiated the existence of a "Black-Hundred danger," that they rejected an agreement with the Cadets and backed the Bolshevik slogan—Down with the hegemony of the Cadets!

It meant also that the Mensheviks rejected their own tactics and openly recognized the Bolshevik tactics.

2*

And lastly, it meant that the Mensheviks had stopped dragging at the tail of the Cadets and now dragged at the tail of the Bolsheviks.

Finally, the elections took place and it turned out that not a single one of the Black Hundreds was elected in St. Petersburg!

That is how the correctness of the Bolshevik tactics was proved in St. Petersburg.

That is how the Mensheviks sustained defeat.

Chveni Tskhovreba
(*Our Life*),[12] No. 1,
February 18, 1907
Unsigned

Translated from the Georgian

THE AUTOCRACY OF THE CADETS
OR THE SOVEREIGNTY OF THE PEOPLE?

Who should take power during the revolution? Which classes should take the helm of social and political life? The people, the proletariat and peasantry!—the Bolsheviks answered, and thus they answer now. In their opinion, the victory of the revolution means the establishment of the dictatorship (sovereignty) of the proletariat and peasantry with the object of winning an eight-hour day, of confiscating all the landlords' land and of setting up a democratic regime. The Mensheviks reject the sovereignty of the people and, until lately, did not give a straight answer to the question as to who should take power. But now that they have obviously turned towards the Cadets they are more boldly stating that power must be taken by the Cadets and not by the proletariat and the peasantry. Listen to this:

"The dictatorship of the proletariat and peasantry is . . . a paradox" (an incongruity) . . . it is "an inclination towards Socialist-Revolutionary views" (see the Menshevik organ *Na Ocheredi*,[13] No. 4, pp. 4-5, article by *Potresov*).

True, that outstanding Marxist, K. Kautsky, clearly says that the democratic dictatorship of the proletariat and peasantry is essential; but who is K. Kautsky

to contradict Potresov? Everybody knows that Potresov
is a true Marxist and Kautsky is not!

Another Menshevik adds:

"The slogan of a responsible ministry will become the slogan
of the struggle for power, the struggle to transfer power from
the bureaucracy to the people" (see *ibid.*, p. 3, article by
Koltsov).

In Koltsov's opinion, as you see, the slogan of a responsible ministry must become the slogan of the people's
struggle, that is, the proletariat and the peasantry must
fight under that slogan and no other, and must shed their
blood not for a democratic republic, but for a Cadet ministry.

This, then, is what the Mensheviks call conquest of
power by the people.

Think of it! It turns out that the dictatorship of
the proletariat and peasantry is harmful, but the
dictatorship of the Cadets is beneficial! As much as to
say: We don't want the sovereignty of the people, we
want the autocracy of the Cadets!

Yes, indeed! It is not for nothing that the Cadets,
the enemies of the people, are praising the Mensheviks! . . .

Dro (Time),[14] No. 2,
March 13, 1907
Unsigned

Translated from the Georgian

THE PROLETARIAT IS FIGHTING, THE BOURGEOISIE IS CONCLUDING AN ALLIANCE WITH THE GOVERNMENT

"The Prussian bourgeoisie was not, as the French of 1789 had been . . . It had sunk to the level of a sort of *social estate* . . . inclined from the very beginning to betray the people and compromise with the crowned representative of the old society."

That is what Karl Marx wrote about the Prussian liberals.

And indeed, even before the revolution had really unfolded, the German liberals started to make a deal with the "supreme power." They soon concluded this deal, and then, jointly with the government, attacked the workers and peasants. How bitingly and aptly Karl Marx exposed the duplicity of the liberals is well known:

"Without faith in itself, without faith in the people, grumbling at those above, trembling before those below, egoistic towards both sides and conscious of its egoism, revolutionary in relation to the conservatives and conservative in relation to the revolutionists, distrustful of its own mottoes, intimidated by the world storm, exploiting the world storm; no energy in any respect, plagiarism in every respect; base because it lacked originality, original in its baseness; haggling with its own desires, without initiative, without a world-historical calling; an execrable old man, . . . sans eyes, sans ears, sans teeth, sans everything—such was the Prussian bourgeoisie that found itself at the helm of the Prussian state after the March Revolution" (see *Neue Rheinische Zeitung*).[15]

Something similar to this is taking place here, in the course of the Russian revolution.

The point is that our bourgeoisie also differs from the French bourgeoisie of 1789. Our liberal bourgeoisie has been even more prompt and outspoken than the German bourgeoisie in declaring that it would "conclude an agreement with the supreme power" against the workers and peasants. The liberal-bourgeois party, the so-called Cadets, started secret negotiations with Stolypin behind the back of the people long ago. What was the object of these negotiations? What had the Cadets to talk about with the "field court-martial" minister if, in fact, they were not betraying the interests of the people? Concerning this, the French and English newspapers wrote not long ago that the government and the Cadets were entering into an alliance with the object of curbing the revolution. The terms of this secret alliance are as follows: The Cadets are to drop their oppositional demands and in return the government will appoint several Cadets to ministerial posts. The Cadets took offence and protested that it was not true. But, in fact, it turned out that it was true, it turned out that the Cadets had *already* concluded an alliance with the Rights and the government.

What does the recent voting in the Duma show if not that the Cadets are in alliance with the government? Recall the facts: the Social-Democrats introduce a motion to set up a commission to deal with the starving peasantry. They want the matter of helping the famine-stricken to be taken up by the people themselves apart from the deputies and the bureaucracy, and that the people themselves should expose "the heroic deeds" of the Gurkos and Lidvals.[16] This is good, this is desirable, because all this will strengthen the connections between the deputies and the people; all this will give the sullen discontent of the people a conscious character. Clearly, whoever was really serving the interests of the people would unfailingly support the proposal of the Social-Democrats as a measure beneficial to the people. But what did the Cadets do? Did they support the Social-Democrats? No! In conjunction with the Octobrists[17] and the Black Hundreds they unanimously voted down the Social-Democrats' proposal. If your proposal were carried out it would give rise to a popular movement and for that reason it is harmful, said the Cadet leader *Hessen* in reply to the Social-Democrats (see *Parus*,[18] No. 24). I am entirely in agreement with you, gentlemen, you are right—said *Stolypin*, giving the Cadets their due (*ibid.*). As a result, the Social-Democrats were supported only by the Socialist-Revolutionaries, the Popular Socialists and the majority of the Trudoviks.

Thus, the Duma split up into two camps: the camp of the enemies of the people's movement and the camp of the supporters of the people's movement. In the first camp are the Black Hundreds, the Octobrists, Stolypin, the Cadets and others. In the second camp are the Social-Democrats, the Socialist-Revolutionaries, the Popular Socialists, the majority of the Trudoviks, and others.

What does this show if not that the Cadets have *already* entered into an alliance with the government?

As is evident, the Bolsheviks' tactics, which sow distrust towards the Cadets, the traitors to the people, and call for a struggle against them, are justified.

But that is not all. The point is that the abovementioned rumours disseminated by the French and English newspapers have been fully confirmed. During the past few days the newspapers of the capital have been reporting from "reliable sources" that the Cadets have already struck a bargain with the government. And just imagine! It appears that the terms of this bargain have been ascertained even down to details. True, the Cadets deny it, but this is nothing but hypocrisy. Listen to this:

"*Segodnya*[19] reports from most reliable sources that Stolypin's speech in the State Duma yesterday did not in the least come as a surprise to the Cadets and the Octobrists. Preliminary negotiations concerning it had been going on all day between the Prime Minister, Kutler . . . and Fyodorov, who represented the Right Centre. A definite agreement between these persons was reached in the editorial offices of *Slovo*,[20] which Count Witte also intended to visit. . . . In main outline the agreement amounts to the following: 1) The Cadets will openly break off all connections with the Left parties and occupy a strictly central position in the Duma. 2) The Cadets will abandon part of their agrarian programme and make it approximate to the programme of the Octobrists. 3) The Cadets will for a time refrain from insisting on equal rights for the nationalities. 4) The Cadets will support the foreign loan. In return for this, the Cadets are promised: 1) Immediate legalization of the Cadet Party. 2) . . . The Cadets will be offered the portfolios of the Ministries of Land Settlement and Agriculture, Public Education, Commerce and Industry, and Justice. 3) Partial amnesty. 4) Support for the Cadet bill to abolish the field courtsmartial" (see *Parus*, No. 25).

That is how the matter stands.

While the people are fighting, while the workers and peasants are shedding their blood in order to crush the reaction, the Cadets are concluding an alliance with the reaction in order to curb the people's revolution!

That is what the Cadets are!

That, it appears, is why they want to "save" the Duma!

That is why they did not support the Social-Democrats' proposal to set up a famine commission!

The Menshevik thesis that the Cadets are democratic thus collapses.

The Menshevik tactics of supporting the Cadets thus collapse: after this, supporting the Cadets means supporting the government!

The Bolshevik view that at a critical moment we shall be supported only by the politically-conscious representatives of the peasants, such as the Socialist-Revolutionaries and others, is justified.

Clearly, we must also support them against the Cadets.

Or perhaps the Mensheviks think of continuing to support the Cadets? . . .

Dro (Time), No. 6,
March 17, 1907
Unsigned

Translated from the Georgian

COMRADE G. TELIA[21]

In Memoriam

Excessive eulogy of departed comrades has become a custom in our Party circles. The hushing up of the weak sides and the exaggeration of positive sides is a characteristic feature of obituary notices today. That, of course, is an unwise custom. We do not wish to follow it. We wish to say only what is true about Comrade G. Telia; we want to present Telia to our readers as he was in reality. And reality tells us that Comrade G. Telia, an advanced working man and an active Party worker, was a man of irreproachable character and of inestimable value for the Party. All that which most of all characterizes the Social-Democratic Party—thirst for knowledge, independence, undeviating progress, staunchness, industry and moral strength—all combined in the person of Comrade Telia. Telia personified the best features of the proletarian. That is not an exaggeration. The following brief biography of him will prove this.

Comrade Telia was not a "scholar." He learned to read and write by his own efforts and became class conscious. Leaving the village of Chagani (Telia was born in the village of Chagani, Kutais Uyezd), he obtained a job as a domestic servant in Tiflis. Here he learned to speak Russian and acquired a passion for

reading books. He quickly grew tired of being a domestic servant and soon got a job in the carpenters'
shop at the railway workshops. These workshops rendered
Comrade Telia a great service. They were his school;
there he became a Social-Democrat; there he was steeled
and became a staunch fighter; there he came to the front
as a capable and class-conscious worker.

In 1900-01 Telia already stood out among the advanced workers as an esteemed leader. He had known no
rest since the demonstration in Tiflis in 1901.[22] Ardent
propaganda, the formation of organizations, attendance
at important meetings, persevering effort in socialist
self-education—to that he devoted all his spare time.
He was hunted by the police, who searched for him "with
lanterns," but it only served to redouble his energy and
ardour in the struggle. Comrade Telia was the inspirer
of the 1903 demonstration (in Tiflis).[23] The police were
hot on his heels, but, notwithstanding this, he hoisted
the flag and delivered a speech. After that demonstration he passed entirely underground. In that year, on
the instructions of the organization, he began to "travel"
from one town to another in Transcaucasia. In that same
year, on the instructions of the organization, he went
to Batum to organize a secret printing plant, but he was
arrested at the Batum station with the equipment for
this printing plant in his possession and soon after he
was sent to the Kutais prison. That marked the beginning of a new period in his "restless" life. The eighteen
months of imprisonment were not lost on Telia. The
prison became his second school. Constant study, the
reading of socialist books and participation in discussions markedly increased his stock of knowledge. Here

his indomitable revolutionary character, which many of his comrades envied, was definitely moulded. But the prison also left on him the impress of death, this prison infected him with a fatal disease (consumption), which carried our splendid comrade to his grave.

Telia was aware of the fatal state of his health, but this did not daunt him. The only thing that troubled him was "sitting in idleness and inaction." "How I long for the day when I shall be free and do what I want to do, see the masses again, put myself in their embrace and begin to serve them!"—that is what our comrade dreamed of during his confinement in jail. The dream came true. Eighteen months later he was transferred to the "little" Kutais prison, from which he forthwith made his escape and appeared in Tiflis. At that time a split was taking place in the Party. Comrade Telia then belonged to the Mensheviks, but he did not in the least resemble the "official" Mensheviks who regard Menshevism as their "Koran," who regard themselves as the faithful and the Bolsheviks as infidels. Nor did Telia resemble those "advanced" workers who pose as "born Social-Democrats," and being utter ignoramuses shout in their comical way: We are workers—we don't need any knowledge! The characteristic feature of Comrade Telia was precisely that he rejected factional fanaticism, that he utterly despised blind imitation and wanted to think everything out for himself. That is why, after escaping from prison, he at once pounced upon the books: *Minutes of the Second Congress*, Martov's *State of Siege*, and Lenin's *What Is To Be Done?* and *One Step Forward*. It was a sight to see Telia, his face pale and emaciated, poring over these books and to hear him say with a smile: "I can see it's not such an easy matter to decide whether to be a Bolshevik or a Menshevik; until I have studied these books my Menshevism is built on sand." And so, after studying the necessary literature, after pondering over the controversies between the Bolsheviks and the Mensheviks, after weighing everything up, and only after that, Comrade Telia said: "Comrades, I am a Bolshevik. As it looks to me, whoever is not a Bolshevik is certainly betraying the revolutionary spirit of Marxism."

After that he became an apostle of revolutionary Marxism (Bolshevism). In 1905, on the instructions of the organization, he went to Baku. There he set up a printing plant, improved the work of the district organizations, was an active member of the leading body and wrote articles for *Proletariatis Brdzola*[24]—such was the work Comrade Telia performed. During the well-known police raid he, too, was arrested, but here too he "slipped away" and again hastened to Tiflis. After working in the leading organization of Tiflis for a short time he attended the All-Russian Conference of Bolsheviks in Tammerfors in 1905. His impressions of that conference are interesting. He viewed the Party's future with great hope and he used to say with glistening eyes: I shall not begrudge my last ounce of strength for this Party. The unfortunate thing, however, was that immediately on his return from Russia he took to his bed, never to rise from it again. Only now did he commence serious literary activity. During his illness he wrote: "What We Need" (see *Akhali Tskhovreba*),[25] "Old and New Corpses" (a reply to Archil Jordjadze),

"Anarchism and Social-Democracy,"* "Why We Are Called Blanquists," and others.

A few days before he died he wrote to us that he was working on a pamphlet on the history of Social-Democracy in the Caucasus, but cruel death prematurely tore the pen out of the hand of our tireless comrade.

Such is the picture of Comrade Telia's short but stormy life.

Amazing capabilities, inexhaustible energy, independence, profound love for the cause, heroic determination and apostolic talent—that is what characterized Comrade Telia.

Men like Telia are met with only in the ranks of the proletariat; only the proletariat gives birth to heroes like Telia; and the proletariat will take revenge on the accursed system to which our comrade, *the working man G. Telia*, fell a victim.

Dro (*Time*), No. 10,
March 22, 1907
Signed: *Ko.* . . .
Translated from the Georgian

---

* The last two pamphlets could not be printed as the manuscripts were seized by the police during a raid.

THE ADVANCED PROLETARIAT
AND THE FIFTH PARTY CONGRESS

The preparations for the congress are drawing to a close.[26] The relative strength of the different groups is gradually becoming revealed. It is becoming apparent that the industrial districts largely support the Bolsheviks. St. Petersburg, Moscow, the Central Industrial region, Poland, the Baltic region and the Urals—these are the regions where the Bolsheviks' tactics are trusted. The Caucasus, the trans-Caspian region, South Russia, several towns in the areas where the Bund[27] has influence, and the peasant organizations of the Spilka[28]—these are the sources from which the Menshevik comrades draw their strength. South Russia is the only industrial area where the Mensheviks enjoy confidence. The rest of the Menshevik strongholds are for the most part centres of small industry.

It is becoming apparent that the Mensheviks' tactics are mainly the tactics of the backward towns, where the development of the revolution and the growth of class consciousness are frowned upon.

It is becoming apparent that the Bolsheviks' tactics are mainly the tactics of the advanced towns, the industrial centres, where the intensification of the revolution and the development of class consciousness are the main focus of attention. . . .

At one time Russian Social-Democracy consisted of a handful of members. At that time it bore the character of a movement of intellectuals and was unable to influence the proletarian struggle. Party policy was then directed by one or two individuals—the voice of the proletarian membership of the party was drowned. ... The situation is entirely different today. Today we have a magnificent party—the *Russian Social-Democratic Labour Party*, which has as many as 200,000 members in its ranks, which is influencing the proletarian struggle, is rallying around itself the revolutionary democracy of the whole of Russia, and is a terror to "the powers that be." And this magnificent party is all the more magnificent and splendid for the reason that its helm is in the hands of the general membership and not of one or two "enlightened individuals." That was most clearly revealed during the Duma elections, when the general membership rejected the proposal of the "authoritative" Plekhanov and refused to have a "common platform" with the Cadets. True, the Menshevik comrades insist on calling our party a party of intellectuals, but that is probably because the majority in the party is not Menshevik. But if the German Social-Democratic Party, which with a proletariat numbering 18,000,000 has a membership of only 400,000, has the right to call itself a proletarian party, then the Russian Social-Democratic Party, which with a proletariat numbering 9,000,000 has a membership of 200,000, also has the right to regard itself as a proletarian party. ...

Thus, the Russian Social-Democratic Party is magnificent also because it is a genuine proletarian party, which is marching towards the future along its own road, and is critical of the whispered advice of its old "leaders."

In this respect the recent conferences in St. Petersburg and Moscow are instructive.

At both conferences the workers set the keynote; at both conferences workers comprised nine-tenths of the delegates. Both conferences rejected the obsolete and inappropriate "directives" of the "old leaders" like Plekhanov. Both conferences loudly proclaimed the necessity of Bolshevism. And thus Moscow and St. Petersburg expressed their lack of confidence in the Menshevik tactics and recognized the necessity of the hegemony of the proletariat in the present revolution.

St. Petersburg and Moscow speak for the entire class-conscious proletariat. Moscow and St. Petersburg are leading all the other towns. From Moscow and St. Petersburg came the directives during the January and October actions; they led the movement during the glorious December days. There can be no doubt that they will give the signal for the impending revolutionary onslaught.

And St. Petersburg and Moscow adhere to the tactics of Bolshevism. The tactics of Bolshevism alone are proletarian tactics—that is what the workers of these cities say to the proletariat of Russia. . . .

Dro (Time), No. 25,
April 8, 1907
Unsigned

Translated from the Georgian

MUDDLE...

The "publicists" of *Lakhvari*[29] are still unable to define their tactics. In their first issue they wrote: We are supporting only the "progressive steps" of the Cadets, but not the Cadets themselves. Commenting on this we said that it was amusing sophistry, since the Mensheviks voted for the Cadet candidates to the Duma and not only for their "steps"; they helped to get into the Duma Cadets as such and not only their "steps," and they helped to elect a Cadet as such as President of the Duma and not only his "steps"—and this clearly confirms the fact that the Mensheviks supported the Cadets. This is so obvious and the Mensheviks have talked so much about supporting the Cadets, that denial of the fact has only raised a laugh. . . .

Now, having "pondered" over the matter a little, they are talking differently: true, "during the elections we supported the Cadets" (see *Lakhvari*, No. 3), but this was only during the elections; in the Duma we are supporting not the Cadets but only their "steps"; you, they say, "do not distinguish between tactics in the Duma and tactics during elections." In the first place, "tactics" which safeguard you from doing stupid things only in the Duma but prompt you to do stupid things during elections are very funny tactics. Secondly, is it not true that the Mensheviks helped to elect a Cadet as President

of the Duma? Under what category of tactics should
we place helping to elect a Cadet as President—"tactics in the Duma" or tactics outside the Duma? We
think that Golovin was elected President of the Duma
in the Duma, and not president of the street in the
street.

Clearly, the Mensheviks pursued the same tactics
in the Duma as they pursued outside the Duma. These
are the tactics of supporting the Cadets. If they deny
it now, it is because they have fallen victims to muddle.

Supporting the Cadets does not mean creating a reputation for the Cadets; if it does, then you are creating
a reputation for the Socialist-Revolutionaries by supporting them—says *Lakhvari*. What comical fellows those
"Lakhvarists" are! Apparently it does not occur to them
that any support that Social-Democracy lends a party
creates a reputation for that party! That is why they
have been so lavish in their promises of every kind of
"support.". . . Yes, dear comrades, by supporting the
Socialist-Revolutionaries, Social-Democracy creates a
reputation for them in the eyes of the people, and this
is exactly why such support is permissible *only in exceptional cases, and as a means of defeating the Cadets*. Supporting the Socialist-Revolutionaries is by no means
ideal, it is an inevitable evil, resorted to in order
to curb the Cadets. You, however, supported the very
Cadets who are betraying the workers and peasants;
the Socialist-Revolutionaries are superior to them because
they side with the revolution. . . .

"The Cadets, for example, demanded universal
suffrage. It turns out that this demand is a great evil,
because it is a Cadet demand" (*ibid.*).

Well, aren't they comical? You see, it turns out that universal suffrage is a "Cadet demand"! The Tiflis Mensheviks, it turns out, do not know that universal suffrage is not a Cadet demand, but the demand of revolutionary democracy, which Social-Democracy advocates more consistently than anyone else! No, comrades, if you cannot even understand that the Cadets are not revolutionary democrats; if you cannot even understand that the fight against them in· order to strengthen the hegemony of the proletariat is the question of the day for us; if you cannot even distinguish between what you said yesterday and what you are saying today—then you had better put your pens aside, get yourselves out of the muddle you are in, and only after that launch into "criticism. ". . .

By the holy Duma, that would be better!

Dro (Time), No. 26,
April 10, 1907
Unsigned

Translated from the Georgian

OUR CAUCASIAN CLOWNS

The Menshevik newspaper *Lakhvari* flew into a rage over our articles. Evidently our accusations hit the mark. It makes, of course, a very amusing spectacle. . . .

What's it all about?

We wrote that the Duma's swing to the right does not surprise us. Why? Because the Duma is dominated by the liberal bourgeoisie, and this bourgeoisie is entering into an alliance with the government and breaking with the workers and peasants. Hence the weakness of the Duma. And the fact that the workers and revolutionary peasants are not dragging at the tail of the anti-revolutionary Duma; the fact that they are indeed breaking with the Duma majority—shows that the people of our country are more politically conscious than the French people were in the eighteenth century. Hence again the weakness of the Duma. That is how we explained the Duma's weakness and its swing to the right.

It turns out that on reading this explanation the Mensheviks' hearts sank into their boots and they howled in horror:

"No, if the explanation offered by the Bolsheviks were true, we would have to shrug our shoulders and say that it is all up with the Russian revolution" (see *Lakhvari*, No. 6).

Poor fellows! They believe in their own revolution-ariness less than they believe in that of the Cadets! The liberals are betraying the revolution—hence, the revolution has grown weaker! The workers and revolutionary peasants, it appears, are a mere cypher. Woe to you if you have no more penetration than that!

They are not even faithful to themselves. For example, eighteen months ago, the same Mensheviks wrote something different in their newspaper *Skhivi:*[30]

"The December strike repelled the bourgeoisie from the revolution and *made it conservative.* The further development of the revolution must proceed *against the liberals.* Will the revolution be able to do this? That will depend upon who will be the driving force of the revolution. *Here, too, of course, the proletariat is the leader of the revolution.* It will be unable to carry the revolution to the end unless it has a powerful and faithful ally, and this *ally is the peasantry, and only the peasantry*" (see *Skhivi,* No. 12).

Yes, that is what the Mensheviks said when they were adhering to the standpoint of Social-Democracy....

But now, having turned their backs on Social-Democracy, they are singing a different song and are proclaiming the liberals as the hub of the revolution, as the saviours of the revolution.

And after all this they have the effrontery to assure us that the Caucasian Mensheviks are not clowns, that they do not deck themselves in Social-Democratic apparel in order to cover up their Cadet natures!

"How did it happen," the Mensheviks ask, "that in the First Duma the Cadets acted more boldly, demanded a ministry responsible to the Duma, etc.? How is it to be explained that on the day after the Duma was dispersed the Cadets signed the Vyborg manifesto?

"Why are they not behaving in the same way today?
"To this question the political philosophy of the Bolsheviks *provides no reply, nor can it do so*" (*ibid.*).

It is no use trying to console yourselves, poor frightened comrades. We answered that question long ago: the present Duma is more colourless because the proletariat is now more politically conscious and united than it was in the period of the First Duma, and this is pushing the liberal bourgeoisie to the side of reaction. Get that well into your minds once and for all, pro-liberal comrades: *the more consciously the proletariat fights the more counter-revolutionary the bourgeoisie becomes.* That is our explanation.

And how do you explain the colourlessness of the Second Duma, dear comrades?

For example: In No. 4 of *Lakhvari* you write that the Duma's weakness and colourlessness are due to "the people's lack of political consciousness and organization." You yourselves say that the First Duma was "bolder,"—it follows, therefore, that at that time the people were "politically conscious and organized." The Second Duma is more colourless—hence, this year the people are less "politically conscious and organized" than they were last year, and hence, the revolution and the political consciousness of the people have receded! Is this not what you wanted to say, comrades? Is this not how you want to justify your gravitation towards the Cadets, dear friends?

Woe to you and to your muddled "logic" if you think of continuing to remain clowns. . . .

Dro (Time), No. 29,
April 13, 1907
Unsigned

Translated from the Georgian

THE DISPERSION OF THE DUMA
AND THE TASKS OF THE PROLETARIAT

The Second Duma has been dispersed.[31] It was not merely dissolved, it was shut up with a bang—exactly like the First Duma. Here we have the "dispersion manifesto" with the hypocrite tsar's "sincere regret" at the dispersion. We also have a "new electoral law" which practically nullifies the franchise for the workers and peasants. We even have a promise to "renovate" Russia with the aid, of course, of shootings and a Third Duma. In short, we have everything we had only recently, when the First Duma was dispersed. The tsar has briefly re-enacted the dispersion of the First Duma.

In dispersing the Second Duma the tsar did not act idly, without an object in view. With the aid of the Duma he wanted to establish contact with the peasantry, to transform it from an ally of the proletariat into an ally of the government and, by making the proletariat stand alone, by isolating it, to cripple the revolution, to make its victory impossible. For that purpose the government resorted to the aid of the liberal bourgeoisie, which still exercised some influence over the ignorant masses of the peasants; and through this bourgeoisie it wanted to establish contact with the vast masses of the peasants. That is how it wanted to utilize the Second State Duma.

But the opposite happened. The very first sessions of the Second Duma showed that the peasant deputies distrusted not only the government but also the liberal-bourgeois deputies. This distrust grew as a consequence of a series of votes which were taken and it finally reached the stage of open hostility towards the deputies of the liberal bourgeoisie. Thus, the government failed to rally the peasant deputies around the liberals and, through them, around the old regime. The government's design—to establish contact with the peasantry through the Duma and to isolate the proletariat—was frustrated. The opposite happened: the peasant deputies more and more rallied around the proletarian deputies, around the Social-Democrats. And the more they moved away from the liberals, from the Cadets, the more resolutely did they draw closer to the Social-Democratic deputies. This greatly facilitated the task of rallying the peasants around the proletariat outside the Duma. The result was not the isolation of the proletariat, but the isolation of the liberal bourgeoisie and the government from the peasants—the proletariat consolidated its backing by the vast masses of the peasantry—it was not the revolution that was thrown out of gear, as the government wanted, but the counter-revolution. In view of this, the existence of the Second Duma became increasingly dangerous for the government. And so it "dissolved" the Duma.

In order more effectively to prevent the peasants and the proletariat from coming together, in order to rouse hostility towards the Social-Democrats among the ignorant masses of the peasants and to rally them around itself, the government resorted to two measures.

First, it attacked the Social-Democratic group in the Duma, falsely accused its members of calling for an immediate insurrection and made it appear as if they were chiefly responsible for the dispersion of the Duma, as much as to say: we would not have dispersed your "nice little Duma," dear peasants, but the Social-Democrats threatened us with an insurrection, and so we were obliged to "dissolve" the Duma.

Second, the government promulgated a "new law" which reduces the number of peasant electors by half, doubles the number of landlord electors, gives the latter the opportunity to elect peasant deputies at general meetings, reduces the number of workers' electors also by nearly half (124 instead of 237), reserves for the government the right to redistribute voters "according to locality, various qualifications and nationality," destroys all possibility of conducting free election propaganda, etc., etc. And all this has been done in order to prevent revolutionary representatives of the workers and peasants from getting into the Third Duma, in order to fill the Duma with the liberal and reactionary representatives of the landlords and factory owners, to get the peasants misrepresented by making possible the election of the most conservative peasant candidates in spite of the wishes of the peasants, and thereby to deprive the proletariat of the opportunity of openly rallying the broad masses of the peasants around itself—in other words, to have an opportunity for an open rapprochement with the peasantry.

This is the idea behind the dispersion of the Second State Duma.

Evidently, the liberal bourgeoisie understands all this and, by the agency of its Cadets, is helping the government. It struck a bargain with the old regime already in the Second Duma and tried to isolate the proletariat by flirting with the peasant deputies. On the eve of the dispersion, the Cadet leader Milyukov called upon his party to rally all and sundry around the "Stolypin government," to enter into an agreement with it, and declare war on the revolution, that is to say, on the proletariat. And Struve, the second Cadet leader, after the Duma was already dispersed, defended "the idea of surrendering" the Social-Democratic deputies to the government, called upon the Cadets openly to take the road of fighting the revolution, to merge with the counter-revolutionary Octobrists and, after isolating the restless proletariat, to wage a struggle against it. The Cadet party is silent—which means that it agrees with its leaders.

Evidently, the liberal bourgeoisie is aware of the gravity of the present situation.

All the more clearly, therefore, is the proletariat faced with the task of overthrowing the tsarist regime. Just think! There was the First Duma. There was the Second Duma. But neither the one nor the other "solved" a single problem of the revolution, nor, indeed, could either of them "solve" these problems. Just as before, the peasants are without land, the workers are without the eight-hour day, and all citizens are without political freedom. Why? Because the tsarist regime is not yet dead, it still exists, dispersing the Second Duma after it dispersed the First, organizing the counter-revolution, and trying to break up the revolutionary forces, to divorce the vast masses of the peasants from the proletarians. Meanwhile, the subterranean forces of the revolution—the crisis in the towns and famine in the rural districts—are continuing their work, rousing more and more the broad masses of the workers and peasants, and more and more persistently demanding a solution of the fundamental problems of our revolution. The exertions of the tsarist regime serve only to aggravate the crisis. The efforts of the liberal bourgeoisie to divorce the peasants from the proletarians are only intensifying the revolution. Clearly, it will be impossible to satisfy the broad masses of the workers and peasants unless the tsarist regime is overthrown and a Popular Constituent Assembly is convened. It is no less clear that the fundamental problems of the revolution can be solved only in alliance with the peasantry against the tsarist regime and against the liberal bourgeoisie.

To the overthrow of the tsarist regime and the convocation of a Popular Constituent Assembly—this is what the dispersion of the Second Duma is leading to.

War against the treacherous liberal bourgeoisie and close alliance with the peasantry—this is what the dispersion of the Second Duma means.

The task of the proletariat is consciously to take this path and worthily to play the part of leader of the revolution.

Bakinsky Proletary, No. 1,   Reprinted from the newspaper
June 20, 1907
Unsigned

THE LONDON CONGRESS OF THE RUSSIAN SOCIAL-DEMOCRATIC LABOUR PARTY

(*Notes of a Delegate*)[32]

The London Congress is over. In spite of the expectations of liberal hacks, such as the Vergezhskys[33] and Kuskovas,[34] the congress did not result in a split, but in the further consolidation of the Party, in the further unification of the advanced workers of all Russia in one indivisible party. It was a real all-Russian unity congress, for at this congress our Polish comrades, our comrades of the Bund, and our Lettish comrades were for the first time most widely and fully represented, for the first time they took an active part in the work of the Party congress and, consequently, for the first time most directly linked the fate of their respective organizations with the fate of the entire Party. In this respect the London Congress greatly contributed to the consolidation and strengthening of the Russian Social-Democratic Labour Party.

Such is the first and an important result of the London Congress.

But the importance of the London Congress is not confined to this. The point is that, in spite of the wishes of the liberal hacks we have referred to, the congress ended in the victory of "Bolshevism," in the victory of revolutionary Social-Democracy over the opportunist wing of our Party, over "Menshevism." Everybody, of course, is aware of the disagreements among us on the role of the different classes and parties in our revolution and of our attitude towards them. Everybody knows, too, that in a number of pronouncements the official centre of the Party, which is Menshevik in composition, took a stand in opposition to the Party as a whole. Recall, for example, the case of the Central Committee's slogan of a responsible Cadet ministry, which the Party rejected in the period of the First Duma; the case of the same Central Committee's slogan of "resumption of the session of the Duma" after the First Duma was dispersed, which was also rejected by the Party; and the case of the Central Committee's well-known call for a general strike in connection with the dispersion of the First Duma, which was also rejected by the Party. . . . It was necessary to put an end to that abnormal situation. And to do this it was necessary to sum up the actual victories the Party had achieved over the opportunist Central Committee, the victories which fill the history of our Party's internal development during the whole of the past year. And so the London Congress summed up all these victories of *revolutionary* Social-Democracy and sealed the victory by adopting the tactics of that section of Social-Democracy.

Consequently, the Party will henceforth pursue the strictly class policy of the socialist proletariat. The red flag of the proletariat will no longer be hauled down before the spellbinders of liberalism. A mortal blow has been struck at the vacillation characteristic of intellectuals, which is unbecoming to the proletariat.

Such is the second and no less important result of the London Congress of our Party.

The actual unification of the advanced workers of all Russia into a single all-Russian party under the banner of *revolutionary* Social-Democracy—that is the significance of the London Congress, that is its general character.

We shall now pass to a more detailed characterization of the congress.

I

THE COMPOSITION OF THE CONGRESS

In all about 330 delegates were present at the congress. Of these, 302 had the right to vote; they represented over 150,000 Party members. The rest were consultative delegates. The distribution of the delegates according to groups was approximately as follows (counting only those with right to vote): Bolsheviks 92, Mensheviks 85, Bundists 54, Poles 45 and Letts 26.

As regards the social status of the delegates (workers or non-workers) the congress presented the following picture: manual workers 116 in all, office and distributive workers 24, the rest were non-workers. The manual workers were distributed among the different groups as follows: Bolshevik group 38 (36 per cent), Menshevik group 30 (31 per cent), Poles 27 (61 per cent), Letts 12 (40 per cent) and Bundists 9 (15 per cent). Professional revolutionaries were distributed among the groups as follows: Bolshevik group 18 (17 per cent), Menshevik group 22 (22 per cent), Poles 5 (11 per cent), Letts 2 (6 per cent), Bundists 9 (15 per cent).

We were all "amazed" by these statistics. How is this? The Mensheviks had shouted so much about our Party consisting of intellectuals; day and night they had been denouncing the Bolsheviks as intellectuals; they had threatened to drive all the intellectuals out of the Party and had all the time been reviling the professional revolutionaries—and suddenly it turned out that they had far fewer workers in their group than the Bolshevik "intellectuals" had! It turned out that they had far more professional revolutionaries than the Bolsheviks! But we explained the Menshevik shouts by the proverb: "The tongue ever turns to the aching tooth."

Still more interesting are the figures of the composition of the congress showing the "territorial distribution" of the delegates. It turned out that the large groups of Menshevik delegates came mainly from the peasant and handicraft districts: Guria (9 delegates), Tiflis (10 delegates), Little-Russian peasant organization "Spilka" (I think 12 delegates), the Bund (the overwhelming majority were Mensheviks) and, by way of exception, the Donets Basin (7 delegates). On the other hand, the large groups of Bolshevik delegates came exclusively from the large-scale industry districts: St. Petersburg (12 delegates), Moscow (13 or 14 delegates), the Urals (21 delegates), Ivanovo-Voznesensk (11 delegates), Poland (45 delegates).

Obviously, the tactics of the Bolsheviks are the tactics of the proletarians in big industry, the tactics of those areas where class contradictions are especially clear and the class struggle especially acute. Bolshevism is the tactics of the real proletarians.

On the other hand, it is no less obvious that the tactics of the Mensheviks are primarily the tactics of the handicraft workers and the peasant semi-proletarians, the tactics of those areas where class contradictions are not quite clear and the class struggle is masked. Menshevism is the tactics of the semi-bourgeois elements among the proletariat.

So say the figures.

And this is not difficult to understand: it is impossible to talk seriously among the workers of Lodz, Moscow or Ivanovo-Voznesensk about blocs with the very same liberal bourgeoisie whose members are waging a fierce struggle against them and who, every now and again, "punish" them with partial dismissals and mass lockouts. There Menshevism will find no sympathy; there Bolshevism, the tactics of uncompromising proletarian class struggle, is needed. On the other hand, it is extremely difficult to inculcate the idea of the class struggle among the peasants of Guria or say, the handicraftsmen of Shklov, who do not feel the sharp and systematic blows of the class struggle and, therefore, readily agree to all sorts of agreements against the "common enemy." There Bolshevism is not yet needed; there Menshevism is needed, for there an atmosphere of agreements and compromises pervades everything.

No less interesting is the national composition of the congress. The figures showed that the majority of the Menshevik group were Jews (not counting the Bundists, of course), then came Georgians and then Russians. On the other hand, the overwhelming majority of the Bolshevik group were Russians, then came Jews (not counting Poles and Letts, of course), then Georgians, etc. In this connection one of the Bolsheviks (I think it was Comrade Alexinsky[35]) observed in jest that the Mensheviks constituted a Jewish group while the Bolsheviks constituted a true-Russian group and, therefore, it wouldn't be a bad idea for us Bolsheviks to organize a pogrom in the Party.

It is not difficult to explain this composition of the different groups: the main centres of Bolshevism are the areas of large-scale industry, purely Russian districts with the exception of Poland, whereas the Menshevik districts are districts with small production and, at the same time, Jewish, Georgian, etc., districts.

As regards the different trends revealed at the congress, it must be noted that the formal division of the congress into five groups (Bolsheviks, Mensheviks, Poles, etc.) retained a certain validity, inconsiderable it is true, only up to the discussion on questions of principle (the question of the non-proletarian parties, the labour congress, etc.). When these questions of principle came up for discussion the formal grouping was in fact cast aside, and when a vote was taken the congress, as a rule, divided into two parts: Bolsheviks and Mensheviks. There was no so-called centre, or marsh, at the congress. Trotsky proved to be "pretty but useless." All the Poles definitely sided with the Bolsheviks. The overwhelming majority of the Letts also definitely supported the Bolsheviks. The Bund, the overwhelming majority of whose delegates in fact always supported the Mensheviks, formally pursued an extremely ambiguous policy, which, on the one hand, raised a smile, and on the other, caused irritation. Comrade Rosa Luxemburg aptly characterized the policy of the Bund when she said that the Bund's policy was not the policy of a mature political organization that influenced the masses, but the policy of shopkeepers who are eternally looking forward to, and hopefully expecting, a drop in the price of sugar tomorrow. Of the Bundists, only 8 to 10 delegates supported the Bolsheviks, and then not always.

In general, predominance, and rather considerable predominance, was on the side of the Bolsheviks.

Thus, the congress was a Bolshevik congress, although not sharply Bolshevik. Of the Menshevik resolutions only the one on guerilla actions was carried, and that by sheer accident: on that point the Bolsheviks did not accept battle, or rather, they did not wish to fight the issue to a conclusion, purely out of the desire to "give the Menshevik comrades at least one opportunity to rejoice.". . .

II

THE AGENDA.
REPORT OF THE CENTRAL COMMITTEE.
REPORT OF THE GROUP IN THE DUMA

As regards political trends at the congress, its proceedings can be divided up into two parts.

First part: debates on formal questions, such as the agenda of the congress, the reports of the Central Committee and report of the group in the Duma, i.e., questions of profound political significance, but linked, or being linked, with the "honour" of this or that group, with the idea "not to offend" this or that group, "not to cause a split"—and for that reason called formal questions. This part of the congress was the most stormy, and absorbed the largest amount of time.

This was due to the fact that considerations of principle were forced into the background by "moral" considerations ("not to offend") and, consequently, no strictly defined groups were formed; it was impossible to tell at once "who would win," and in the hope of winning over the "neutral and polite," the groups plunged into a furious struggle for predominance.

Second part: discussion on questions of principle, such as the question of the non-proletarian parties, the labour congress, etc. Here "moral" considerations were absent, definite groups were formed in conformity with strictly defined trends of principle; the relation of forces between the groups was revealed at once, and for that reason this part of the congress was the calmest and most fruitful— clear proof that keeping to principle in discussion gives the best guarantee that the proceedings of a congress will be calm and fruitful.

We shall now pass to a brief characterization of the first part of the congress proceedings.

After a speech by Comrade Plekhanov, who opened the congress and in his speech urged the necessity of agreements "as occasion arises" with "the progressive elements" of bourgeois society, the congress elected a presidium of five (one from each group), elected a credentials committee and then proceeded to draw up the agenda. It is characteristic that at this congress, just as they did at last year's Unity Congress, the Mensheviks furiously opposed the Bolsheviks' proposal to include in the agenda the questions of the present situation and of the class tasks of the proletariat in our revolution. Is the revolutionary tide rising or subsiding and, accordingly, should we "liquidate" the revolution or carry it through

to the end? What are the proletariat's class tasks in our
revolution which sharply distinguish it from the other
classes in Russian society? Such are the questions which the
Menshevik comrades are afraid of. They flee from them
like shadows from the sun; they do not wish to bring to
light the roots of our disagreements. Why? Because the
Menshevik group itself is split by profound disagreements
on these questions, because Menshevism is not an integral
trend; Menshevism is a medley of trends, which are
imperceptible during the factional struggle against
Bolshevism but which spring to the surface as soon as
current questions and our tactics are discussed from the
point of view of principle. The Mensheviks do not wish
to expose this inherent weakness of their group. The
Bolsheviks were aware of this, and in order to keep
the discussions closer to principles, insisted on the
inclusion of the above-mentioned questions in the agenda.
Realizing that keeping to principles would kill them, the
Mensheviks became stubborn; they hinted to the "polite
comrades" that they would be "offended," and so the
congress did not include the question of the present
situation, etc., in the agenda. In the end, the following
agenda was adopted: report of the Central Committee,
report of the group in the Duma, attitude towards the
non-proletarian parties, the Duma, the labour congress,
the trade unions, guerilla actions, crises, lockouts and
unemployment, the International Congress at Stuttgart,[36]
and organizational questions.

The chief speakers on the report of the Central Committee were Comrade Martov (for the Mensheviks)
and Comrade Ryadovoi[37] (for the Bolsheviks). Strictly

speaking, Martov's report was not a serious elucidation
of facts, but a sentimental story about how the innocent
Central Committee set to work to guide the Party and then
the group in the Duma, and how the "awful" Bolsheviks
hindered it in its work by pestering it with their principles.
Martov justified the Central Committee's slogans of a
responsible Cadet ministry, "resumption of the session
of the Duma," etc., etc., which the Party subsequently
rejected, on the plea that the situation was indefinite
and that it was impossible to advance different slogans
in a period of lull. And he justified the Central Committee's misguided call for a general strike, and later
for partial actions immediately after the dispersion of
the First Duma, also on the plea that the situation
was indefinite and that it was impossible to define precisely the mood of the masses. He spoke very little about
the part the Central Committee played in the split in
the St. Petersburg organization.[38] But he spoke too much
about the conference of military and combat organizations that was convened on the initiative of a certain
group of Bolsheviks, and which, in Martov's opinion,
caused disruption and anarchy in the Party organizations.
At the end of his report Martov called upon the congress
to bear in mind the difficulties connected with the work
of guiding the Party in view of the exceptionally compli-
cated and confused situation, and asked it not to be
severe in its criticism of the Central Committee. Evidently, Martov himself realized that the Central Committee had grave sins to answer for.

Comrade Ryadovoi's report was of an entirely different character. He expressed the opinion that it was
the duty of the Central Committee of the Party: 1) to

defend and carry out the Party programme, 2) to carry out the tactical directives given it by the Party Congress, 3) to safeguard the integrity of the Party, and 4) to co-ordinate the positive activities of the Party. The Central Committee had not carried out any one of these duties. Instead of defending and carrying out the Party programme, the Central Committee, in connection with the well-known agrarian appeal of the First Duma,[39] instructed the Social-Democratic group in the Duma, with a view to ensuring the unity of the opposition and winning over the Cadets, not to try to secure the inclusion in the Duma's appeal of the well-known point of our agrarian programme on the confiscation of all (landlords') land, but to confine itself to a simple statement about alienating the land without saying whether compensation should be paid or not.

Just think of it! The Central Committee issued instructions to throw out the extremely important point in the Party programme on the confiscation of the land! The Central Committee violated the Party programme! The Central Committee as the violator of the programme—can you imagine anything more disgraceful?

To proceed. Instead of carrying out at least the directives of the Unity Congress, instead of systematically intensifying the struggle between the parties in the Duma with the object of introducing greater political consciousness in the class struggle outside the Duma, instead of pursuing the strictly class, independent policy of the proletariat—the Central Committee issued the slogans of a responsible Cadet ministry, "resumption of the session of the Duma," "for the Duma against the camarilla," etc., etc., slogans which obscured the struggle of the

Party in the Duma, glossed over the class antagonisms outside the Duma, obliterated all distinction between the militant policy of the proletariat and the compromising policy of the liberal bourgeoisie, and adapted the former to the latter. And when Comrade Plekhanov, a member of the editorial board of the Central Organ and, consequently, of the Central Committee, went even further on the road of compromise with the Cadets and proposed that the Party should enter into a bloc with the liberal bourgeoisie, abandoning the slogan of a Constituent Assembly and issuing the slogan acceptable to the liberal bourgeoisie of a "sovereign Duma," the Central Committee, far from protesting against Comrade Plekhanov's sally which disgraced the Party, even agreed with it, although it did not dare to express its agreement officially.

That is how the Central Committee of the Party violated the elementary requirements of the independent class policy of the proletariat and the decisions of the Unity Congress!

A Central Committee which obscures the class consciousness of the proletariat; a Central Committee which subordinates the policy of the proletariat to the policy of the liberal bourgeoisie; a Central Committee which hauls down the flag of the proletariat before the charlatans of Cadet liberalism—this is what the Menshevik opportunists have brought us to!

We shall not dilate on the fact that far from safeguarding the unity and discipline of the Party the Central Committee systematically violated them by taking the initiative in splitting the St. Petersburg organization.

Nor do we wish to dilate on the fact that the Central Committee has not co-ordinated the Party's activities—this is clear enough as it is.

How is all this, all these mistakes of the Central Committee, to be explained? Not, of course, by the fact that there were "awful" people in the Central Committee, but by the fact that Menshevism, which then predominated in the Central Committee, is incapable of guiding the Party, is utterly bankrupt as a political trend. From this point of view, the entire history of the Central Committee is the history of the failure of Menshevism. And when the Menshevik comrades reproach us and say that we "hindered" the Central Committee, that we "pestered" it, etc., etc., we cannot refrain from answering these moralizing comrades: yes comrades, we "hindered" the Central Committee in its violation of our programme, we "hindered" it in its adaptation of the tactics of the proletariat to the tastes of the liberal bourgeoisie, and we will continue to hinder it, for this is our sacred duty. . . .

That is approximately what Comrade Ryadovoi said.

The discussion showed that the majority of the comrades, even some Bundists, supported Comrade Ryadovoi's point of view. And if, after all, the Bolshevik resolution, which noted the mistakes of the Central Committee, was not carried, it was because the consideration "not to cause a split" strongly influenced the comrades. Nor, of course, was the Menshevik vote of confidence in the Central Committee carried. What was carried was simply a motion to pass to the order of the day without appraising the activities of the Central Committee. . . .

———

The discussion on the report of the group in the Duma was, in general, a repetition of the discussion on the preceding question. That is understandable; the group in the Duma acted under the direct guidance of the Central Committee and, naturally, criticism or defence of the Central Committee was at the same time criticism or defence of the group in the Duma.

Of interest were the remarks of Comrade Alexinsky, the second reporter (the first reporter being Comrade Tsereteli), to the effect that the slogan of the group in the Duma, the majority of which was Menshevik, the slogan of unity of the opposition in the Duma, of not splitting the opposition and of the need to march with the Cadets—this Menshevik slogan went completely bankrupt in the Duma, as Comrade Alexinsky put it, because on the most important questions, such as the budget, the army, etc., the Cadets sided with Stolypin, and the Menshevik Social-Democrats were obliged to fight hand in hand with the peasant deputies against the government and the Cadets. The Mensheviks were, in fact, obliged to admit the failure of their position and carry out in the Duma the Bolshevik slogan that the peasant deputies must be won for the struggle against the Rights and the Cadets.

No less interesting were the remarks of the Polish comrades to the effect that it was impermissible for the group in the Duma to agree to joint meetings with the Narodovtsy,[40] those Black Hundreds of Poland, who have more than once in the past organized the massacre of Socialists in Poland and are continuing to do so now. To this, two leaders of the Caucasian Mensheviks,[41] one after another, replied that the important thing for the group in the Duma was not what the various parties did at home, but how they were behaving in the Duma, and that in the Duma the Narodovtsy were behaving more or less like liberals. It follows, therefore, that parties must be judged not by what they *do* outside the Duma, but by what they *say* in the Duma. Opportunism cannot go further than that. . . .

Most of the speakers agreed with the point of view expressed by Comrade Alexinsky, but, for all that, no resolution was adopted on this question either; once again from the consideration "not to offend." The congress set aside the question of the resolution and passed straight on to the next question.

III

THE NON-PROLETARIAN PARTIES

From formal questions we pass to questions of principle, to the questions of our disagreements.

Our disagreements on tactics centre around the questions of the probable fate of our revolution, and of the role of the different classes and parties in Russian society in this revolution. That our revolution is a bourgeois revolution, that it must end in the rout of the feudal and not of the capitalist system, and that it can culminate only in a democratic republic—on this, everybody seems to be agreed in our Party. Further, that, on the whole, the tide of our revolution is rising and not subsiding, and that our task is not to "liquidate" the revolution but to carry it through to the end—on this too, formally at least, everybody is agreed, for the Mensheviks, as a group, have so far not said anything to the contrary. But how is our revolution to be carried through to the end? What is the role of the proletariat, of the peasantry and of the liberal bourgeoisie in this revolution? With what combination of fighting forces would it be possible to carry through this revolution to the end? Whom shall we march with, whom shall we fight? etc., etc. This is where our disagreements begin.

The opinion of the Mensheviks. Since ours is a bourgeois revolution, only the bourgeoisie can be the leader of the revolution. The bourgeoisie was the leader of the great revolution in France, it was the leader of revolutions in other European countries—it must be the leader of our Russian revolution too. The proletariat is the principal fighter in the revolution, but it must march behind the bourgeoisie and push it forward. The peasantry is also a revolutionary force, but it contains too much that is reactionary and, for that reason, the proletariat will have much less occasion to act jointly with it than with the liberal-democratic bourgeoisie. The bourgeoisie is a more reliable ally of the proletariat than the peasantry. It is around the liberal-democratic bourgeoisie, as the leader, that all the fighting forces must rally. Hence, our attitude towards the bourgeois parties must be determined not by the revolutionary thesis: together with the peasantry against the government and the liberal bourgeoisie, with the proletariat at the head— but by the opportunist thesis: together with the entire opposition against the government, with the liberal bourgeoisie at the head. Hence the tactics of compromising with the liberals.

Such is the opinion of the Mensheviks.

The opinion of the Bolsheviks. Ours is, indeed, a bourgeois revolution, but this does not mean that our liberal bourgeoisie will be its leader. In the eighteenth century the French bourgeoisie was the leader of the French revolution, but why? Because the French proletariat was weak, it did not come out independently, it did not put forward its own class demands, it had neither class consciousness nor organization, it then dragged at the tail of the bourgeoisie and the bourgeoisie used it as a tool for its bourgeois aims. As you see, the bourgeoisie was then not in need of an ally in the shape of the tsarist regime against the proletariat—the proletariat itself was the ally and servant of the bourgeoisie—and that is why the latter could then be revolutionary, even march at the head of the revolution. Something entirely different is observed here in Russia. The Russian proletariat can by no means be called weak: for several years already it has been acting quite independently, putting forward its own class demands; it is sufficiently armed with class consciousness to understand its own interests; it is united in its own party; its party is the strongest party in Russia, with its own programme and principles of tactics and organization; led by this party, it has already won a number of brilliant victories over the bourgeoisie. . . . Under these circumstances, can our proletariat be satisfied with the role of tail of the liberal bourgeoisie, the role of a miserable tool in the hands of this bourgeoisie? Can it, must it march behind this bourgeoisie and make it its leader? Can it be anything else than the leader of the revolution? And see what is going on in the camp of our liberal bourgeoisie: our bourgeoisie is terrified by the revolutionary spirit of the proletariat; instead of marching at the head of the revolution it rushes into the embrace of the counter-revolution and enters into an alliance with it against the proletariat. Its party, the Cadet party, openly, before the eyes of the whole world, enters into an agreement with Stolypin, votes for the budget and the army for the benefit of tsarism and against the people's revolution. Is it not clear that the Russian liberal bourgeoisie is an anti-revolutionary force against which the most relentless war must be waged? And was not Comrade Kautsky right when he said that where the proletariat comes out independently the bourgeoisie ceases to be revolutionary? . . .

Thus, the Russian liberal bourgeoisie is anti-revolutionary; it cannot be the driving force of the revolution, and still less can it be its leader; it is the sworn enemy of the revolution and a persistent struggle must be waged against it.

The only leader of our revolution, interested in and capable of leading the revolutionary forces in Russia in the assault upon the tsarist autocracy, is the proletariat. The proletariat alone will rally around itself the revolutionary elements of the country, it alone will carry through our revolution to the end. The task of Social-Democracy is to do everything possible to prepare the proletariat for the role of leader of the revolution.

This is the pivot of the Bolshevik point of view.

To the question: who, then, can be the reliable ally of the proletariat in the task of carrying through our revolution to the end, the Bolsheviks answer—the only ally of the proletariat, to any extent reliable and powerful, is the revolutionary peasantry. Not the treacherous liberal bourgeoisie, but the revolutionary peasantry will fight side by side with the proletariat against all the props of the feudal system.

Accordingly, our attitude towards the bourgeois parties must be determined by the proposition: together with the revolutionary peasantry against tsarism and the liberal bourgeoisie, with the proletariat at the head. Hence the necessity of combating the hegemony (leadership) of the Cadet bourgeoisie and, consequently, the impermissibility of compromising with the Cadets.

Such is the opinion of the Bolsheviks.

It was within the framework of these two positions that the speeches of the reporters—Lenin and Martynov—and of all the other speakers revolved.

Comrade Martynov touched the final depths of "profundity" of the Menshevik point of view by categorically denying that the proletariat should assume hegemony, and also by categorically defending the idea of a bloc with the Cadets.

The other speakers, the vast majority of them, expressed themselves in the spirit of the Bolshevik position.

Of exceptional interest were the speeches of Comrade Rosa Luxemburg, who conveyed greetings to the congress on behalf of the German Social-Democrats and expounded the views of our German comrades on our disagreements. (Here we link together the two speeches R. L. delivered at different times.) Expressing her complete agreement with the Bolsheviks on the questions of the role of the proletariat as the leader of the revolution, the role of the liberal bourgeoisie as an anti-revolutionary force, etc., etc., Rosa Luxemburg criticized the Menshevik leaders Plekhanov and Axelrod, called them opportunists, and put their position on a par with that of the Jaurèsists in France. I know, said Luxemburg, that the Bolsheviks, too, have certain faults and fads, that they are somewhat too rigid, but I fully understand and excuse them: one cannot help being rigid in face of the diffuse and jellylike mass of Menshevik opportunism. The same excessive rigidity was observed among the Guesdists[42] in France, whose leader, Comrade Guesde, stated in a well-known election poster: "Don't let a single bourgeois dare to vote for me, for in Parliament I will defend only the interests of the proletarians against all the bourgeois." In spite of this, in spite of this sharpness, we German Social-Democrats always took the side of the Guesdists in their struggle against the traitors to Marxism, against the Jaurèsists. The same must be said about the Bolsheviks, whom we German Social-Democrats will support in their struggle against the Menshevik opportunists. . . .

That approximately is what Comrade R. Luxemburg said.

Still more interesting was the famous letter the Central Committee of the German Social-Democratic Party sent to the congress, and which Rosa Luxemburg read. It is interesting because, by advising the Party *to fight* liberalism, and recognizing the special role played by the Russian proletariat as the leader of the Russian revolution, by the same token it recognized all the main propositions of Bolshevism.

Thus, it became clear that the German Social-Democratic Party, the most tried and tested and the most revolutionary party in Europe, openly and clearly supported the Bolsheviks, as true Marxists, in their struggle *against* the traitors to Marxism, *against* the Mensheviks.

Of interest also are several passages in the speech
delivered by Comrade Tyszka, the representative of the
Polish delegation in the Presidium. Both groups assure
us, said Comrade Tyszka, that they stand firmly by the
point of view of Marxism. It is not easy for everybody to
understand who it is that really stands by this point of
view, the Bolsheviks or the Mensheviks. . . . "We stand
by the point of view of Marxism"—came an interruption
from several Mensheviks on the "Left." "No, comrades,"
retorted Tyszka, "you do not stand by it, you *lie down*
on it, for all the helplessness you display in leading the
class struggle of the proletariat, the fact that you can
learn by rote the great words of the great Marx but are
unable to apply them—all this shows that you do not
stand by but lie down on the point of view of Marxism."

Aptly put!

Indeed, just take the following fact. The Mensheviks
often say that it is the task of Social-Democracy
always and everywhere to convert the proletariat
into an independent political force. Is this true? Absolutely true! These are the great words of Marx, which
every Marxist should always remember. But how do
the Menshevik comrades apply them? Are they helping
actually to separate the proletariat from the mass of
bourgeois elements which surround it and to form it into
an independent, self-reliant class? Are they rallying the
revolutionary elements around the proletariat and preparing the proletariat for the role of leader of the revolution? The facts show that the Mensheviks are doing
nothing of the kind. On the contrary, the Mensheviks
advise the proletariat to enter more often into agreements
with the liberal bourgeoisie—and thereby they are

helping not to separate the proletariat as an independent class, but to fuse it with the bourgeoisie. The Mensheviks advise the proletariat to renounce the role of leader of the revolution, to cede that role to the bourgeoisie, to follow the bourgeoisie—thereby they are helping to convert the proletariat not into an independent political force, but into an appendage of the bourgeoisie. . . . That is to say, the Mensheviks are doing the very opposite of what they should be doing from the standpoint of the correct Marxist proposition.

Yes, Comrade Tyszka was right when he said that the Mensheviks do not stand by but lie down on the point of view of Marxism. . . .

At the end of the discussion two draft resolutions were submitted: a Menshevik and a Bolshevik resolution. Of these two, the draft submitted by the Bolsheviks was adopted as a basis by an overwhelming majority of votes.

Then came amendments to the draft. About eighty amendments were moved, mainly to two points in the draft: on the point concerning the proletariat as the leader of the revolution, and the point on the Cadets as an anti-revolutionary force. That was the most interesting part of the discussion, for here the complexions of the different groups were revealed in special relief. The first important amendment was moved by Comrade Martov. He demanded that the words "proletariat as the *vanguard*" be substituted for the words "proletariat as the *leader* of the revolution." In support of his amendment he said that the word "vanguard" expressed the idea more precisely. He was answered by Comrade Alexinsky who said that it was not a matter of precision, but of the two opposite points of view that were reflected in this, for "vanguard"

and "leader" are two totally different concepts. To be
the vanguard (the advanced detachment) means fighting
in the front ranks, occupying the points most heavily
under fire, shedding one's blood, but at the same time
being led by others, in this case by the bourgeois democrats;
the vanguard never leads the general struggle, the vanguard is always led. On the other hand, to be a leader
means not only fighting in the front ranks *but also leading
the general struggle, directing* it towards its goal. We
Bolsheviks do not want the proletariat to be led by the
bourgeois democrats, we want the proletariat itself to
lead the whole struggle of the people and direct it
towards the democratic republic.

As a result, Martov's amendment was defeated.

All the other amendments of a similar nature were
also defeated.

Another group of amendments was directed against
the point about the Cadets. The Mensheviks proposed
that it be recognized that the Cadets have not yet taken
the path of counter-revolution. But the congress refused to accept this proposal and all amendments of that
kind were rejected. The Mensheviks further proposed
that in certain cases at least technical agreements with the
Cadets be permitted. The congress also refused to accept
this proposal and defeated all amendments of that kind.

At last the resolution as a whole was voted on and
it turned out that 159 votes were cast for the Bolshevik
resolution, 104 against, the rest abstaining.

The congress adopted the resolution of the Bolsheviks
by a large majority.

From that moment, the point of view of the Bolsheviks became the point of view of the Party.

Furthermore, this vote produced two important results.

First, it put an end to the formal and artificial division of the congress into five groups (Bolsheviks, Mensheviks, Poles, Letts and Bundists) and introduced a new division based on principles: Bolsheviks (including here all the Poles and a majority of the Letts) and Mensheviks (including nearly all the Bundists).

Second, the vote provided the most precise figures showing how the worker delegates were distributed among the groups: it turned out that in the Bolshevik group there were not 38 but 77 workers (38 plus 27 Poles plus 12 Letts), and that in the Menshevik group there were not 30 workers but 39 (30 plus 9 Bundists). The Menshevik group turned out to be a group of intellectuals.

IV

THE LABOUR CONGRESS

Before describing the discussion on the labour congress it is necessary to know the history of this question.* The fact of the matter is that this question is extremely confused and unclear. Whereas on the other points of our disagreements we already have two sharply defined trends in the Party, Bolshevik and Menshevik, on the question of the labour congress we have not two but a whole heap of

---

* This is all the more necessary because the Menshevik comrades who have migrated to the editorial offices of bourgeois newspapers are spreading fables about the past and present of this question (see the article "A Labour Congress," from the pen of a prominent Menshevik, published in *Tovarishch* and reprinted in *Bakinsky Dyen*[43]).

trends, extremely unclear and contradictory. True, the Bolsheviks take a united and definite stand: they are opposed to a labour congress altogether. But among the Mensheviks utter chaos and confusion reign; they have split up into numerous groups, each one singing its own song and paying no heed to the others. Whereas the St. Petersburg Mensheviks, headed by Axelrod, propose that a labour congress be convened for the purpose of *forming a party*, the Moscow Mensheviks, headed by El, propose that it should be convened not for the purpose of forming a party, but *with the object of forming a non-party "All-Russian Workers' League."* The Mensheviks from the South go still further and, headed by Larin,[44] call for the convocation of a labour congress with the object of forming not a party, and not a "Workers' League," *but a wider "Toilers' League"* which, in addition to all the proletarian elements, could embrace also the Socialist-Revolutionary, semi-bourgeois "toiler" elements. I shall not dwell on other, less influential, groups and persons, like the Odessa and trans-Caspian groups, or like those half-witted "authors" of a comical pamphlet who call themselves "Brodyaga" and "Shura."[45]

Such is the confusion that reigns in the ranks of the Mensheviks.

But how is the labour congress to be convened? How is it to be organized? In connection with what is it to be convened? Who is to be invited to it? Who is to take the initiative in convening it?

The same confusion reigns among the Mensheviks on all these questions as on the question of the object of the congress.

While some of them propose that the election of delegates to the congress should be made to coincide with the Duma elections and that the labour congress be thus organized by "unauthorized means," others propose to trust to the government's "connivance" or, in the last resort, to apply for its "permission," while still others advise that the delegates be sent abroad—even if they number three or four thousand—and that the labour congress be held underground there.

While some Mensheviks propose that only definitely formed workers' organizations be allowed to send representatives to the congress, others advise inviting representatives of the entire organized and unorganized proletariat, which numbers not less than ten millions.

While some Mensheviks propose that the labour congress be convened on the initiative of the Social-Democratic Party with the participation of intellectuals, others advise that the Party and the intellectuals be thrust aside, and that the congress be convened only on the initiative of the workers themselves, without the participation of any intellectuals.

While some Mensheviks insist on a labour congress being convened immediately, others propose that it be postponed indefinitely, and that, meanwhile, only agitation in favour of the idea of a labour congress be conducted.

But what is to be done with the existing Social-Democratic Labour Party which has been leading the proletarian struggle for several years already, which has united 150,000 members in its ranks, which has already held five congresses, etc., etc.! "Send it to the devil?" Or what?

In answer to this, all the Mensheviks, from Axelrod to Larin, declare unanimously that *we have no proletarian party*. "The whole point is that we have no party," said the Mensheviks at the congress. "*All we have is an organization of petty-bourgeois intellectuals*," which must be replaced by a party with the aid of a labour congress. That is what Comrade Axelrod, the Menshevik reporter, said at the Party congress.

But wait! What does that mean? Does it mean that all the congresses our Party has held, from the first (1898) to the latest (1907), in the organization of which the Menshevik comrades took a most energetic part, that all the colossal expenditure of proletarian money and effort involved in the organization of these congresses—and for which the Mensheviks are as much responsible as the Bolsheviks—does it mean that all this was mere deception and hypocrisy?!

Does it mean that all the fighting appeals the Party has issued to the proletariat, appeals which the Mensheviks also signed, that all the strikes and insurrections of 1905, 1906 and 1907, which flared up with the Party at their head, and often on the Party's initiative, that all the victories achieved by the proletariat headed by our Party, that the thousands of proletarian victims who fell in the streets of St. Petersburg, Moscow, and elsewhere, who were immured in Siberia and who perished in prison *for the sake of* the Party, and *under the banner* of the Party— that all that was just a farce and a deception?

So we have no party? We have only "an organization of petty-bourgeois intellectuals"?

Of course, that was a downright lie; an outrageous, brazen lie.

That, evidently, explains the boundless indignation which the above-mentioned statement by Axelrod roused among the worker delegates from St. Petersburg and Moscow. They jumped to their feet and energetically answered the reporter Axelrod: "You, who spend your time abroad, are bourgeois, not we. We are workers, and we have our Social-Democratic Party, and we will not allow anyone to defame it. ". . .

But let us suppose that a labour congress is held; let us imagine that it has already been held. The existing Social-Democratic Party therefore has been put into the archives, a labour congress has been convened in some way or another, and we want to organize at it a league of "workers" or "toilers," whatever it may be. Well, what next? What programme will this congress adopt? What will be the complexion of the labour congress?

Some Mensheviks answer that the labour congress could adopt the programme of Social-Democracy, with certain deletions, of course; but they at once add that it might not adopt the programme of Social-Democracy and that this, in their opinion, would not be particulàrly harmful to the proletariat. Others answer more emphatically as follows: Since our proletariat is strongly imbued with petty-bourgeois tendencies, in all probability the labour congress will adopt not a Social-Democratic but a *petty-bourgeois democratic programme*. At the labour congress the proletariat will lose the Social-Democratic programme, but instead it will acquire a workers' organization that will unite all the workers in one league. That is what, for example, N. Cherevanin, the head of the Moscow Mensheviks, says (see "Problems of Tactics").[46]

And so: "A workers' league without a Social-Democratic programme"—such is the probable result of a labour congress.

That, at all events, is what the Mensheviks themselves think.

Evidently, while they disagree with one another on certain questions concerning the objects of the labour congress and the methods of convening it, the Mensheviks are agreed among themselves on the point that "we have no party, all we have is an organization of petty-bourgeois intellectuals, *which ought to be put into the archives.*". . .

It was within this framework that Axelrod's report revolved.

It became evident from Axelrod's report that agitation for a labour congress would practically and inevitably amount to agitation *against* the party, a war against it.

And the practical work of convening the labour congress would also inevitably amount to practical work in disorganizing and undermining our present party.

And yet the Mensheviks—through the mouth of their reporter, and also in their draft resolution—requested the congress *to prohibit agitation* against attempts to organize a labour congress, i.e., against attempts leading to disorganization of the Party.

It is interesting to note that, running through the speeches of the Menshevik speakers (with the exception of Plekhanov, who said nothing about the labour congress), were the slogans: "Down with the Party, down with Social-Democracy—long live the non-party principle, long live the non-Social-Democratic 'Workers' League.'" These slogans were not openly advanced by the speakers, but they ran as an undertone through their speeches.

It is not without reason that all the bourgeois writers, from the Syndicalists and Socialist-Revolutionaries to the Cadets and Octobrists—all so ardently express themselves in favour of a labour congress; after all, they are all enemies of our Party, and the practical work of convening a labour congress might considerably weaken and disorganize the Party. Why should they not welcome "the idea of a labour congress"?

The Bolshevik speakers said something entirely different.

The Bolshevik reporter, Comrade Lindov,[47] after briefly characterizing the main trends among the Mensheviks, proceeded to trace the conditions which gave rise to the idea of a labour congress. Agitation for a labour congress began in 1905, before the October days, during the repressions. It ceased during the October-November days. During the subsequent months of fresh repression, agitation for a labour congress revived. During the period of the First Duma, in the days of relative freedom, the agitation subsided. Then, after the dispersion of the Duma, it grew again, etc. The conclusion to be drawn is clear: in the period of relative freedom, when the Party is able to expand freely, there is naturally no ground for agitation for a labour congress with the object of forming "a broad non-party party." On the other hand, during periods of repression, when the influx of new members into the Party gives way to an exodus, agitation for a labour congress, as an artificial measure for widening the narrow party, or replacing it by "a broad non-party party," finds some ground. But it goes without saying that no artificial measures will be of any avail, for what is needed for the actual expansion of the Party is political freedom and not a labour congress, which itself needs such freedom.

To proceed. The idea of a labour congress, taken concretely, is fundamentally false, for it rests not on facts, but on the false proposition that "we have no party." The point is that we have a proletarian party which loudly proclaims its existence, and whose existence is felt only too well by the enemies of the proletariat—the Mensheviks are fully aware of this—and precisely because we already have such a party, the idea of a labour congress is fundamentally false. Of course, if we did not have a party numbering over 150,000 advanced proletarians in its ranks, and leading hundreds of thousands of fighters, if we were only a tiny handful of uninfluential people as the German Social-Democrats were in the 'sixties, or the French Socialists in the 'seventies of the last century, we ourselves would try to convene a labour congress with the object of squeezing a Social-Democratic Party out of it. But the whole point is that we already have a party, a real proletarian party, which exercises enormous influence among the masses, and to convene a labour congress, to form a fantastic "non-party party," we would, inevitably, first of all have to "put an end" to the existing party, we would first of all have to wreck it.

That is why, in practice, the work of convening a labour congress must inevitably amount to a work of disorganizing the Party. And whether success could ever be achieved in forming "a broad non-party party" in place of it, and indeed, whether such a party ought to be formed, is questionable.

That is why the enemies of our Party, the Cadets and Octobrists, and the like, so heartily praise the Mensheviks for their agitation in favour of a labour congress.

That is why the Bolsheviks think that the work of convening a labour congress would be dangerous, would be harmful, for it would discredit the Party in the eyes of the masses and subject them to the influence of bourgeois democracy.

That is approximately what Comrade Lindov said.

For a labour congress and against the Social-Democratic Party? Or, for the Party and against a labour congress?

This is how the question stood at the congress.

The Bolshevik worker delegates understood the question at once and vigorously came out "in defence of the Party": "We are Party patriots," they said. "We love our Party, and we shall not allow tired intellectuals to discredit it."

It is interesting to note that Comrade Rosa Luxemburg, the representative of German Social-Democracy, entirely agreed with the Bolsheviks. "We German Social-Democrats," she said, "cannot understand the comical dismay of the Menshevik comrades who are groping for the masses when the masses themselves are looking for the Party and are irresistibly pressing towards it."...

The discussion showed that the vast majority of the speakers supported the Bolsheviks.

At the end of the discussion two draft resolutions were submitted to a vote: a Bolshevik draft and a Menshevik draft. Of these two, the Bolshevik draft was accepted as a basis. Nearly all amendments on points of principle were rejected. Only one more or less important amendment was accepted, viz., against restricting freedom to discuss the question of a labour congress. The resolution as a whole stated that "the idea of convening a labour congress leads to the disorganization of the Party," "to the subjection of the broad masses of the workers to the influence of bourgeois democracy," and, as such, is harmful to the proletariat. Moreover, the resolution drew a strict distinction between a labour congress and Soviets of Workers' Deputies and their congresses which, far from disorganizing the Party and competing with it, strengthen the Party by following its lead and helping it to solve practical problems in periods of revolutionary upsurge.

Finally the resolution as a whole was adopted by a majority of 165 votes against 94. The rest of the delegates abstained from voting.

Thus, the congress rejected the idea of a labour congress as harmful and anti-Party.

The voting on this question revealed to us the following important fact. Of the 114 worker delegates who took part in the voting, only 25 voted for a labour congress. The rest voted against it. Expressed in percentages, 22 per cent of the worker delegates voted for a labour congress, while 78 per cent voted against it. What is particularly important is that of the 94 delegates who voted for a labour congress, only 26 per cent were workers and 74 per cent were intellectuals.

And yet the Mensheviks shouted all the time that the idea of a labour congress was a workers' idea, that it was only the Bolshevik "intellectuals" who were opposing the convocation of a congress, etc. Judging by this vote, one should rather admit that, on the contrary, the idea of a labour congress is the idea of intellectual dreamers. . . .

Apparently, even the Menshevik workers did not vote for the labour congress: of the 39 worker delegates (30 Mensheviks plus 9 Bundists) only 24 voted for a labour congress.

Baku, 1907

First published in the
Bakinsky Proletary, Nos. 1 and 2,
June 20 and July 10, 1907

Signed: *Koba Ivanovich*

MANDATE TO THE SOCIAL-DEMOCRATIC DEPUTIES IN THE THIRD STATE DUMA

*Adopted at a Meeting of the Delegates
of the Workers' Curia in the City of Baku,
September 22, 1907[48]*

The Social-Democratic deputies in the State Duma must form a separate group which, as a Party organization, must be most closely connected with the Party, and must submit to its guidance and to the directives of the Central Committee of the Party.

The main task of the Social-Democratic group in the State Duma is to facilitate the proletariat's class education and class struggle both for the emancipation of the working people from capitalist exploitation and for the fulfilment of the part of political leader which it is called upon to play in the present bourgeois-democratic revolution in Russia.

For this purpose, the group must under all circumstances pursue its own proletarian class policy, which distinguishes Social-Democracy from all other organizations and revolutionary parties, from the Cadets to the Socialist-Revolutionaries. It must not under any circumstances sacrifice this task to the aim of conducting joint oppositional action with any other political parties or groups in the Duma.

Our deputies must systematically expose in the Duma the entire counter-revolutionary nature both of the Black-Hundred landlord parties and of the treacherous,

liberal-monarchist, bourgeois, Cadet Party. On the other
hand, they must strive to wrest the peasant petty-
bourgeois parties (Socialist-Revolutionaries, Popular
Socialists and Trudoviks) from the liberals, push them on
to the path of consistent democratic-revolutionary policy,
and lead them in the struggle both against the Black
Hundreds and against the Cadet bourgeoisie. At the same
time, the Social-Democratic group must combat the
reactionary, pseudo-socialist utopias in which the
Socialist-Revolutionaries, Popular Socialists and others
clothe what are in fact petty-bourgeois demands, and
with the aid of which they obscure the purely proletarian,
socialist class consciousness of the working class. From
the floor of the Duma our group must tell the entire
people the whole truth about the revolution through
which we are passing. It must loudly proclaim to the
people that in Russia their emancipation cannot be
achieved by peaceful means, that the only path to
freedom is the path of a nation-wide struggle against
the tsarist regime.

The slogan which Social-Democracy advances, and for
which it must call upon the masses to launch another
open struggle, is for a Constituent Assembly freely elected by the whole people on the basis of universal, direct,
equal and secret suffrage, an assembly which will put
an end to the tsarist autocracy and establish a democratic
republic in Russia. No other slogans, such as a responsible ministry, etc., advanced by the liberal bourgeoisie
in opposition to the proletarian slogans, can be accepted
and supported by the Social-Democratic group.

In taking part in the daily legislative and other activities of the State Duma, the Social-Democratic group

must pursue its constant tasks of criticism and agitation and not pursue the object of direct legislation; and it must explain to the people that such legislation is ephemeral and futile so long as real power remains entirely in the hands of the autocratic government.

By working in the Third State Duma in this way, the Social-Democratic group will facilitate the revolutionary struggle which the proletariat, and the peasantry along with it, are at present waging against the tsarist autocracy outside the Duma.

Published in leaflet form
in September 1907

Reprinted from the leaflet

BOYCOTT THE CONFERENCE![49]

The question whether to participate in or to boycott the conference with the oil owners is not a question
of principle for us, but one of practical expediency. We
cannot lay down a hard and fast rule to boycott every
conference, as certain embittered and not quite sane "individuals" propose. Nor can we lay down a hard and fast
rule to participate in every conference, as our Cadet-like
comrades manage to do. We must approach the question
of participation or boycott from the point of view of
living facts, and of facts alone. It may turn out that,
given certain facts, certain conditions, our task of uniting the masses will make our participation imperative
—and in that case we must certainly participate. Given
other conditions, however, that same task may render
a boycott imperative—and in that case we must certainly boycott the conference.

Furthermore, to avoid confusion, we must first of
all define the concepts with which we are operating.
What does "participating" in a conference mean? What
does "boycotting" a conference mean? If, in formulat-
ing common demands, electing delegates, etc., etc., at
meetings, our aim is not to prevent the conference from
being held, but, on the contrary, to go to the conference
in order, submitting to and relying on its standing
orders, to negotiate with the oil owners and in the

end reach an agreement of some kind—we must describe such behaviour on our part as participation in the conference. But if, in drawing up demands, electing delegates to formulate these demands better, and in popularizing and publishing the demands that have been formulated, our aim is not to participate in the proceedings of a conference with the oil owners, but to prevent the conference from being held, to frustrate any agreement with the oil owners *before a fight* (we think an agreement *after a fight*, especially after a successful fight, is essential)—then we must describe our conduct as boycotting the conference; active boycotting, of course, because it will result in the prevention of the conference.

Under no circumstances must tactics towards a conference be confused with tactics towards the Duma. The object of participating in or boycotting a conference is to prepare the ground for an improvement of the conditions prevailing *in the oil fields*, whereas the object of going into or boycotting the Duma is to *improve* general conditions *in the country*. The fate of a conference is determined wholly and *exclusively* by the proletariat in the given locality, for, if the proletariat does not participate, the conference automatically falls through, whereas the issue whether to go into or to boycott the Duma is determined not by the proletariat alone, but also by the peasantry. And finally, an active boycott of a conference (its prevention) can be conveniently carried out without active operations, and this is not the case with the results of boycotting the Duma.

After these general remarks, we shall proceed to the concrete question of boycotting the forthcoming conference.

The history of the economic struggle waged by the Baku workers may be divided into two periods.

The first period is the period of struggle up to recent times, during which the principal roles were played by the mechanics, while the oil workers[50] simply and trustfully followed the mechanics as their leaders and were as yet unconscious of the enormously important part they played in production. The tactics pursued by the oil owners during that period may be described as the tactics of flirting with the mechanics, tactics of systematic concessions to the mechanics, and of equally systematic ignoring of the oil workers.

The second period opens with the awakening of the oil workers, their independent entry on to the scene, and the simultaneous pushing of the mechanics into the background. But this entry bore the character of a burlesque, for 1) it went no further than the shameful demand for bonuses, and 2) it was tinged with the most fatal distrust towards the mechanics. The oil owners are trying to take advantage of the changed situation and are changing their tactics. They are no longer flirting with the mechanics; they are no longer trying to cajole the mechanics, for they know perfectly well that the oil workers will not always follow them now; on the contrary, the oil owners themselves are trying to provoke the mechanics to go on strike *without the oil workers*, in order, thereby, to demonstrate the relative weakness of the mechanics and make them submissive. Parallel with this, the oil owners, who previously had paid no attention to the oil workers, are now most brazenly flirting with them and treating them to bonuses. In this way they are trying completely to divorce the oil workers from the mechanics, utterly to corrupt them, to infect them with slavish faith in the oil owners, to replace the principle of uncompromising struggle by the "principle" of haggling and obsequious begging, and thus make all real improvement impossible.

It was with these objects in view that the forthcoming conference was "thought up."

Hence it is obvious that the immediate task of the advanced comrades is to launch a desperate struggle to win over the oil workers, a struggle to rally the oil workers around their comrades the mechanics *by imbuing their minds with utter distrust of the oil owners, by obliterating from their minds the pernicious prejudices in favour of haggling and begging.* We must loudly and sharply tell (not only in words but with facts!) the masses of the oil workers who have come on to the scene for the first time, and in such a clumsy and burlesque fashion at that ("beshkesh,"[51] etc.), that improvements in conditions of life are not granted from above, nor as a result of haggling, but are obtained from below, by means of a general struggle jointly with the mechanics.

Only if we have this task in mind can we correctly settle the question of the conference.

And so, we think that participation in the forthcoming conference, a call for co-operation between the oil owners and the workers with the object of drawing up a binding agreement now, before a general struggle, when there is still the partial struggle, when the general struggle still lies ahead, when the oil owners are handing out bonuses right and left, divorcing the oil workers from the mechanics and corrupting their

newly awakened consciousness, we think that *"to go to
the conference"* in such a situation means not obliterating but still more strongly ingraining "beshkesh" prejudices in the minds of the masses. It means imbuing
the minds of the masses not with distrust of the oil owners,
but with trust in them. It means not rallying the oil
workers around the mechanics, not drawing them nearer
to the mechanics, but abandoning them for a time, throwing them back into the clutches of the capitalists.

Of course, "it's an ill wind that blows nobody any
good." At the present moment a conference may also be
of *some* use in the organizational sense, in the sense of
"extending the struggle," as Comrade *Kochegar*[52] expresses
it. But if the harm caused by the conference undoubtedly exceeds this *some* use, then the conference must
undoubtedly be cast aside like useless lumber. For if
Comrade *Kochegar* is ready "to go to the conference"
mainly on the grounds that this conference "organizes"
and "extends the struggle," then we simply cannot understand why it would not be right "to go to the conference"
also when the tide of the movement is rising, on the
eve of a general struggle, at the beginning of a general
struggle that is being organized. What is there to be
afraid of? At such a time "general organization" and
"extension of the struggle" are especially necessary, are
they not? At such a time the masses should least of
all fall for concessions from above, should they not? But
the whole point is that electing delegates in itself does
not mean organizing the masses. The whole point is that
to organize (in *our* and not in the Gapon sense of the
term, of course) means *first of all* developing consciousness of the *irreconcilable* antagonism between the capi-

talists and the workers. So long as *that* consciousness exists, all the rest will come of itself.

This is exactly what the forthcoming conference cannot do.

In view of this, the only tactics in keeping with our task under present conditions are the tactics of boycotting the conference.

The boycott tactics best of all develop consciousness of the irreconcilable antagonism between the workers and the oil owners.

The boycott tactics, by shattering "beshkesh" prejudices and divorcing the oil workers from the oil owners, rally them around the mechanics.

The boycott tactics, by imbuing distrust of the oil owners, best of all emphasize in the eyes of the masses the necessity of fighting as the only means of improving their conditions of life.

That is why we must launch a boycott campaign: organize works meetings, draw up demands, elect delegates for the better formulation of common demands, distribute the demands in printed form, explain them, bring them to the masses again for final endorsement, etc., etc., and we must do all this under the slogan of boycott in order, after popularizing the common demands and utilizing the "legal possibilities," to boycott the conference, make a laughingstock of it, and thereby emphasize the necessity of a struggle for common demands.

And so—boycott the conference!

Gudok, No. 4,
September 29, 1907
Signed: *Ko*. . . .   Reprinted from the newspaper

BEFORE THE ELECTIONS

Messrs. the oil owners have retreated. Only recently they stated through the editor of their newspaper, *Neftyanoye Delo*,[53] that the trade unions in Baku are "an adventitious element standing apart from the workers." In obedience to their will, the authorities posted up notices inviting the workers to elect delegates to an organizing committee, wishing thereby to remove the trade unions from the leadership of the campaign. That was the case yesterday. But now, on January 7, the factory inspector has informed the trade union secretaries that the oil owners have held a meeting at which they decided to request the City Governor to grant the trade unions permits to hold meetings in the oil fields and at the works.

Messrs. the capitalists are afraid of the growing influence of the trade unions; they would like to see the workers in a state of disunity and disorganization, and with this object they refuse to recognize even the oil field and works commissions. But we have now compelled them to admit that the task of guiding the settlement of one of the most important questions of working-class life, the question of a conference and a collective agreement, is and must be the task of the trade unions.

We have compelled them to recognize the leading role played by the trade unions, despite the fact that Messrs. the Dashnaktsakans[54] and Socialist-Revolutionaries came to the aid of Messrs. the oil owners and the authorities in their struggle against the workers' organizations.

Messrs. the Dashnaktsakans hurriedly responded to the call of the City Governor and immediately proceeded with the elections, in pursuit of their own ends, of course—to evade the conditions demanded by the trade unions for the conduct of the campaign, and above all the principal condition—recognition of the workers' organizations.

But Messrs. the oil owners were not satisfied with the hurried activity of the Dashnaktsakans. The latter had a following only among the workers employed by the smaller firms, such as Abiyants, Raduga, Ararat, Pharos and others, and at the big Armenian firms elections took place only at two or three.

The workers employed by the Caspian-Black Sea Company, Nobel's, Kokorev's, Born's, Shibayev's, Asadullayev's, the Moscow-Caucasus Company, and other firms, passed resolutions protesting against these elections and refused to take part in them until permits were issued to the trade unions.

The workers employed at the largest and most influential firms clearly and definitely expressed their will, and thereby answered not only Messrs. the oil owners, but also those "friends" of theirs who are fond of talking too eloquently about nothing.

By their resolutions the workers clearly and definitely confirmed the fact that the conditions demanded by the trade unions were not the inventions of "leaders," as the Socialist-Revolutionaries assert in their pamphlet *Why We Are Not Going to the Conference.*

The authorities, the oil owners and the Dashnaktsakans are trying to counteract the growing influence of the trade unions. The workers are expressing their confidence in the trade unions and their agreement with the conditions which the trade unions are demanding.

The workers are not and must not be scared by the words "conference" and "negotiations," any more than they are scared by the prospect of negotiations and of putting forward demands on the eve of a strike. The presentation of demands sometimes removes the necessity of a strike to settle a dispute. Most often, the opposite happens. But in order that "negotiations" may unfold before the workers the whole picture of the present state of affairs, in order that the campaign around the conference may render the workers inestimable service by securing the wide presentation and public discussion of all questions affecting the workers' lives, the conditions demanded by the trade unions, which will be included in the instructions to the elected delegates, must be conceded.

No negotiations are "terrible" if they are conducted in sight of the masses of the workers. The conditions that are demanded ensure the possibility of the wide participation of all the workers in the discussion of all the questions connected with the conference.

Conferences of the Shendrikov type, of sad memory, have been buried forever.

We have succeeded in persuading the comrades "associated" with the mechanics' union to follow our lead and to abandon the slogan of "a conference at all costs." And they have decided to boycott the elections if the principal condition, recognition of the leading importance of the trade unions, is not conceded. And we shall see to it that there will be no more supporters of boycott "at all costs." A conference, and what is the chief thing, a campaign around the conference, will be acceptable to the workers if the necessary conditions for it are provided.

The workers, by the resolutions they passed recently, have confirmed the correctness of our position.

Permits have been issued to us. Hence, we have obtained from the authorities and the oil owners recognition of the leading role of the unions.

The majority of the workers employed by the larger firms have declared in favour of participating in the elections on the conditions that we have indicated.

We can now calmly and confidently proceed with the election of delegates who, we advise, should be given the following instructions: let the sixteen representatives whom you elect be such as will demand, as an absolute condition for conducting negotiations in the organizing committee, the recognition *primarily* of the following points:

1) The date of the conference to be decided by the delegates of the workers and employers as equal parties, i.e., by mutual agreement.

2) The general assembly of delegates, elected at the rate of one for every hundred workers, to remain in session until the end of the conference, to meet

periodically, and, as circumstances demand, to discuss the reports of the workers' representatives at the conference and to give them guiding instructions.

3) Delegates to have the right to organize meetings at works, oil fields and workshops to discuss the terms of the agreement demanded and offered.

4) The executives of the oil industry workers' and mechanics' trade unions to have the right to send to the conference with the oil owners representatives with right of voice but not of vote, and also to have the right to report to all conference committees, delegate meetings, works and oil field meetings, etc.

5) Representatives on the organizing committee are to be elected by the Delegate Council as a whole, without division according to craft. Negotiations in the organizing committee are also to be conducted as a whole (a single agreement for all the workers).

Gudok, No. 14,   Reprinted from the newspaper
January 13, 1908
Unsigned

MORE ABOUT A CONFERENCE
WITH GUARANTEES

The conference campaign is at its height. The election of delegates is drawing to a close. The Delegate Council will meet in the near future. Is there to be a conference or not? With what guarantees (conditions) is a conference desirable? How are these guarantees to be understood? Such, primarily, are the questions with which the Delegate Council will deal.

What should be our line of conduct on the Delegate Council?

We repeat that conferences with the oil owners are not a novelty for us. We had a conference in 1905. We had a second in 1906. What did we get out of these conferences? What did they teach us? Was it worth while holding them?

At that time, and again quite recently, we were told that conferences *by themselves*, without any conditions, unite the masses. The facts, however, have shown that neither of the two past conferences united the masses, nor could they do so—only elections were held, and with this all the "uniting" ended.

Why?

Because in organizing the past conferences there was not even a hint of any kind of *freedom of speech and assembly*, it was impossible to assemble the masses at the works—in the oil fields—and in their living quarters, to draw up instructions on each point, and generally to intervene actively in all the affairs of the conference. Consequently, the masses were obliged to remain idle; only the representatives were active, far away from the masses of the workers. But we have known for a long time that the masses can be organized only during action. . . .

Further—because there was no *Delegate Council* acting freely as a permanent organ of the workers all the time the conference was in session, uniting around itself the workers in all firms and districts, drawing up the demands of these workers, and controlling the workers' representatives on the basis of these demands. The oil owners would not permit the formation of such a Delegate Council, while the initiators of the conference meekly resigned themselves to this.

This is quite apart from the fact that at that time there were no such centres of the movement as the *trade unions*, which could rally the Delegate Council around themselves and direct it along the path of the class struggle. . . .

At one time we were told that a conference, even *by itself*, could satisfy the demands of the workers. But the experience of the first two conferences has refuted this assumption too, for when our representatives at the first conference began to talk about the workers' demands, the oil owners interrupted them and said that "this is not on the agenda of the conference," that the function of the conference was to discuss the "supply of liquid fuel for industry," and not demands of any

kind. When our representatives at the second conference demanded that representatives of the unemployed
also be allowed to take part, the oil owners again
interrupted them and said that they had no authority to
deal with demands of that kind. With that our representatives were thrown out by the scruff of the neck. And when
some of the comrades raised the question of backing our
representatives by means of a general struggle—it turned out
that such a struggle was impossible because the capitalists
had arranged both conferences in the slack season favourable for themselves, in the winter, when navigation on
the Volga was closed, when the price of oil products
was dropping and, consequently, when it was quite senseless even to think of a victory for the workers.

That is how "worth while" the two previous conferences were.

Clearly, a conference *by itself*, a conference without
a free Delegate Council, a conference without the participation and guidance of the unions, and moreover
one called in the winter—in short, *a conference without
guarantees*—is merely an empty sound. Far from uniting
the workers and facilitating the achievement of our
demands, such a conference can only disorganize the
workers and put off the satisfaction of our demands, for
it feeds the workers on empty promises, while giving
them nothing.

That is what the two preceding conferences have
taught us.

That is why the class-conscious proletariat boycotted
the third conference in November 1907.

Let this be remembered by those individual comrades
in the mechanics' union who are agitating for a conference

without guarantees, in spite of the entire experience
of the previous conferences, in spite of the will of
the majority of the proletariat in the oil industry,
*and, lastly, in spite of the agreement reached between the
unions*!

Let them remember this and not violate this agreement.

But does this mean that we must wave aside all conferences?

No, it does not!

To the remarks of the boycottist Socialist-Revolutionaries that we must not go to the conference because
our enemy, the bourgeoisie, is inviting us to it, we can
answer only with a laugh. After all it is the same enemy,
the bourgeoisie, who invites us to go to work in the
factories, at the works, or in the oil fields. Should we
therefore boycott the factories, works or oil fields only
because our enemy, the bourgeoisie, invites us to them?
If we did, we might all die of starvation! If that argument were sound, it would mean that all the workers
have taken leave of their senses by going to work on the
invitation of the bourgeoisie!

As for the statement made by the Dashnaktsakans
that we must not go to the conference because it is a
bourgeois institution—we need not pay any attention
whatever to this absurd statement. After all, present-
day social life is also a bourgeois "institution," the
factories, works and oil fields are all bourgeois "institutions," organized "in the image of" the bourgeoisie,
and for the benefit of the bourgeoisie. Shall we boycott
all these merely because they are bourgeois? If so, where
shall we migrate to, to Mars, Jupiter, or perhaps to the

castles in the air built by the Dashnaktsakans and
Socialist-Revolutionaries? . . .*

No, comrades! We must not turn our backs on the
positions of the bourgeoisie, we must face and storm
them! We must not leave the bourgeoisie in possession of
their positions, we must capture them, step by step, and
eject the bourgeoisie from them! Only those who live in
castles in the air can fail to understand this simple truth!

We shall not go to the conference if we do not receive
in advance the guarantees we demand. But if we
obtain the guarantees we demand, we shall go to the
conference in order, by relying on these guarantees,
to transform the conference from a begging instrument
into a weapon in the further struggle, in the same way as
we go to work, after certain necessary conditions are
satisfied, in order to transform the factories, works and
oil fields from an arena of oppression into an arena of
emancipation.

By organizing a conference with guarantees won by
the workers, and by calling upon the mass of fifty thousand workers to elect a Delegate Council and to draw
up our demands, we shall lead the working-class movement in Baku on to a new road of struggle advantageous to
it, on to the road of an organized and class-conscious and
not of a spontaneous (disunited) and beshkesh movement.

---

* That the boycottist stand taken by Messrs. the Dashnaktsakans and Socialist-Revolutionaries is utterly inconsistent and un-
realistic is proved by the very fact that they themselves are favourably inclined towards a conference between the typographical
workers and their employers, and towards a collective agreement
between them. Furthermore, individual members of these parties
are even permitted to take a hand in this matter.

7*

That, properly speaking, is what we expect from a conference with guarantees; that is why we say: *a conference with guarantees, or no conference at all!*[55]

Let the gentlemen who supported the old type of conference agitate against guarantees; let them extol conferences without guarantees; let them flounder in the Zubatov marsh—the proletariat will drag them out of the marsh and teach them to walk through the wide fields of the class struggle!

Let Messrs. the Dashnaktsakans and Socialist-Revolutionaries "soar"; let them boycott the organized action of the workers from their lofty heights. The class-conscious proletariat will pull them down to this sinful earth and compel them to bow their heads before a conference with guarantees!

Our object is clear: to gather the proletariat around the Delegate Council and to rally the latter around the unions for the achievement of our common demands, for the improvement of our conditions of life.

Our road is clear: from a conference with guarantees to the satisfaction of the vital needs of the proletariat in the oil industry.

In due time we shall call upon the Delegate Council to fight both the marsh-dweller supporters of a conference and the fairy-tale fantasies of the Socialist-Revolutionary and Dashnak boycottists.

A conference with certain guarantees, or a conference is unnecessary!

Gudok, No. 17,   Reprinted from the newspaper
February 3, 1908
Unsigned

WHAT DO OUR RECENT STRIKES TELL US?

Characteristic of the January and February strikes are certain new features, which introduce new elements into our movement. One of these features—the defensive character of the strikes—has already been mentioned in *Gudok*.[56] But that is an external feature. Of much greater interest are the other, internal features, which throw a clear light on the development of our movement. We have in mind the character of the demands, the methods of waging the strikes, the new methods of struggle, etc.

The first thing that strikes one is the content of the demands. It is characteristic that in a considerable number of the strikes no demands for bonuses were put forward (at Nobel's, Motovilikha, Molot, Mirzoyev's, Adamov's and others). Where demands for bonuses were put forward, the workers, ashamed to fight only for "beshkesh," tried to put them at the end of their lists of demands (at Pitoyev's and others). Evidently, the old beshkesh habits are breaking down. "Beshkesh" is beginning to lose importance in the eyes of the workers. From petty-bourgeois demands (for bonuses), the workers are passing to proletarian demands: dismissal of the more arrogant managers (at Nobel's, Molot, Adamov's), reinstatement of discharged comrades (at Mirzoyev's), extension of the rights of the oil field and works commission (at Nobel's, Mirzoyev's). In this respect, the strike at Mirzoyev's is of special interest.[57] The workers at this firm demand recognition of the commission and the reinstatement of discharged comrades as a guarantee that the firm will not discharge a single worker in future without the consent of the commission. The strike has already lasted two weeks, and is being conducted with rare solidarity. One must see these workers, one must know with what pride they say: "We are not fighting for bonuses, or for towels and soap, but for the rights and the honour of the workers' commission"—one must know all this, I say, to realize what a change has taken place in the minds of the workers.

The second feature of the recent strikes is the awakening and activity of the masses of the oil workers. The point is that up to now the oil workers had to follow the mechanics, and they did not always follow them willingly; they rose independently only for bonuses. Moreover, a certain hostility towards the *mechanics* existed among them, and this was fanned by the provocative beshkesh policy of the oil owners (the Bibi-Eibat Company last year, and Lapshin's recently). The recent strikes show that the passivity of the oil workers is receding into the past. It was they who started the strike at Nobel's (in January) and the mechanics followed their lead; the strike at Mirzoyev's (in February) was also inspired by the oil workers. It goes without saying that with the awakening activity of the oil workers, their hostility towards the mechanics is waning. The oil workers are beginning to go hand in hand with the mechanics.

Of still greater interest is the third feature—the friendly attitude of the strikers towards our union and, in general, the relatively well-organized way in which the strikes were conducted. Characteristic, first of all, is the absence of yard-long' lists of demands, which hindered the successful conduct of strikes (recall the strike at the Caspian Company last year); now only a few important demands capable of uniting the masses are put forward (at Nobel's, Mirzoyev's, Motovilikha, Molot, and Adamov's). Secondly, hardly any of these strikes take place without the active intervention of the union: the workers consider it necessary to invite representatives of the union (at Kokorev's, Nobel's, Molot, Mirzoyev's, and others). The rivalry that formerly existed between the oil field and works commissions on the one hand and the union on the other is becoming a thing of the past. The workers are beginning to regard the union as their own offspring. Instead of being the union's competitors, the oil field and works commissions are becoming its supporters. This explains the larger degree of organization observed in the recent strikes.

From this follows the fourth feature—the relative success of the recent strikes, or rather, the fact that partial strikes do not fail so often, and then not always completely. We have in mind primarily the strike at Kokorev's. We think that the strike at Kokorev's marked a turning point in the development of our methods of struggle. It and several other strikes (at Pitoyev's and Motovilikha) show that, given 1) the organized conduct of the strikes, 2) the active intervention of the union, 3) a certain amount of perseverance and 4) the right choice of the moment for launching the struggle, partial strikes may be far from fruitless. At all events, it has become clear that those who "on principle" cry: "Down with partial strikes!" are advancing a risky slogan which is not sufficiently justified by the facts of the recent movement. On the contrary, we think that, given leadership by the union and the right choice of the moment to launch the struggle, partial strikes can be converted into a very important factor in uniting the proletariat.

Such, in our opinion, are the most important internal features of the recent strikes.

Gudok, No. 21,   Reprinted from the newspaper
March 2, 1908
Signed: *K. Kato*

THE CHANGE IN THE OIL OWNERS' TACTICS

Not so long ago—just a few months back—our oil owners were "talking" about "European-style" relations between workers and employers.

At that time they tried to behave in a conciliatory manner. This is understandable: the incessant preaching of the "meditative" Rin on the divine origin of collective agreements, the growing wave of partial strikes, the oil owners' expectations of being able to "regulate production" by means of a "European-style" conference, and the pressure exercised to some extent by the authorities—all this put the oil owners in a conciliatory, "European" mood.

"Down with the anarchy of strikes!"—exclaimed Rin.

"Long live order!" responded the oil owners, in harmony with Rin.

And it looked as if "order" was being introduced. The number of repressive actions on the part of the employers seemed to diminish. The number of strikes also diminished. The oil owners "found it necessary to come to terms" (see *Neftyanoye Delo*, December).

But then the campaign began. The workers emphatically rejected the old, backstage type of conference. The overwhelming majority of them expressed themselves in favour of a conference with guarantees. Thereby, the workers expressed a definite desire to utilize the conference to the utmost, to convert it into a weapon of organized, conscious struggle.

Well, what has happened?

We no longer hear any talk about "European-style" relations. About "expectations" of being able to "regulate production" we hear not a word. The "anarchy of strikes" no longer frightens the oil owners; on the contrary, they themselves are driving the workers towards "anarchy" by attacking them, by robbing them of their gains, by discharging advanced comrades, etc., etc.

Evidently, the oil owners no longer find it necessary to come to terms. They prefer to attack.

Already at their congress at the end of January the oil owners launched their attack upon the workers. They gagged the representatives of the unions. They buried the question of workers' settlements. They decided to "cancel" the questions of schools, medical aid, etc. They deprived the workers of the right to participate in the management of the people's halls.

By all these measures the oil owners made it felt that they were taking a "new," "non-European" path, the path of open attacks upon the workers.

The Council of the Congress is continuing the "work" of their congress. It launched an attack on the workers by introducing the "ten-kopek hospital levy." This is apart from the minor orders of the Council, which bear the impress of the same change in the oil owners' tactics.

Then followed the usual "intensification" of reprisals in the shape of the cancellation of previously won oil field and works rights, reduction of staffs, discharge of advanced workers, lockouts, etc.

They reduced the oil field and works commissions to a cipher. The conflicts over the commission at Rothschild's (Balakhany), the Caspian Company, Shibayev's (Balakhany), Born's (Balakhany), Biering's, Mirzoyev's and the Naphtha Producers' Association clearly prove this.

On the pretext of "reducing staffs" they are "kicking out" the most influential comrades, especially the council delegates. The incidents that have occurred at the Caspian Company, at Born's, Mukhtarov's (Balakhany), Shibayev's (Balakhany), Lapshin's (Bibi-Eibat) and Malnikov's leave no room for doubt on this score.

The lockout at Wotan's crowns the "new" tactics of the oil owners.

By all these measures they are driving the workers on to the path of spontaneous and anarchic outbursts, which exhaust the workers.

Still more characteristic are the forms of the repressive actions taken against strikers. We have in mind the firm of Mirzoyev's, or more exactly, the manager of that firm, Mr. Markarov, who is inciting Moslems armed with rifles against the Armenian strikers and is thus creating the conditions for Armenian-Tatar conflicts.

Such is the change that has taken place in the oil owners' tactics.

Evidently, the oil owners no longer want "European conditions."

Seeing no prospect of the conference being "successful," losing hope of being able to "regulate production" by means of a conference alone, without satisfying the principal demands of the workers, seeing the conference changing from an instrument of disruption into an instrument for organizing the mass of 50,000 workers—the oil owners want, in one way or another, to free themselves from the conference by postponing it indefinitely or, at least, devitalizing it.

With that object in view they are resorting to a system of repressive measures, provoking the workers to premature action, breaking up the growing general movement into separate partial movements, and pushing the workers from the broad road of the class struggle into the crooked back streets of group conflicts.

With the aid of all these measures they want to divert the workers' attention from a conference with guarantees, to discredit in the eyes of the workers the Delegate Council, which might unite them, to prevent the workers from uniting and thereby prevent them from preparing to win their demands.

By acting in this way they want to provoke the as yet unorganized workers to take premature general action, which may provide them with the opportunity of "utterly" crushing the workers and ensuring "uninterrupted" production of oil for a long time to come.

Such is the significance of the change in the oil owners' tactics.

What should be our tactics in view of all that has been said above?

The oil owners are attacking us, taking advantage of our lack of organization. Consequently, our task is to rally around our union and defend ourselves from their blows by every means in our power.

Efforts are being made to provoke us into spontaneous, partial outbursts with the object of splitting up our general movement—consequently, we must not fall into the oil owners' trap, we must refrain, as far as possible, from partial strikes, we must not split up the general movement.

Efforts are being made to deprive us of the instrument of our unity, to rob us of the Delegate Council, by indefinitely postponing the conference and provoking us to premature general action. Consequently, it is our duty to demand the immediate convocation of the Delegate Council, to set to work to draw up the workers' demands and, in the course of this work, to rally the masses around the Delegate Council.

After strengthening the Delegate Council and rallying the mass of 50,000 workers around it, we shall not find it difficult to deal properly with the non-European schemes of Messrs. the oil owners.

Gudok, No. 22,   Reprinted from the newspaper
March 9, 1908
Unsigned

WE MUST PREPARE!

The executive of the oil industry workers' union has decided to take measures to secure the speedy convocation of the Delegate Council.[58]

In this the executive was prompted by the numerous statements from workers who are refusing to wait any longer and are demanding the immediate convocation of the Delegate Council.

The mechanics' union has decided to act along the same lines.

In the last few days both unions submitted the necessary statement to the Senior Factory Inspector.

It must be assumed that the question will soon be decided one way or another.

How the possessors of power and capital will answer the statement of the unions we, of course, cannot yet tell.

They may yield to the workers and immediately convene the Delegate Council and then, in all probability, the conference arrangements will take their "normal course."

On the other hand, they may procrastinate and not give a definite answer for the time being.

In either case, we must be prepared for every contingency so as to prevent the oil owners from deceiving the workers.

We must be ready to confront the oil owners fully armed at any moment.

For this we must immediately set to work to draw up demands.

We are going to a conference with guarantees, but with what shall we come before the oil owners if not with demands approved by the entire mass of the oil proletariat? Let us then draw up the workers' demands on wages, working hours, workers' settlements, people's halls, medical assistance, etc.

Our union has already set to work. In the columns of *Gudok* it has expressed its opinion on the questions of settlements, medical assistance, people's halls and schools. The union has already issued these demands in the form of a pamphlet entitled *Materials for the Conference*.

But that is not enough.

All these demands must be submitted to the masses, so that they can discuss them and pass their opinion, for only their opinion is binding on them.

The union, moreover, has not yet worked out the questions of wages and working hours. Consequently, we must proceed immediately to draw up demands on these questions too.

With this object, our union will elect a special commission to draw up demands.

This commission will establish contact with the council delegates and the oil field and works commissions of the four districts with the object of jointly working out with them the urgent questions affecting our daily life.

Later, general meetings will be held at the works, oil fields and in living quarters, at which the demands will be finally endorsed.

That should be our plan of work in preparation for a conference with guarantees.

Only by drawing up demands and making them known among the masses shall we be able to rally these masses around the Delegate Council.

By rallying the masses around their Council, we shall be able to safeguard them against surprises that may be sprung on them by the oil owners.

Not flabby philosophizing about "concretizing" the points of the guarantees (see *Promyslovy Vestnik*[59]), nor frivolous outcries about "the coming of spring" (remember the Socialist-Revolutionaries), but persevering effort in drawing up the workers' demands—that is what above all should occupy us in face of impending events.

And so, let us more energetically prepare for a conference with guarantees!

Gudok, No. 23,   Reprinted from the newspaper
March 16, 1908
Unsigned

ECONOMIC TERRORISM
AND THE LABOUR MOVEMENT

The workers' struggle does not always and everywhere assume the same form.

There was a time when in fighting their employers the workers smashed machines and set fire to factories. Machines are the cause of poverty! The factory is the seat of oppression! Therefore, smash and burn them!— said the workers at that time.

That was the period of unorganized, *anarchist-rebel conflicts*.

We know also of other cases where the workers, disillusioned with incendiarism and destruction, adopted "more violent forms"—killing directors, managers, foremen, etc. It is impossible to destroy all the machines and all the factories, said the workers at that time, and besides, it is not in the workers' interests to do so, but it is always possible to frighten the managers and knock the starch out of them by means of terrorism— therefore, beat them up, terrify them!

This was the period of individual *terroristic conflicts* stemming from the economic struggle.

The labour movement sharply condemned both these forms of struggle and made them a thing of the past.

This is understandable. There is no doubt that the factory is indeed the seat of exploitation of the workers, and the machine still helps the bourgeoisie to extend this exploitation, but this does not mean that the machine and the factory are in themselves the cause of poverty. On the contrary, it is precisely the factory and the machine that will enable the proletariat to break the chains of slavery, abolish poverty and vanquish all oppression—all that is needed is that the factories and machines be transformed from the private property of individual capitalists into the public property of the people.

On the other hand, what would our lives become if we set to work to destroy and burn the machines, factories and railways? It would be like living in a dreary desert, and the workers would be the first to lose their bread! . . .

Clearly, we must not smash up the machines and factories, *but gain possession of them, when that becomes possible, if we are indeed striving to abolish poverty.*

That is why the labour movement rejects anarchist-rebel conflicts.

There is no doubt that economic terrorism also has some apparent "justification," in so far as it is resorted to in order to intimidate the bourgeoisie. But what is the use of this intimidation if it is transient and fleeting? That it can only be transient is clear from the one fact alone that it is impossible to resort to economic terrorism always and everywhere. That is the first point. The second point is: Of what use to us is the fleeting fear of the bourgeoisie and the concessions this fear may wring from it if we have not behind us a powerful, mass, workers' organization, which will always be ready to fight for the workers' demands and be capable of retaining the concessions we have won? Indeed facts tell us convincingly that economic terrorism kills the desire for such an organization, robs the workers of the urge to unite and come out independently—since they have terrorist heroes who are able to act for them. Should we cultivate the spirit of independent action among the workers? Should we cultivate the desire for unity among the workers? Of course we should! But can we resort to economic terrorism if it kills the desire for both among the workers?

No, comrades! It is against our principles to terrorize the bourgeoisie by means of individual, stealthy acts of violence. Let us leave such "deeds" to the notorious terrorist elements. We must come out *openly* against the bourgeoisie, we must keep it in a state of fear *all the time, until final victory is achieved*! And for this we need not economic terrorism, but a strong mass organization which will be capable of leading the workers into the struggle.

That is why the labour movement rejects economic terrorism.

In view of what has been said above, the resolution recently adopted by the strikers at Mirzoyev's against incendiarism and "economic" assassination is of special interest. In this resolution the joint commission of the 1,500 men at Mirzoyev's, after mentioning the setting fire to a boiler room (in Balakhany) and the assassination of a manager on economic grounds (Surakhany), declares that it "protests against such methods of struggle as assassination and incendiarism" (see *Gudok*, No. 24).

By this the men at Mirzoyev's announced their final rupture with the old, terrorist, rebel tendencies.

By this they resolutely took the path of the true labour movement.

We greet the comrades at Mirzoyev's and call upon all the workers to take the path of the proletarian mass movement as resolutely as they have done.

Gudok, No. 25,   Reprinted from the newspaper
March 30, 1908
Unsigned

THE OIL OWNERS
ON ECONOMIC TERRORISM

The question of economic terrorism continues to engage the attention of the "public."

We have already expressed our opinion on this question and have condemned economic terrorism as harmful for the working class and, therefore, an unsuitable method of struggle.

The workers in the oil fields and at the works have expressed themselves approximately along the same lines.

The oil owners too have, of course, expressed their opinion on this subject. And it turns out that their "views" differ radically from the views expressed by the workers; for while they condemn economic terrorism "emanating from the workers," they say nothing against the same kind of terrorism on the part of the oil owners. We have in mind the well-known leading article on economic terrorism in the well-known organ of the oil owners (see *Neftyanoye Delo*, No. 6, article by Mr. K—za[60]).

Let us discuss this leading article. It is interesting not only as substantiation of the oil owners' "views" but also as an expression of their mood in the present stage of their struggle against the workers. For the sake of convenience the article must be divided into three parts: first, where Mr. K—za raises certain particular points against the workers and their organizations; second, where he deals with the causes of economic terrorism; and third, the measures to combat it.

Let us begin with the particular points. First of all about the men at Mirzoyev's. It is generally known that immediately after the assassination of the manager of the Surakhany oil fields and the fire in the boiler room, the joint commission of the men at Mirzoyev's, on behalf of 1,500 workers, unanimously protested against this method of struggle and denied that there was any connection between the fire and assassination on the one hand and the strike on the other. There would seem to be no grounds for doubting the sincerity of their protest. But K—za thinks otherwise. He, like a carping "critic," nevertheless deems it necessary to throw doubt on the workers' sincerity and says that "the commission is mistaken," that there is a direct connection between the fire and assassination and the strike. And this after the unanimous protest of the representatives of 1,500 workers! What is that if not evidence of a desire to distort the facts, to discredit the workers, to "pillory" them, even if slander has to be resorted to in the process? And after this, is it possible to believe in the sincerity of Mr. K—za, who talks such a lot in his article about "ennobling the criminal will of people."

From the workers at Mirzoyev's Mr. K—za passes to our union. Everybody knows that our union is growing rapidly. One can judge of the enormous influence it exercises among the workers from the mere fact that the entire conference campaign is proceeding under its direct leadership. And *Gudok* merely noted a commonly

known fact when it said that "the influence and importance of the union is growing day by day, that it is
gradually winning the recognition of even the most
backward and uneducated sections of the masses of
workers as the natural leader of their economic struggle."
Yes, all this is a commonly known fact. But our implacable "critic" cares nothing for facts, he "throws doubt"
on all and sundry, he is ready even to deny facts in order
to lower the prestige and dignity of the workers' union
in the eyes of his readers! And, after all this, Mr. K—za
has the effrontery to proclaim himself a supporter of
our union and an advocate of "ennobling the economic
struggle"!

Whoever takes one step must take the next; whoever
rails against our union must also rail against our newspaper, and so Mr. K—za passes on to *Gudok*; and it turns
out that *Gudok* "is not doing all it could do to clear
the atmosphere of the economic struggle of unnecessary
acrimony, dangerous resentment, excessive irritation and
ignorant malice," that *Gudok* does nothing but makes
"forays against other organizations, parties, classes,
newspapers and individuals, and even against its own
brother, *Promyslovy Vestnik*."

That is the song Mr. K—za sings. We could afford
to ignore all this chatter of the celebrated "critic"—
what will a flunkey of capital not chatter about in the
hope of pleasing his master! But so be it! Let us, on
this occasion, devote a few words to the great critic
from Baku. And so, *Gudok* "is not clearing the atmosphere
of the struggle of unnecessary acrimony, dangerous resentment.". . . Let us assume that all this is true. But, in the
sacred name of capital, tell us what can introduce more

acrimony and resentment—the printed word of *Gudok* or the actual deeds of the oil owners, who are systematically discharging workers, introducing the ten-kopek hospital levy, depriving the workers of the people's halls, resorting to the services of cochis,[61] beating up workers, etc.? Why does not Mr. K—za, this "devoted" champion of the idea of "ennobling the economic struggle," find it necessary to say even a single word about the activities of the oil owners which incense and embitter the workers? After all, the "dark" elements which are likely to resort to economic terrorism do not read our paper, they are more likely to be incensed and embittered by the repressive measures, big and small, of the oil owners—that being the case, why does Mr. K—za, who has so much to say against *Gudok*, say nothing at all about the "dark deeds" of Messrs. the oil owners? And is it not clear after this that Mr. K—za's insolence knows no bounds?

Secondly, where does Mr. K—za get the idea that *Gudok* has not tried "to clear the atmosphere of the economic struggle of unnecessary acrimony and dangerous resentment"? What about *Gudok's* agitation against economic terrorism and the stay-in strike, against anarchist-rebel strikes and in favour of organized strikes, against partial actions and in favour of the general class defence of our interests? What is that if not "clearing the atmosphere of the struggle of unnecessary acrimony and dangerous resentment"? Is Mr. K—za really unaware of all this? Or perhaps, in playing the role of capital's advocate, he considers it necessary to pretend that he does not know? But if that is the case, why all this fine talk about "morality" and "human conscience"?

Gudok makes "forays against other organizations, parties, classes, newspapers, individuals, and even against *Promyslovy Vestnik*," says Mr. K—za, continuing his indictment. Quite right, Mr. K—za, you have accidentally spoken the truth! *Gudok* does, indeed, wage a struggle against other classes and their organs. But can you demand anything else from a newspaper of the workers, who are exploited by all the other classes and groups? Stop playing the part of "innocent angel" and tell us straight, without equivocation: do you really not know that *Neftyanoye Delo*, the organ of the oil owners, and its master, the Council of the Congress, were established precisely for the purpose of making "forays" against the working class, against the workers' Party, and against the workers' newspapers? Have you really forgotten the recent instructions issued by the Council of the Congress to impose a ten-kopek levy, to raise the prices of meals, to reduce the number of schools and hutments, to deprive the workers of the people's halls, etc.? And is not *Neftyanoye Delo*, the organ of the oil owners, trying to justify these Asiatic instructions? Or perhaps these are not "forays" against the workers, but the "ennobling of the criminal will," regulation of the economic struggle, etc.? How else do you want a workers' newspaper to act towards the oil owners who are exploiting the workers, towards their organization, which is fooling the workers, towards their organ, which is corrupting the workers, and towards Mr. K—za, for example, who is making comical efforts to find "philosophical" justification for the Asiatically barbarous *steps* of the oil owners? Does Mr. K—za really fail to understand the necessity of the class struggle between the workers and the employers? Of course: Mr. K—za understands all this perfectly well: he himself is waging a struggle against the proletariat and its organizations! But, firstly, he opposes the struggle waged by the workers, but not a struggle in general; secondly, the oil owners, it appears, are not fighting, but only "ennobling the struggle"; thirdly, K—za is not opposed to the workers, no—he is entirely for the workers for the benefit . . . of the oil owners; fourthly, after all K—za "gets paid," and this, too, must be taken into consideration, you know. . . .

Evidently, Mr. K—za's effrontery can successfully compete with his "conscience" in its capacity to stretch as circumstances require.

That is how the matter stands in Mr. K—za's leading article as regards his particular points against the proletariat and its organizations.

* * *

Let us now pass to the second part of his article. In it the author speaks of the causes of economic terrorism. It "transpires" that the cause is the "darkness of the minds" and the "criminal will" of the backward sections of the working class. This "darkness," this "criminality," in their turn, are due to the fact that the workers' unions and newspapers are not conducting sufficiently energetic enlightening and ennobling activities among the workers. Of course, adds Mr. K—za, "the programmes (of the unions?) do not approve of economic terrorism," but mere "disapproval in the programme is not enough, once we see that life has taken the wrong road. Here an active struggle must be waged . . . by all parties and unions" "against the evil which has arisen." To explain what he means, Mr. K—za goes on to say: "Only when . . . all friends of the workers, irrespective of their party affiliation, wage an energetic struggle against . . . economic terrorism, *and only then*, will assassination disappear," etc.

And so, the workers' minds are dark, and that is why they often resort to assassination; but their minds are dark because their unions and newspapers make no effort to "enlighten and ennoble" them—hence, the workers' unions and newspapers are to blame for everything.

Such is the song Mr. K—za sings.

We shall not dwell on the confusion that reigns in Mr. K—za's head about economic terrorism—we have in mind his ignorant statement that economic terrorism is a programmatic question. We only wish to make the following observations: 1) If, in mentioning "programmatic terrorism," Mr. K—za talks about unions, does he really not know that the unions in Russia do not have any programmes? Every working man knows that! 2) If, however, he has parties in mind, does he really not know what every schoolboy knows, that economic terrorism is not a question of programme, but a question of tactics? Why then all this palaver about a programme? We are surprised that Messrs. the oil owners were unable to hire a better, or at least a less ignorant "ideologist."

Nor shall we dwell on the other, this time muddled (and not only ignorant!) statement of Mr. K—za's that, as regards economic terrorism, "life has taken the wrong road" and that "we" must fight against life. We shall merely observe that our cause would be in a bad way if it was life that had taken the wrong road, *and not individuals who have dropped behind life.* The strength of our agitation lies precisely in the fact that life itself, all-powerful, developing life, is demanding a struggle against economic terrorism. If Mr. K—za fails to understand this, we advise him to migrate to another planet. There, perhaps, he will be able to apply his muddled theory about fighting against developing life. . . .

Let us rather pass to Mr. K—za's "analysis."

First of all we would like to ask: does Mr. K—za really think that it is the workers' unions and newspapers that are the cause of economic terrorism?

What does "enlightening" the workers mean? It means teaching the workers to wage a class-conscious systematic struggle! (Mr. K—za agrees with this!) But who else could engage in this task if not the workers' unions and newspapers with their oral and printed agitation in favour of an organized struggle?

What does "ennobling" the economic struggle mean? It means directing it against the *system*, but under no circumstances against *persons*! (Even K—za agrees with this!) But who engages in this task, except the workers' unions and newspapers?

But do not the oil owners reduce this struggle against the working class to a struggle against individual workers, singling out and discharging the most class conscious of them?

If Mr. K—za is really convinced of the justice of his charge against the workers' unions and newspapers, why does he offer his advice to these unions and newspapers? Does he really not know that organizations "which make forays against other classes, news-papers, individuals," etc., will not follow his advice? Why does he waste his time pounding water in a mortar?

Obviously, he himself does not believe his accusation.

And if, in spite of this, Mr. K—za talks against the unions, he does so only in order to divert the attention of his readers from the real cause, to conceal the real "culprits" from them.

But no, Mr. K—za! You will not succeed in conceal-ing from your readers the real causes of economic ter-rorism.

Not the workers and their organizations, but the activ-ities of Messrs. the oil owners, which incense and embit-ter the workers, are the real cause of "economic assassi-nations."

You point to the "darkness" and "ignorance" of certain sections of the proletariat. But where are "dark-ness" and "ignorance" to be combated if not in schools and at lectures? Why, then, are Messrs. the oil owners cutting down the number of schools and lectures? And why do not you, the "sincere" advocate of the struggle against "darkness," raise your voice against the oil owners who are depriving the workers of schools and lectures?

You talk about "ennobling" habits. Why then, my dear sir, were you quiet when Messrs. the oil owners deprived the workers of the people's halls, those centres of popular entertainment?

You sing about "ennobling the economic struggle," but why were you silent when the hirelings of capital killed the working man Khanlar[62] (at the Naphtha

Producers' Association), when Born's, the Caspian Company, Shibayev's, Mirzoyev's, Molot, Motovilikha, Biering's, Mukhtarov's, Malnikov's and other firms discharged their most advanced workers, and when workers at Shibayev's, Mukhtarov's, Molot, Runo, Kokorev's in Bibi-Eibat, and other firms were beaten up?

You talk about the workers' "criminal will," about "unnecessary acrimony," etc., but where were you hiding when Messrs. the oil owners infuriated the workers, incensed the most sensitive and most easily inflamed of them—the temporary workers and the unemployed? And do you know, my dear sir, that it was precisely that section of the workers which was doomed to starvation by the notorious ten-kopek hospital levy and the raising of the price of meals in the canteens run by the Council of the Congress?

You talk about the horrors of "blood and tears" called forth by economic terrorism, but do you know how much blood and tears is shed when large numbers of workers are injured and can find no place in the hospitals run by the Council of the Congress? Why are Messrs. the oil owners reducing the number of hutments? And why are you not shouting about it as much as you are shouting against the workers' unions and newspapers?

You sing about "conscience," and so forth; but why is your crystal clear conscience silent about all these reprisals which Messrs. the oil owners are carrying out?

You say . . . but enough! It should be obvious that the main cause of "economic assassinations" is not the workers and their organizations, but the activities of Messrs. the oil owners, which incense and embitter the workers.

It is no less clear that Mr. K—za is a miserable hireling of Messrs. the oil owners who throws all the blame upon the workers' organizations and thus tries to justify the actions of his masters in the eyes of the "public."

*   *   *

Let us now pass to the third part of Mr. K—za's article.

In the third part of his article Mr. K—za speaks about measures to combat economic terrorism, and his "measures" are fully in keeping with his "philosophy" "about the causes" of economic terrorism.

Let us hear what the great philosopher from Baku has to say:

"An active struggle must be waged against the evil that has arisen, and the slogan of this struggle must be issued. This slogan, to be accepted by all parties and organizations, unions, and circles, must now be: 'Down with economic terrorism!' Only when we boldly hoist the pure white flag bearing this slogan, and only then . . . will assassinations disappear."

Thus philosophizes Mr. K—za.

As you see, Mr. K—za remains faithful to his god capital to the end.

Firstly, he removed (philosophically removed!) all "blame" for "economic assassinations" from the oil owners and laid it on the workers, their unions and newspapers. In this way he fully "justified" in the eyes of so-called "society" the *Asiatically* aggressive tactics of Messrs. the oil owners. . . .

Secondly—and most important for the oil owners— he "invented" the cheapest method of combating "assas-

sinations," a method that will involve no expenditure
for the oil owners—intensified agitation by the unions
and newspapers against economic terrorism. By this he
once again emphasized that the oil owners should not
yield to the workers, should not incur "expenditure."

Both cheap and easy! Messrs. the oil owners may
exclaim on hearing Mr. K—za's proposal.

Of course, Messrs. the oil owners could "conveniently
flout" the opinion of so-called "society," but what
objection can they have to a K—za coming along and
justifying them in the eyes of "society" in the interests
of "the human conscience"?

On the other hand, why should they not rejoice when,
after this justification, the same K—za comes along and
proposes the "surest" and cheapest means of combating
economic terrorism? Let the unions and newspapers
agitate freely and unhindered, so long as it does not
affect the pocket of the oil owners. Well, isn't that
liberal? ... Why should they not, after this, send
Mr. K—za, their "Warbling Brigand," on to the literary
stage?

And yet, it is sufficient to think a little, it is sufficient only to adopt the point of view of the class-
conscious workers, to see at once the utter absurdity of
the measure Mr. K—za proposes.

Here it is by no means a matter of the unions
and newspapers alone; the unions and newspapers have
long been conducting agitation against economic terrorism,
and yet "assassinations" have not ceased. It is much
more a matter of the activities of Messrs. the oil owners,
which incense and embitter the workers, of the economic
repressive measures, big and small, the *Asiatically* aggres-

sive tactics of Messrs. the oil owners, which foster, and will continue to foster, the "economic assassinations" with which we are concerned.

Tell me, if you please: what can *agitation alone* by the unions and newspapers do, even if those unions and newspapers are very influential, *in face of the incensing activities* of Messrs. the oil owners who are robbing the workers of one gain after another, thereby pushing the least class conscious of them on to the path of "economic assassinations"? Clearly, anti-terrorist agitation alone, even if conducted under a "pure white flag," is powerless to abolish it.

Obviously, more profound measures than simple agitation are needed to cause the "disappearance" of "economic assassinations"; and what is primarily needed is that the oil owners should drop their repressive measures, big and small, and satisfy the just demands of the workers. . . . Only when the oil owners abandon their *Asiatically* aggressive tactics of lowering wages, taking away the people's halls, reducing the number of schools and hutments, collecting the ten-kopek hospital levy, raising the price of meals, systematically discharging advanced workers, beating them up, and so forth, only when the oil owners definitely take the path of cultured European-style relations with the masses of the workers and their unions and regard them as a force "on an equal footing"— only then will the ground for the "disappearance" of "assassinations" be created.

All this is so clear that it needs no proof.

But Mr. K—za fails to understand it; indeed, he cannot, or more correctly, does not wish to understand it, because it is "unprofitable" for Messrs. the oil owners; for it would involve them in a certain amount of expenditure, and it would reveal the whole truth about those who are "guilty" of economic "assassinations.". . .

The only conclusion to be drawn is that K—za is a flunkey of capital.

But what follows from this, from K—za's role as a flunkey?

What follows is that Mr. K—za is not expressing his own views, but the views of the oil owners who "inspire" him. Consequently, K—za's article expresses not his own philosophy, but the philosophy of Messrs. the oil owners. Obviously, it is the oil owners who are speaking through the mouth of K—za; K—za is merely conveying their "thoughts, wishes and sentiments."

In this, and this alone, lies the interest of Mr. K—za's article that we are discussing.

K—za as Koza*, K—za as a "personality," is an absolute nonentity for us, imponderable matter of no value whatever. K—za has no grounds whatever for complaining that *Gudok* makes "forays" against his "personality"; we assure Mr. K—za that *Gudok* was never interested in his so-called "personality."

But K—za as an impersonal something, K—za as the absence of "personality," K—za as the mere expression of the opinion and sentiments of Messrs. the oil owners is certainly of some value to us. It is from this aspect that we are examining both K—za himself and his article.

It is obvious that Mr. K—za is not singing for nothing. The fact that in the first part of his article he fu-

---

* Koza—the Russian for goat.—*Tr*.

riously attacks the unions and tries to discredit them, that in the second part of his article he accuses the unions of cultivating economic terrorism, but says not a word about the Asiatic instructions issued by the oil owners, and that in the third part of his article he points to anti-terroristic agitation as the only measure with which to combat "assassinations," leaving aside the aggressive tactics of his masters,—all that shows that the oil owners do not intend to make any concessions to the masses of the workers.

The oil owners will attack, the oil owners must attack, but you workers and unions, be good enough to retreat—this is what Mr. K—za's article tells us, this is what the oil owners tell us through the mouth of their "Warbling Brigand."

Such is the moral to be drawn from Mr. K—za's article.

It remains for us workers, our organizations and newspapers, to keep a close eye on Messrs. the oil owners, not to allow ourselves to be provoked by their outrageous actions, but to continue firmly and calmly along the path of converting our spontaneous struggle into a strictly class struggle, which systematically leads to a definite goal.

As for the hypocritical screeching of various hirelings of capital, we can afford to ignore them.

Gudok, Nos. 28, 30 and 32,   Reprinted from the newspaper
April 21, May 4 and 18, 1908
Signed: *K. Kato*

9*

FLUNKEY "SOCIALISTS"

One of the newspapers published in Tiflis is a Georgian-language one which calls itself *Napertskali*.[64] It is a new and at the same time a very old paper, for it is the continuation of all the Menshevik newspapers published in Tiflis since the time of *Skhivi* of 1905. *Napertskali* is edited by an old group of Menshevik opportunists. But that is not the only point, of course. The main point is that the opportunism of this group is something exceptional, something fabulous. Opportunism is lack of principle, political spinelessness. We declare that no Menshevik group has displayed such crass spinelessness as is displayed by the Tiflis group. In 1905 this group recognized the role of the *proletariat* as the leader of the revolution (see *Skhivi*). In 1906 it changed its "position" and declared that "it is no use relying on the workers . . . the initiative can come only from the *peasants*" (see *Skhivi*). In 1907 it changed its "position" again and stated that "leadership of the revolution must belong to the liberal bourgeoisie" (see *Azri*[65]), etc., etc.

But never has the above-mentioned group's lack of principle attained such a shameless degree as now, in the summer of 1908. We have in mind the appraisal in the columns of *Napertskali* of the murder of that spiritual enslaver of the dispossessed, the so-called Exarch. The story of this murder is well known. A certain group killed the Exarch, and also a captain of gendarmes who was returning with a report from "the scene of the crime," and then attacked a procession of hooligans who were accompanying the body of the Exarch. Obviously, this was not a hooligan group, but nor was it a revolutionary group, for no revolutionary group would commit such an act at the present time, when our forces are being mustered, and thus jeopardize the cause of uniting the proletariat. The attitude of Social-Democracy towards groups of this kind is commonly known: ascertaining the conditions which give rise to such groups, and combating these conditions, it at the same time wages an ideological and organizational struggle against these groups, discredits them in the eyes of the proletariat and dissociates the proletariat from them. But that is not what *Napertskali* does. Without ascertaining or explaining anything, it belches a few banal liberal phrases against terrorism in general, and then goes on to advise, and not only advise but order its readers to do nothing more nor less than *report* such groups to the police, to *betray* them to the police! This is disgraceful, but, unfortunately, it is a fact. Listen to what *Napertskali* says:

"To haul the murderers of the Exarch before a court—such is the only means of wiping this stain from oneself forever. . . . Such is the duty of the advanced elements" (see *Napertskali*, No. 5).

Social-Democrats in the role of voluntary police informers—this is what the Menshevik opportunists in Tiflis have brought us to!

The political spinelessness of the opportunists is no mysterious growth. It springs from the irresistible striving to adapt oneself to the tastes of the bourgeoisie, a striving to please the "masters" and earn their praise. Such is the psychological basis of the opportunist tactics of adaptation. And so, to stand well with the "gentry," to please them, or at all events to avert their wrath over the murder of the Exarch, our Menshevik opportunists grovel like flunkeys before them and take upon themselves the function of police sleuths!

Tactics of adaptation could not go further than that!

HYPOCRITICAL ZUBATOVITES

Among the cities in the Caucasus which produce original types of opportunism is Baku. In Baku there is a group which is still more to the right and, therefore, more unprincipled than the Tiflis group. We do not mean *Promyslovy Vestnik*, which has entered into unlawful cohabitation with the bourgeois *Segodnya*; enough has been written about that paper in our press. We are referring to the Shendrikovite *Pravoye Delo* group, the progenitors of the Baku Mensheviks. True, this group has long ceased to exist in Baku; to escape the wrath of the Baku workers and their organizations it had to migrate to St. Petersburg. But it sends its screeds to Baku, it writes only about Baku affairs, it is seeking for supporters precisely in Baku, it is striving to "win" the Baku proletariat. It will not be amiss, therefore, to talk about this group. Before us lies a copy of *Pravoye Delo*, No. 2-3. We turn over the pages and before our eyes unfolds the old picture of the old, shady gang, Messrs. the Shendrikovs.[66] Here is Ilya Shendrikov, the well-known "handshaker" of Mr. Junkovsky, a veteran of backstage intrigue. Here also is Gleb Shendrikov, former Socialist-Revolutionary, former Menshevik, former "Zubatovite," and now in retirement. And here is the celebrated chatterbox, the "immaculate" Klavdia Shendrikova, a pleasant lady in all respects. Nor is there a lack of "followers" of various types, like the Groshevs and Kalinins, who played a part in the movement some time ago, but who are now behind the times and are living only on their reminiscences. Even the shade of the late Lev rises before us. . . . In short, the picture is complete!

But who needs all this? Why are these inglorious shadows of the gloomy past thrust upon the workers? Are they calling upon the workers to set fire to the derricks? Or to vilify the Party and trample it in the mire? Or to go to the conference without the workers and then strike a shady bargain with Mr. Junkovsky?

No! The Shendrikovs want to "save" the Baku workers! They "see" that after 1905, i.e., after the workers had driven out the Shendrikovs, "the workers find themselves on the brink of a precipice" (see *Pravoye Delo*, p. 80); and so the Shendrikovs produced *Pravoye Delo* in order to "save" the workers, to lead them out of the "blind alley." To achieve this they propose that the workers should return to the past, abandon the gains of the last three years, turn their backs on *Gudok* and *Promyslovy Vestnik*, give up the existing unions, send Social-Democracy to the devil, and after expelling all the non-Shendrikovites from the workers' commissions, unite around *conciliation boards*. Strikes are no longer needed, nor are illegal organizations—all that the workers need are conciliation boards, on which the Shendrikovs and Gukasovs[67] will "settle questions" with Mr. Junkovsky's permission. . . .

That is how they want to lead the Baku labour movement out of the "blind alley."

That is exactly what is proposed by Mr. K—za, the chameleon from *Neftyanoye Delo* (see *Neftyanoye Delo*, No. 11).

But is not this the way the workers were "saved" by Zubatov in Moscow, by Gapon in St. Petersburg, and by Shayevich in Odessa? And did they not all turn out to be mortal enemies of the workers?

Upon whom, then, do these hypocritical "saviours" want to work their daylight swindle?

No, Messrs. the Shendrikovs, although you, along with K—za, assert that the Baku proletariat is "not yet mature," that it yet "has to pass its matriculation examination" (before whom?) (see *Pravoye Delo*, p. 2), you will not succeed in fooling it!

The Baku proletariat is sufficiently politically conscious to be able to tear off your masks and put you in your proper place!

Who are you? Where do you come from?

You are not Social-Democrats, for you grew up and are living in conflict with Social-Democracy, in conflict with the Party principle!

Nor are you trade unionists, for you trample in the mire the workers' unions, which are naturally permeated with the spirit of Social-Democracy!

You are just Gaponites and Zubatovites, hypocritically wearing the mask of "friends of the people"!

You are enemies within the camp and, therefore, the most dangerous enemies of the proletariat!

Down with the Shendrikovites! Turn your backs on the Shendrikovites!

That is our answer to your *Pravoye Delo*, Messrs. the Shendrikovs!

And that is how the Baku proletariat will respond to your hypocritical advances to them! . . .

Bakinsky Proletary, No. 5, July 20, 1908

Signed: *Ko. . . .*

Reprinted from the newspaper

THE CONFERENCE AND THE WORKERS

The conference campaign has been suspended. Negotiations between the parties have been interrupted.[68] The old but eternally new conference has again been prevented from meeting. The Delegate Council, the organizing committee, the drawing up of demands, reports to the masses, the *broad* union of the workers around their commissions, of the commissions around the trade unions and of the latter around Social-Democracy— all this has been interrupted and made a thing of the past. Forgotten also is the old hypocritical talk about "regulating production" by means of a conference, and about "ennobling the relations" between the workers and the employers. Mr. Junkovsky, that old clown from Tiflis, announces that the "show" is over. Mr. Kara-Murza, that dissipated flunkey of capital, applauds him. The curtain falls, and we get the old familiar picture: the oil owners and the workers are in their former positions, waiting for further storms, for new conflicts.

But there is something "incomprehensible" here. Only yesterday the oil owners were imploring the workers to agree to a conference with a view to putting an end to "the anarchy of partial strikes," to "come to terms" with them, while the authorities, in the person of the notorious Junkovsky, invited influential workers to meet them, arranged official negotiations with them, urged upon them the advantages of a collective agreement. But suddenly a sharp change took place— a conference was declared to be superfluous, a collective agreement harmful and "the anarchy of partial strikes" desirable!

What does it mean? How is this "queer" situation to be explained? Who is "to blame" for the prevention of the conference?

The workers are to blame, of course, answers Mr. Junkovsky: We had not yet started negotiations, but they already came out with a demand in the form of an ultimatum about the unions. Let the workers abandon their unions and then we shall have a conference. If they do not, we do not want a conference!

We agree, the oil owners respond in chorus. It is indeed the workers who are to blame. Let them abandon their unions. We do not want any unions!

They are quite right; indeed the workers are to blame, says the "mechanics' union," the union without workers, echoing the enemies of the workers. Why should not the workers abandon their unions? Would it not be better first to bargain a little after abandoning our demands, and then to talk about demands?

Yes, that's right, assents *Promyslovy Vestnik*, the newspaper without readers, backing the union without workers. Respectable workers first bargain and then talk about ultimatums; first they surrender their positions and then win them back again. The Baku workers lacked this respectability, they proved to be too disreputable, almost boycottists.

We knew it, we foresaw it all long ago, the Dash-naks and Socialist-Revolutionaries observe with profundity. Had the workers shouted boycott, had they completely abandoned the unions, and had they plunged into a strike without any preparation and rallying of some sort of broad masses, they would have understood that a conference was impossible without "land and freedom," and that "by struggle you will achieve your rights." [69] . . .

That is what the "friends" and the enemies of the Baku proletariat say.

Does the unsoundness of these accusations against the Baku proletariat need any proof? It is enough to bring the Dashnaks and the Socialist-Revolutionaries, who accuse the workers of *being enamoured* with the conference, face to face with the mechanics and oil owners who accuse these very same workers of *boycotting* the conference—it is enough, I say, to contrast these mutually exclusive views to see at once the utter absurdity and falsity of the above-mentioned accusations. . . .

But in that case, who is really "to blame" for the prevention of the conference?

Let us briefly review the history of the conference. This is not the first time that the oil owners have invited the workers to a conference—this is the fourth conference we have seen (1905, 1906, 1907, 1908). On every occasion it was the oil owners who first called for a conference, and on every occasion the authorities helped them "to come to terms" with the workers, to conclude a collective agreement. The oil owners were pursuing their own objects: in return for minor concessions they wanted to guarantee themselves against strikes and ensure the uninterrupted bailing of oil. The authorities were still more interested in the maintenance of "peace and quiet" in the oil kingdom, quite apart from the fact that very many members of the government own shares in the big oil firms, that the taxes on the oil industry constitute one of the most important items of revenue in the state budget, that Baku crude oil feeds "home industry" and, consequently, the slightest hitch in the oil industry inevitably affects the state of industry in Russia.

But this is not all. Apart from everything already said above, peace in Baku is important for the government because the mass actions of the Baku proletariat—both the oil industry workers and the marine workers connected with them—have a contagious effect on the proletariat in other cities. Recall the facts. The first general strike in Baku in the spring of 1903 marked the beginning of the celebrated July strikes and demonstrations in the South-Russian towns.[70] The second general strike in November and December 1904[71] served as the signal for the glorious January and February actions all over Russia. In 1905, after quickly recovering from the Armenian-Tatar massacres, the Baku proletariat again rushed into battle, infecting with its enthusiasm "the whole Caucasus." Lastly, beginning with 1906, after the retreat of the revolution in Russia, Baku remains "irrepressible," to this day actually enjoys certain liberties, and every year celebrates proletarian May Day better than any other place in Russia, rousing feelings of noble envy in other towns. . . . After all this, it is not difficult to understand why the authorities tried not to incense the Baku workers, and on each occasion supported the oil owners in their attempts to confer with the workers, "to come to terms," to conclude a collective agreement.

On every occasion, however, we Bolsheviks answered with a boycott.

Why?

Because the oil owners wanted to confer and conclude an agreement not with the masses, and not in sight of the masses, but with a handful of individuals behind the backs of the masses. They know perfectly well that only in this way can the many thousands of oil industry workers be deceived.

What is the essence of *our* conference? Our conference means negotiations between the oil proletariat and the oil bourgeoisie regarding demands. If the negotiations are successful, the conference will end in a collective agreement for a certain period and binding on both parties. *Speaking generally*, we have no objection to a conference, because under certain conditions it *can* unite the workers into a single whole on the basis of common demands. But a conference can unite the workers only: 1) if the masses take a most active part in it, freely discuss their demands, control their representatives, etc.; 2) if the masses have the opportunity to back their demands by a general strike if necessary. Can the workers actively confer, discuss demands, etc., without a certain amount of freedom to meet in the oil fields and at the works, without a Delegate Council that can meet freely, without the leadership of the unions? Of course not! Is it possible to back one's demands in the winter, when navigation is closed and shipment of oil ceases, when the employers can resist a general strike longer than in any other part of the year? Again no! And yet, all the conferences we have had up till now were called precisely in the winter, and were offered without freedom to discuss demands, without a free Delegate Council, and without the intervention of the unions; the masses of the workers and their organizations were carefully removed from the stage, the whole business was placed in the hands of a handful of Shendrikov-minded "individuals." It was like saying to the workers: gentlemen, elect your delegates and then disperse to your homes! A conference *without* the workers, a conference *to deceive* the workers—that is what we were offered during three years. *Such* conferences deserve only to be boycotted, and we Bolsheviks proclaimed a boycott of them....

The workers did not at once understand all this and, therefore, in 1905, went to the first conference. But they were obliged to leave the conference, to disrupt it.

The workers were again mistaken, in 1906, in going to the second conference. But they were again obliged to abandon the conference, to disrupt it again.

All this shows that life itself censured and rectified the workers' mistakes, compelling the workers to take the path of boycotting backstage, fraudulent, Shendrikov type of conferences.

The Mensheviks who invited the workers to go to *such* conferences unconsciously helped the oil owners to deceive the workers....

But in 1907 things took a different turn. The experience of the two conferences on the one hand, and the intensified agitation of the Bolsheviks on the other, had its effect. The workers met the proposal of the authorities and the oil owners to hold a conference (the third!) with an emphatic refusal.

This opened a new phase in the Baku labour movement. . . .

But does that mean that the workers were afraid of a conference? Of course not. Why should they, who had gone through tremendous strikes, be afraid of negotiations with the oil owners?

Does it mean that the workers ran away from a collective agreement? Of course not. Why should they, who had known the "December agreement," be afraid of a collective agreement?

By boycotting the conference in November 1907 the workers said, in effect, that they were sufficiently mature not to permit their enemies to fool them any longer with a backstage Shendrikov type of conference.

And so, when the authorities and the oil owners, haunted by the spectre of a boycott, asked us under what conditions we would agree to a conference, we answered: only on the condition that the masses of the workers and their unions take the widest possible part in the entire proceedings of the conference. Only when the workers are able 1) freely to discuss their demands, 2) freely to assemble a Delegate Council, 3) freely to utilize the services of their unions and 4) freely to choose the moment for opening the conference—only then will the workers agree to a conference. And the cornerstone of our demands was recognition of the unions. These points were called guarantees. Here, for the first time, was issued the celebrated formula: *a conference with guarantees or no conference at all!*

Were we thereby false to the tactics of boycotting the old Shendrikov type of conference without the workers? Not by one iota! The boycott of the old type of conference remained in full force—all we did was to proclaim a new type of conference, a conference with guarantees, and only such a conference!

Does the correctness of these tactics need proof? Does it need proof that only by means of these tactics would we be able to convert the conference from an instrument for deceiving the workers into an instrument for uniting them around the unions in one vast army numbering many thousands and capable of standing up for its demands?

Even the Mensheviks, the mechanics' union and *Promyslovy Vestnik* were unable to take a stand against this position and, following our example, they proclaimed the point about the unions to be an ultimatum. We are in possession of documents showing that the Mensheviks refused to agree not only to a conference, but also to the election of delegates unless the point about the unions was conceded, and unless permits were issued to the unions. All this took place *before* the negotiations in the organizing committee, *before* the Delegate Council, *before* the election of delegates. Now, of course, they can say that "ultimatums can be presented only *at the end* of negotiations," that *"from the very beginning"* they "fought against the presentation of demands in the form of an ultimatum" (see *Promyslovy Vestnik*, No. 21), but these are the usual and long-known "somersaults" of the spineless opportunists in the Menshevik camp, which prove once again the consistency of our tactics!

Even the Socialist-Revolutionaries and Dashnaks, who had anathemized "anything and everything connected with a conference," even they "bowed their heads" before our tactics and decided to take part in the preparatory work connected with the conference!

The workers understood that our position was correct, and the overwhelming majority of them voted for it. Of the 35,000 workers canvassed, only 8,000 voted for the Socialist-Revolutionaries and Dashnaks (a boycott under all circumstances), 8,000 voted for the Mensheviks (a conference under all circumstances), and 19,000 voted for our tactics, the tactics of a conference with guarantees.

Thus, the workers rejected the Menshevik tactics, the tactics of a conference without the workers, without guarantees. The workers also rejected the tactics of the Dashnaks and Socialist-Revolutionaries, the tactics of an imaginary boycott and an unorganized general strike. The workers declared for a conference with guarantees, for systematically utilizing the entire proceedings of the conference with the object of organizing a general strike.

Herein lies the secret of the prevention of the conference!

The oil owners, with one voice, declared for a conference without guarantees. In this way they approved of the Mensheviks' tactics. We assert that this is the best possible proof that the stand taken by the Mensheviks was wrong.

As, however, the workers rejected a conference without guarantees, the oil owners changed their tactics and . . . prevented the conference, boycotted it. In this way they expressed their solidarity with the tactics of the

Dashnaks and Socialist-Revolutionaries. We assert that this is the best possible proof that the stand taken by the Dashnaks and the Socialist-Revolutionaries was unsound.

The tactics of the Baku proletariat proved to be the only correct tactics.

That is why the oil bourgeoisie is attacking these tactics with all its might. The oil bourgeoisie fully approves of the Menshevik proposal for a conference without guarantees, and in the last resort it clutches at the Dashnak-Socialist-Revolutionary proposal for a boycott; but it will not at any price make peace with the Baku proletariat, which has declared for a conference with guarantees!

This is understandable. Picture to yourself the following: certain points are conceded—the guarantees; the workers' demands are discussed on the widest possible scale; the Delegate Council becomes more and more firmly established among the masses; in the course of drawing up their demands the masses rally around their Council and through it around their unions; the masses, 50,000 strong, organized in a single army, present demands to the oil owners; the oil owners are obliged to surrender without a fight, or else reckon with the possibility of a thoroughly organized general strike, to take place at a time least convenient for them—is that profitable for the oil bourgeoisie? After this, how can the bourgeois pets on *Neftyanoye Delo* and *Baku*[72] help yapping and mewing? So—down with the conference, since it cannot be held without those cursed guarantees—say the oil owners, preventing the conference.

That is the cause of the prevention of the conference by the authorities and the oil owners.

That is what the history of the conference tells us.

But *Promyslovy Vestnik*, forgetting all this, goes on singing about the "tactlessness of the leaders," fatuously repeating and chewing the cud over the leading articles in *Baku* and *Neftyanoye Delo*! Even the Georgian newspaper of the Tiflis Mensheviks found it necessary to "raise its voice" and sing second to the Baku Cadets![73] Miserable echoes!

But what should be our tactics in the new situation?

The oil owners have prevented the conference. They are provoking a general strike. Does that mean that we must immediately respond with a general strike? Of course not! Apart from the fact that the oil owners have already accumulated vast stocks of oil, that they have been long preparing to resist a general strike, we must not forget that we are not yet ready for such a serious struggle. For the time being we must resolutely give up the idea of a general economic strike.

The only expedient form of retreat in the present situation is strikes at individual firms. The Mensheviks who deny the expediency of such strikes almost on "principle" (see L. A. Rin's pamphlet[74]), are profoundly mistaken. The experience of the strikes in the spring shows that, with the active intervention of the unions and of our organization, strikes at individual firms may prove to be one of the surest means of uniting the proletariat. All the more firmly, therefore, should we grasp such means. We must not forget that our organization will grow only to the extent that we actively intervene in all the affairs of the proletarian struggle.

Such is our immediate tactical task.

Having prevented the conference, the authorities now want to abolish completely the so-called "Baku liberties." Does that mean that we must go completely underground and leave the field free for the activities of the dark forces? Of course not! However fiercely the reaction may rage, no matter how much it may wreck our unions and organizations, it cannot abolish the oil field and works commissions without calling forth "anarchy and conflicts" at the works and in the oil fields. It is our duty to strengthen these commissions, to imbue them with the spirit of socialism and to unite them according to the respective firms. To achieve this our works and oil field Party units must systematically come out at the head of these commissions and, in their turn, unite on an interdistrict basis through their representatives also according to the respective firms.

Such are our immediate organizational tasks.

By carrying out these immediate tasks, and thereby strengthening the unions and our organization, we shall be able to weld into one the masses of the oil industry workers numbering many thousands for the forthcoming battles against oil capital.

Published as a supplement to
Bakinsky Proletary, No. 5,
July 20, 1908

Signed: *Koba*

Reprinted from the supplement
to *Bakinsky Proletary*

THE PARTY CRISIS AND OUR TASKS

It is no secret to anyone that our Party is passing through a severe crisis. The Party's loss of members, the shrinking and weakness of the organizations, the latter's isolation from one another, and the absence of co-ordinated Party work—all show that the Party is ailing, that it is passing through a grave crisis.

The first thing that is particularly depressing the Party is the isolation of its organizations from the broad masses. At one time our organizations numbered thousands in their ranks and they led hundreds of thousands. At that time, the Party had firm roots among the masses. This is not the case now. Instead of thousands, tens and, at best, hundreds, have remained in the organizations. As regards leading hundreds of thousands, it is not worth speaking about. True, our Party exercises wide *ideological* influence among the masses; the masses know the Party, the masses respect it. That is what primarily distinguishes the "post-revolution" Party from the "pre-revolution" Party. But that is practically all that the Party's influence amounts to. And yet ideological influence alone is far from enough. The point is that the breadth of *ideological* influence is neutralized by the narrowness of *organizational* consolidation. That is the cause of our organizations' isolation from the broad masses. It is sufficient to point to St. Petersburg, where in 1907 we had about 8,000 members and where we can now scarcely muster 300 to 400, to appreciate at once the full gravity of the crisis. We shall not speak of Moscow, the Urals, Poland, the Donets Basin, etc., which are in a similar state.

But that is not all. The Party is suffering not only from isolation from the masses, but also from the fact that its organizations are not linked up with one another, are not living the same Party life, are divorced from one another. St. Petersburg does not know what is going on in the Caucasus, the Caucasus does not know what is going on in the Urals, etc.; each little corner lives its own separate life. Strictly speaking, we no longer have a single Party living the same common life that we all spoke of with such pride in the period from 1905 to 1907. We are working according to the most scandalously amateurish methods. The organs now published abroad— *Proletary*[75] and *Golos*[76] on the one hand, and *Sotsial-Demokrat*[77] on the other, do not and cannot link up the organizations scattered over Russia, and cannot endow them with a single Party life. Indeed, it would be strange to think that organs published abroad, far removed from Russian reality, can co-ordinate the work of the Party, which has long passed the study-circle stage. True, the isolated organizations have much in common which links them together *ideologically*—they have a common programme, which has stood the test of revolution; they have common practical principles, which have been approved by the revolution, and glorious revolutionary traditions. This is the second important distinction between the "post-revolution" Party and the "pre-revolution" Party. But this is not enough. The point is that the *ideological* unity of the Party organizations does not by a long way save the Party from their want of organizational cohesion and isolation from one another. It is sufficient to point out that not even information by correspondence is kept at anything like a desirable level in the Party. How much more so is this the case as regards linking up the Party in a single organism.

Thus: 1) The Party's isolation from the broad masses, and 2) the isolation of its organizations from one another—that is the essence of the crisis the Party is passing through.

It is not difficult to understand that the cause of all this is the crisis in the revolution itself, the temporary triumph of the counter-revolution, the lull after the various actions, and lastly, the loss of all those semi-liberties which the Party enjoyed during 1905 and 1906. The Party developed, expanded and grew strong while the revolution was progressing, while liberties existed. The revolution retreated, the liberties vanished— and the Party began to ail, the intellectuals began to desert the Party, and later these were followed by the most vacillating of the workers. In particular, the desertion of the intellectuals was accelerated by the ideological growth of the Party, or rather of the advanced workers, who with their complex requirements have outgrown the meagre mental stock-in-trade of the "intellectuals of 1905."

It by no means follows from this, of course, that the Party must vegetate in this state of crisis until future liberties are ushered in, as some people mistakenly think. In the first place, the ushering in of these liberties depends largely upon whether the Party will emerge from the crisis healthy and renovated; liberties do not fall from the skies, they are won thanks, among other things, to the existence of a well-organized workers' Party. Secondly, the universally known laws of the class struggle tell us that the steadily growing organization of the bourgeoisie must inevitably result in a corresponding organization of the proletariat. And everybody knows that the renovation of our Party, as the only workers' party, is a necessary preliminary condition for the growth of the organization of our proletariat as a class.

Consequently, our Party's recovery before liberties are ushered in, its release from the crisis, is not only possible but inevitable.

The whole point is to find ways of bringing about the recovery of the Party, to find means by which the Party 1) will link up with the masses, and 2) unite the organizations now isolated from one another in a single organism.

* * *

And so, how can our Party extricate itself from the crisis; what must be done to achieve this?

Make the Party as legal as possible and unite it around the legal group in the Duma, some say to us. But how can it be made as legal as possible when the most innocuous legal institutions, such as cultural societies, etc., are suffering severe persecution? Can it be done by abandoning its revolutionary demands? But that would mean burying the Party, not renovating it! Moreover, how can the group in the Duma link the Party with the masses when it is itself isolated not only from the masses, but also from the Party organizations?

Clearly, such a solution of the problem serves only to confuse it further and to make it difficult for the Party to extricate itself from the crisis.

Transfer as large a part of the Party functions as possible to the workers themselves and thereby rid the Party of the inconstant intellectual elements, others tell us. There can be no doubt that ridding the Party of useless guests and concentrating functions in the hands of the workers themselves would contribute a great deal to the renovation of the Party. But it is no less clear that the mere "transfer of functions" under the old system of organization, with the old methods of Party work, and with "leadership" from abroad, cannot link the Party up with the masses and weld it into a single whole.

Obviously, half-measures cannot achieve much—we must seek radical means for a radical cure of the ailing Party.

The Party is suffering primarily from its isolation from the masses; it must be linked up with the masses at all costs. But this can be done under our present conditions primarily and mainly on the basis of those questions which are particularly exciting the broad masses. Take, for example, the impoverishment of the masses and the offensive launched by capital. Huge lockouts swept over the workers like a hurricane, and the cutting down of production, arbitrary dismissals, reduction of wages, lengthening of the working day and the capitalist offensive in general are continuing to this day. It can hardly be realized what suffering all this is causing among the workers, how intently it is making them think, what a host of "misunderstandings" and conflicts arise between the workers and the employers, what a mass of interesting questions are arising in the minds of the workers on this basis. Let our organizations, in addition to conducting general political work, constantly intervene in all these minor conflicts, let them link these up with the great class struggle and, backing the masses in their daily protests and demands, demonstrate the great principles of our Party by means of living facts. It should be clear to everybody that only in this way will it be possible to stir the masses who have been "forced to the wall," only in this way will it be possible to "shift" them past the accursed dead point. And "shifting" them past this dead point means precisely—rallying them around our organizations.

The Party committees in the factories and works are the Party organs which could most successfully develop such activities among the masses. The advanced workers in the factory and works committees are the living people who could rally to the Party the masses who are around them. All that is needed is that the factory and works committees should constantly intervene in all the affairs of the workers' struggle, champion their daily interests and link up the latter with the fundamental interests of the proletarian class. To make the factory and works committees the principal bastions of the Party —such is the task.

Further, in pursuit of the same object of drawing closer to the masses, the structure of the other, higher,

Party organizations must be adapted to the task of defending not only the political but also the economic interests of the masses. Not a single branch of industry of any importance must escape the attention of the organization. To achieve this, in building up the organization the territorial principle must be supplemented by the industrial principle, i.e., the factory and works committees in the various branches of industry must be grouped in sub-districts according to industry, and these sub-districts must be linked up territorially in districts, etc. It will not matter if this increases the number of sub-districts—the organization will gain a firmer and more stable foundation, and it will become more closely linked with the masses.

Of still greater importance for overcoming the crisis is the composition of the Party organizations. The most experienced and influential of the advanced workers must find a place in all the local organizations, the affairs of the organizations must be concentrated in their strong hands, and it is they who must occupy the most important posts in the organizations, from practical and organizational posts to literary posts. It will not matter if the workers who occupy important posts are found to lack sufficient experience and training and even stumble at first—practice and the advice of more experienced comrades will widen their outlook and in the end train them to become real writers and leaders of the movement. It must not be forgotten that Bebels do not drop from the skies, they are trained only in the course of work, by practice, and our movement now needs Russian Bebels, experienced and mature leaders from the ranks of the workers, more than ever before,

That is why our organizational slogan must be: "Widen the road for the advanced workers in all spheres of Party activity," "give them more scope!"

It goes without saying that in addition to the will to lead and initiative in leadership, the advanced workers must possess considerable knowledge. We have few workers who possess knowledge. But it is just here that the assistance of experienced and active intellectuals will be of use. Arrangements must be made for higher circles, "discussion groups" for advanced workers, at least one in every district, at which they will systematically "go through" the theory and practice of Marxism. All this would to a very large extent fill the gaps in the knowledge of the advanced workers and help them to become lecturers and ideological leaders in the future. At the same time, the advanced workers must more often deliver lectures at their works and factories to "get the utmost practice," even at the risk of "making a mess of it" in the opinion of their audience. They must once and for all cast aside excessive modesty and stage fright, and arm themselves with audacity, confidence in their own strength. It will not matter if they make mistakes at first; they will stumble once or twice, and then learn to walk independently like "Christ walking on the water."

In short, 1) intensified agitation around daily needs linked with the general class needs of the proletariat, 2) organization and consolidation of the committees in the factories and works as the Party's most important district centres, 3) the "transfer" of the most important Party functions to the advanced workers and 4) the organization of "discussion groups" for the advanced workers—such are the means by which our organizations will be able to rally the broad masses around themselves.

One cannot help observing that life itself is pointing out this path to the overcoming of the Party crisis. The Central District and the Urals have been doing without intellectuals for a long time; there the workers themselves are conducting the affairs of the organizations. In Sormovo, Lugansk (Donets Basin) and Nikolayev, the workers in 1908 published leaflets and in Nikolayev, in addition to leaflets, they published an illegal organ. In Baku the organization has systematically intervened in all the affairs of the workers' struggle and has missed scarcely a single conflict between the workers and the oil owners, while, of course, at the same time conducting general political agitation. Incidentally, this explains why the Baku organization has maintained contact with the masses to this day.

Such is the situation as regards the methods of linking the Party with the broad masses of the workers.

But the Party suffers not only from isolation from the masses. It also suffers from the isolation of its organizations from one another.

Let us pass to this last question.

*
*   *

And so, how can the isolated local organizations be linked up with one another, how can they be linked up in a single well-knit Party, living a common life?

One might think that the general Party conferences that are sometimes arranged would solve the problem, would unite the organizations; or that *Proletary*, *Golos* and *Sotsial-Demokrat*, which are published abroad, would, in the long run, rally and unite the Party. There can be no doubt that both the first and the second are of no little importance in linking up the organizations. At any rate, the conferences and the organs that are published abroad have been until now the only means of linking up the isolated organizations. But in the first place, conferences, arranged very rarely at that, can link up the organizations only for a time and, therefore, not as durably as is required in general: in the intervals between conferences the connections are broken and the old amateurish methods continue as before. Secondly, as regards the organs that are published abroad, apart from the fact that they reach Russia in extremely limited quantities, they naturally lag behind the course of Party life in Russia, are unable to note in time and comment on the questions that excite the workers and, therefore, cannot link our local organizations together by permanent ties. The facts show that since the London Congress, the Party has succeeded in organizing two conferences[78] and in printing scores of issues of the organs published abroad; and yet the work of uniting our organizations in a genuine Party, the work of overcoming the crisis, has made scarcely any headway.

Hence, conferences and organs published abroad, while extremely important for uniting the Party, are, nevertheless, inadequate for overcoming the crisis, for permanently uniting the local organizations.

Evidently, a radical measure is needed.

The only radical measure can be the publication of an all-Russian newspaper, a newspaper that will serve as the centre of Party activity and be published in Russia.

It will be possible to unite the organizations scattered over Russia only on the basis of common Party activity. But common Party activity will be impossible unless the experience of the local organizations is collected at a common centre from which the generalized Party experience can later be distributed to all the local organizations. An all-Russian newspaper could serve as this centre, a centre that would guide, co-ordinate and direct Party activity. But in order that it might really guide the Party's activity it must receive from the localities a constant stream of inquiries, statements, letters, information, complaints, protests, plans of work, questions which excite the masses, etc.; the closest and most durable ties must link the newspaper with the localities; acquiring in this way adequate material, the newspaper must note in time, comment on and elucidate the necessary questions, distil from this material the necessary directions and slogans and bring them to the knowledge of the entire Party, of all its organizations. . . .

If these conditions do not exist there can be no leadership in Party work, and if there is no leadership in Party work the organizations cannot be permanently linked up in a single whole!

That is why we emphasize the necessity of precisely an all-Russian newspaper (and not one published abroad), and precisely a leading newspaper (and not simply a popular one).

Needless to say, the only institution that can undertake to launch and run such a newspaper is the Central Committee of the Party. Even apart from this it is the duty of the Central Committee to guide Party work; but at the present time it is performing this duty unsatisfactorily and, as a result, the local organizations are almost completely divorced from one another. And yet, a well-run all-Russian newspaper could serve as a most effective instrument in the hands of the Central Committee for effectively uniting the Party and guiding Party activity. More than that, we assert that only in this way can the Central Committee be transformed from a fictitious centre into a real, all-Party centre, which will really link up the Party, and really set the tone of its activity. In view of this, the organization and running of an all-Russian newspaper is the direct task of the Central Committee.

Thus, an all-Russian newspaper as an organ that will unite and rally the Party around the Central Committee—such is the task, such is the way of overcoming the crisis through which the Party is passing.

———

Let us sum up all that has been said above. Owing to the crisis in the revolution, a crisis has developed in the Party—the organizations have lost permanent contact with the masses, the Party has been broken up into separate organizations.

Our organizations must be linked up with the broad masses—this is a local task.

The above-mentioned organizations must be linked up with one another, around the Central Committee of the Party—this is a central task.

To carry out the local task, in addition to general political agitation, economic agitation must be conducted around the acute daily needs of the workers; there must be systematic intervention in the workers' struggle;

factory and works Party committees must be formed and consolidated; as many of Party functions as possible must be concentrated in the hands of the advanced workers; "discussion groups" must be organized for the advanced workers for the purpose of training mature workers' leaders equipped with knowledge.

To carry out the central task we must have an all-Russian newspaper that will link the local organizations with the Central Committee of the Party and unite them in a single whole.

Only if these tasks are carried out will the Party be able to emerge from the crisis healthy and renovated; only by fulfilling these conditions can the Party undertake the responsible role of worthy vanguard of the heroic Russian proletariat.

Such are the ways of overcoming the Party crisis.

Needless to say, the more fully the Party utilizes the legal possibilities around it—from the floor of the Duma and the trade unions to co-operative societies and burial funds—the sooner will the task of overcoming the crisis, the task of the renovation and recovery of the Russian Social-Democratic Labour Party, be carried out.

Bakinsky Proletary, Nos. 6 and 7,   Reprinted from the newspaper
August 1 and 27, 1909

Unsigned

THE FORTHCOMING GENERAL STRIKE

The Baku workers are going through hard times. The offensive which the oil owners launched in the spring of last year is still continuing. The gains which the workers won in the past are being taken away from them to the very last. And the workers "have to" keep silent, to bear it "without end."

Wages are being reduced by direct cuts or by the withdrawal of rent allowances, bonuses, etc. The working day is being lengthened, since the three-shift system is being replaced by the two-shift system, and overtime and gang work are becoming practically obligatory. The so-called "reduction of staffs" is continuing as before. Workers, and particularly class-conscious workers, are discharged on trifling pretexts, and often without any pretext at all. "Black-listing" is being applied in the most ruthless manner. The "permanent" worker system is being replaced by the "casual" docket system, under which workers can always be deprived of their livelihood on trifling pretexts. The "system" of fines and beating-up is in full swing. The oil field and works commissions are no longer recognized. The workmen's compensation law is evaded in the most flagrant manner. Medical assistance has been reduced to a minimum.

The "hard-labour law," as the ten-kopek hospital levy is called, continues to operate. Hygiene and sanitation are neglected. Education is in a wretched state. The people's halls have been closed. No evening classes are being conducted. No lectures are being delivered. There are only dismissals without end! The lengths to which the oil owners go in their arrogance is seen from the fact that to avoid paying rent allowances many of the big firms, like the Caspian Company, for example, directly prohibit "their" workers from marrying without the management's permission. And the oil kings do all this with impunity. Conscious of their strength, and seeing the success of their cunningly devised offensive tactics, they continue to torment the workers.

But the success of the oil owners' offensive is not at all accidental; it is wholly determined by many favourable external conditions. First of all, there is the general lull in Russia, the counter-revolutionary situation, which provides a favourable atmosphere for the capitalist offensive. Needless to say, under other circumstances, the oil owners would have been obliged to curb their appetites. Then there is the purely flunkey obsequiousness of the local authorities, headed by the pogromist Martynov, who are ready to do anything to please the oil owners—recall, for example, the "Mirzoyev case." Further, the poor state of organization of the workers due, to a large extent, to the constant flux among the oil workers. Everybody understands how important the oil workers are in the struggle against the oil owners, but it is they who are most closely connected with the rural districts and are least "fit" for an organized struggle. Lastly, there is the system of split wages (which consist, among other things, of bonuses, and of rent, travel, bath, and other allowances), which facilitates cuts. It needs no proof that direct wage cuts are not so easy to carry through as are disguised, partial cuts in the shape of the gradual withdrawal of bonuses and of rent, travel and other allowances, where the illusion is created that the "actual" wage is left untouched.

Naturally, all this, together with the growing experience and organization of the oil owners, greatly facilitates the capitalist offensive in the kingdom of oil.

When this furious offensive of the oil kings will cease, whether there will be a limit to their arrogance, depends upon whether they meet with the powerful and organized resistance of the workers.

So far only one thing is clear, namely, that the oil owners want to smash the workers "completely," to knock the fighting spirit out of them "once and for all," to convert "their" workers into obedient slaves "at all costs." They pursued this aim as far back as the spring of last year when, after preventing the conference, they tried to provoke the workers into an unorganized general strike in order to be able to crush them at one stroke. This is the aim they are pursuing now by maliciously and systematically attacking the workers, and often provoking them to spontaneous actions.

So far the workers are silent, dumbly bearing the blows of the oil owners, while anger accumulates in their breasts. But in view of the fact that, on the one hand, the arrogance of the oil owners is steadily growing, that they are depriving the workers of their last crumbs, reducing the workers to pauperism, tormenting them and provoking them to spontaneous outbreaks, and that, on the other hand, the patience of the workers is steadily running out, giving place to sullen, constantly increasing discontent against the oil owners—in view of all this, we may confidently assert that an outburst of anger on the part of the oil workers is quite inevitable in the near future. One of two things: either the workers will indeed be patient "without end" and sink to the level of slavishly obedient Chinese coolies—or they will rise up against the oil owners and clear the road to a better life. The steadily rising anger of the masses shows that the workers will inevitably take the second path, the path of fighting the oil owners.

The situation in the oil industry is such that it fully permits not only of a defensive struggle by the workers, not only the retention of the old positions, but also the passing to the offensive and the winning of new positions, further increases in wages, further reductions of the working day, etc.

Indeed, since the oil owners' profits are fabulously high at the present time compared with the profits of other employers in Russia and in Europe; since the oil market is not shrinking but, on the contrary, is expanding and spreading to new regions (Bulgaria, for example), since the gushers are steadily increasing in number, and since oil prices are not dropping but, on the contrary, show a tendency to rise—is it not clear that it is quite possible for the workers to break the chains of slavish patience, throw off the yoke of shameful silence, hoist the flag of a counter-offensive against the oil owners and win from them new and better conditions of labour?...

But while remembering all this, we must not forget that the forthcoming general strike will be the most serious, prolonged and stubborn strike that has ever taken place in Baku. It must be borne in mind that in previous strikes we were favoured by 1) the general upsurge in Russia, 2) the relative "neutrality" of the local authorities as a consequence of this, and 3) the inexperience and lack of organization of the oil owners, who lost their heads as soon as a strike broke out. But not one of these three conditions exists now. The general upsurge has given way to a general lull, which encourages the oil owners. The relative "neutrality" of the local authorities has given way to their complete readiness to resort to every means of "pacification." The inexperience and lack of organization of the oil owners has given way to their organization. More than that, the oil owners have become so skilled at fighting that they themselves are provoking the workers to go on strike. They are even not averse to provoking them to go out on a general strike, so long as it is an unorganized one, which would enable them to "crush" the workers "at one stroke."

All this goes to show that the workers have before them a stern and difficult struggle against organized enemies. A fight is inevitable. Victory is possible in spite of numerous unfavourable conditions. All that is necessary is that the workers' struggle should not be spontaneous and sporadic, but organized, systematic and conscious.

Only on this condition can victory be expected.

We cannot tell just when the general strike will begin—in any case it will not begin when it suits the oil owners. So far we know only one thing, namely, that we must at once initiate persevering preparatory work for a general strike and devote to it all our mental capacities, our energy and our courage.

Strengthen our solidarity, our organization—such is the slogan of our preparatory work.

Hence, we must set to work at once to rally the masses of the workers around Social-Democracy, around the unions. First of all, we must put an end to the split in the organization, we must unite the two groups in one body. We must also put an end to the split in the unions and unite them in one strong union. We must revive the oil field and works commissions, imbue them with the spirit of socialism, link them with the masses, and through them link ourselves with the entire army of oil industry workers. We must proceed to draw up common demands that can unite the workers in one powerful army. We must constantly intervene in all the conflicts between the workers and the oil owners and thereby in fact rally the workers around Social-Democracy. In short, we must prepare tirelessly, to the utmost, in order worthily to meet the difficult but glorious forthcoming general strike.

We call for united efforts in the work of preparing for a general economic strike.

Bakinsky Proletary, No. 7,   Reprinted from the newspaper
August 27, 1909
Signed: *K. Ko*. . . .

PARTY NEWS[79]

We publish below the resolution adopted by the Baku Committee on the disagreements on the Editorial Board of *Proletary*. These disagreements are not new. A controversy has long been going on around them in our press abroad. There is even talk about a split in the Bolshevik group. The Baku workers, however, know little or nothing about the nature of these disagreements. We consider it necessary, therefore, to preface the resolution with a few points of explanation.

First of all, about the alleged split in the Bolshevik group. We declare that there is no split in the group, and that there never has been one; there are only disagreements on the question of legal possibilities. Disagreements of that sort have always existed and always will exist in such an active and live group as the Bolshevik group. Everybody knows that at one time there were rather serious disagreements in the group on the question of the agrarian programme, on guerilla actions, and on the unions and the Party, and in spite of that the group did not split, for complete solidarity reigned within the group on other important questions of tactics. The same must be said in the present case. Consequently, the talk about a split in the group is pure fiction.

As regards the disagreements, on the enlarged Editorial Board of *Proletary*,[80] consisting of twelve members, two trends were revealed: the majority on the Board (ten against two) is of the opinion that the legal possibilities in the shape of the unions, clubs, and particularly the floor of the Duma, should be utilized for the purpose of strengthening the Party, that the Party should not recall our group from the Duma but, on the contrary, should help the group to rectify its mistakes and conduct correct, openly Social-Democratic agitation from the floor of the Duma. The minority on the Board (two), around whom the so-called Otzovists and Ultimatumists are grouped, are, on the contrary, of the opinion that the legal possibilities are of no particular value; they look with distrust upon our group in the Duma, do not think it necessary to support the group, and under certain circumstances would not be averse even from recalling it from the Duma.

The Baku Committee is of the opinion that the point of view of the minority on the Editorial Board is not in accord with the interests of the Party and of the proletariat and, therefore, emphatically supports the stand taken by the majority on the Board represented by Comrade Lenin.

RESOLUTION OF THE BAKU COMMITTEE ON THE DISAGREEMENTS ON THE ENLARGED EDITORIAL BOARD OF *PROLETARY*

The Baku Committee discussed the situation on the enlarged Editorial Board of *Proletary* on the basis of the printed documents sent by both sections of the Board and arrived at the following conclusion.

1) As far as the substance of the matter is concerned, the stand taken by the majority on the Editorial Board regarding activities inside and outside the Duma is the only correct one. The Baku Committee believes that only such a stand can be described as truly Bolshevik, Bolshevik in spirit and not only in letter.

2) "Otzovism" as a trend in the group is a result of the underrating of legal possibilities, and of the Duma in particular, which is harmful to the Party. The Baku Committee asserts that under the present conditions of a lull, when other, more important means of conducting open Social-Democratic agitation are absent, using the Duma as a platform can and should be one of the most important branches of Party activity.

3) "Ultimatumism," as a constant reminder to the group in the Duma about Party discipline does not constitute a trend in the Bolshevik group. In so far, however, as it tries to pose as a separate trend, which *confines itself* to demonstrating the rights of the Central Committee in relation to the group in the Duma, "Ultimatumism" is the worst species of "Otzovism." The Baku Committee asserts that constant work by the Central Committee within and with the group can alone make the latter a truly Party and disciplined group. The Baku Committee believes that the facts concerning the Duma group's activities during the past few months clearly prove all this.

4) So-called "god-building" as a literary trend and, in general, the introduction of religious elements into socialism is the result of an interpretation of the principles of Marxism that is unscientific and therefore harmful for the proletariat. The Baku Committee emphasizes that

Marxism took shape and developed into a definite world outlook not as the result of an alliance with religious elements, but as the result of an implacable struggle against them.

5) Proceeding from the foregoing, the Baku Committee is of the opinion that an implacable *ideological* struggle against the above-mentioned trends which group themselves around the minority on the Editorial Board is one of the most urgent and immediate tasks of Party activity.

6) On the other hand, in view of the fact that, notwithstanding the above-mentioned disagreements, both sections of the Editorial Board agree on questions of major importance for the group (appraisal of the current situation, the role of the proletariat and of other classes in the revolution, etc.), the Baku Committee believes that the unity of the group, and hence co-operation between both sections of the Editorial Board, are possible and necessary.

7) In view of this, the Baku Committee disagrees with the organizational policy of the majority on the Editorial Board and protests against any "ejection from our ranks" of supporters of the minority on the Editorial Board. The Baku Committee also protests against the conduct of Comrade Maximov who declared that he would not submit to the decisions of the Editorial Board, thus creating fresh grounds for new and greater friction.

8) As a practical measure for putting an end to the present abnormal situation, the Baku Committee proposes that a conference of Bolsheviks be held parallel with the general Party conference.[81]

On the questions of "the school in X" and the attitude towards the "Left Mensheviks," the Baku Committee refrains from adopting any definite resolutions for the time being owing to the absence of sufficient material.

August 2, 1909

Bakinsky Proletary, No. 7,
August 27, 1909

Reprinted from the newspaper

THE DECEMBER STRIKE
AND THE DECEMBER AGREEMENT

(On the Occasion of the Fifth Anniversary)

Comrades!

Today marks the fifth anniversary of the declaration of the general economic strike in the districts of Baku in December 1904.

In a few days' time we shall see the fifth anniversary of the drafting by the workers and the oil owners of the famous December agreement, our "oil constitution."

We proudly recall those days because they were the days of our victory, days of the defeat of the oil owners!

Before our eyes rises the glorious scene, familiar to us all, when thousands of strikers surrounded the Electric Power offices and dictated the December demands to their delegates, while the representatives of the oil owners, who had taken shelter in the Electric Power offices and were besieged by the workers, "expressed their solidarity," signed the agreement, "agreed to everything.". . .

That was a genuine victory for the poor proletarians over the rich capitalists, a victory which laid the foundations of a "new order" in the oil industry.

Before the December agreement we worked, on the average, eleven hours a day—after the agreement a nine-hour day was established and an eight-hour day was gradually introduced for the workers at the wells.

Before the December agreement we received on the average about eighty kopeks per day—after the agreement wages were raised to a ruble and some kopeks per day.

Before the December strike we received neither rent allowances, nor water, light or fuel—thanks to the strike we obtained all these for the mechanics, and it remained only to extend these benefits to the rest of the workers.

Before the December strike the flunkeys of capital exercised arbitrary power in the oil fields and at the works, and they beat us up and fined us with impunity—thanks to the strike, a definite system, a definite "constitution" was introduced, by virtue of which we were enabled to express our will through our delegates, collectively to reach agreement with the oil owners, and collectively to establish mutual relations with them.

From "amsharas"[82] and "pack animals" we, at one stroke, became men, fighting for a better life!

That is what the December strike and the December agreement gave us!

But that is not all. The main thing the December struggle gave us was confidence in our own strength, confidence in victory, readiness for fresh battles, the consciousness that only "our own right hand" can shiver the chains of capitalist slavery. . . .

After that we made continual progress, increasing wages, extending rent allowances to the oil workers, consolidating the "oil constitution," achieving the partial recognition of the oil field and works commissions, organizing in unions and uniting around Social-Democracy. . . .

But all this did not last long. When the revolution retreated and the counter-revolution gained strength, particularly from the beginning of 1908, the oil owners, hypocritically pleading as an excuse the reduction of output and the shrinking of the oil market, began to withdraw our former gains. They withdrew the bonuses and rent allowances. They introduced the two-shift system and a twelve-hour day in place of the three-shift system and the eight-hour day. They cut down medical assistance. They have already taken away the people's halls, and are taking away the schools, allocating a paltry sum for their maintenance while they spend over 600,000 rubles per annum on the police. On top of all this, beating and fines are being reintroduced, the commissions have been abolished, and the myrmidons of the tsarist government, the servant of big capital, are persecuting the unions. . . .

Thus, during the past two years, not only have we had to give up the idea of further improving our conditions, but our conditions have been made worse; we have been deprived of our former gains and have been thrown back to the old, pre-December times.

And now, on December 13, the fifth anniversary of the victorious December strike, when the oil owners trembled before us and we, attacking, gained new rights— precisely today there rises before us the grave question which is exciting the masses of the oil industry workers: Shall we remain silent much longer, is there a limit to our patience, should we not break the chains of silence and hoist the flag of a general economic strike for our vital demands?

Judge for yourselves! Output this year has reached 500,000,000 poods—a figure not reached in any of the past four years. The price of oil is not dropping at all, for the average price for the year is the same as last year—

twenty-one kopeks. The quantity of gusher oil, which involves no expenditure—is steadily increasing. The market is expanding day by day, abandoning coal and passing over to oil. Oil deliveries are steadily increasing. And yet, the more business.improves for the oil owners, the more "profit" they squeeze out of the workers, the more overbearing do they become to the latter, the more tightly do they squeeze the workers, the more zealously do they discharge class-conscious comrades, and the more determinedly do they deprive us of our last crumbs!

Is it not clear, comrades, that the situation in the oil industry is becoming more and more favourable for a general struggle by the oil industry workers, and that the provocative conduct of the oil owners is inevitably pushing the workers towards such a struggle?

For, comrades, one of two things: either we go on bearing it without end and sink to the level of dumb slaves—or we rise up for a general struggle in support of our common demands.

Our entire past and present, our struggle and our victories, point to the fact that we shall choose the second path, the path of the general strike for higher wages and an eight-hour day, for housing settlements and rent allowances, for people's halls and schools, for medical assistance and compensation for disablement, for the rights of the oil field and works commissions and unions.

And we shall gain our object, comrades, notwithstanding the unprecedented reprisals, notwithstanding the growing organization of the oil owners; we shall bring our masters to their knees as we did five years ago, if we intensify our work in preparation for a general strike, if we strengthen our oil field and works commissions, if we enlarge our unions, and if we rally around Social-Democracy.

Social-Democracy led us to victory in December 1904; it will lead us to future victories through an organized general strike.

This is what the experience of the glorious December struggle tells us.

Let then this day, the opening day of the victorious strike in December 1904, inspire us to make united and persevering efforts to prepare for a general strike!

Let our common feelings for this day serve the oil owners as a grim omen of the coming general strike led by Social-Democracy!

Long Live the Coming General Strike!

Long Live Social-Democracy!

The Baku Committee of the R.S.D.L.P.

December 13, 1909

Published in leaflet form   Reprinted from the leaflet

LETTERS FROM THE CAUCASUS[83]

I

BAKU

THE SITUATION IN THE OIL INDUSTRY

After the country became "pacified" to some extent, after the good harvest in Russia and a revival of activity in the Central Industrial region, the oil industry entered the phase of a minor boom. Owing to the risky nature of partial strikes (because of the cruel political reprisals and the growing organization of the oil owners) arrears of oil output due to strikes dropped to a matter of half a million poods (in 1908 they amounted to 11,000,000 poods and in 1907 to 26,000,000 poods). The absence of strikes and the steady rate of oil bailing served as one of the favourable conditions for increasing the output of gusher oil. The (relative) stability which set in in the oil industry helped it to recover the market it had lost during the past few years. This year oil output rose to 500,000,000 poods—a figure not reached in any of the past four years (last year it amounted to 467,000,000 poods). Thanks to the increased demand for liquid fuel in the Central Industrial region and to the substitution of oil for Donets coal on the South-Eastern, Ryazan-Urals and Moscow-Kazan railways, oil deliveries this year greatly exceed those of last year. Notwithstanding the wailing of the oil owners, the price of oil is not dropping but remains steady, for the average price for the year is the same as that of last year (twenty-one kopeks). And every now and again the heaven-blessed wells burst out in gushers, and it rains oil for the benefit of the oil owners.

In short, "business" is improving for the oil owners.

Meanwhile, economic reprisals, far from subsiding, are steadily increasing. "Bonuses" and rent allowances are being withdrawn. The three-shift system (eight hours' work) is being replaced by the two-shift system (twelve hours' work), while overtime gang work is becoming systematic. Medical assistance and expenditure on schools are being reduced to a minimum (although the oil owners spend over 600,000 rubles per annum on the police!). Canteens and people's halls have already been closed. The oil field and works commissions and the trade unions are absolutely ignored, class-conscious comrades are being discharged as in the old days. Fines and beatings are being reintroduced.

The police and the gendarmerie—the servants of the tsarist regime—are entirely at the service of the oil kings. The inundation of the Baku oil districts with spies and provocateurs, the mass deportation of workers for the slightest conflict with the oil owners, complete destruction of actual "liberties"—Baku's privileges—and arrests after arrests—such is the picture of the "constitutional" activities of the local authorities. This is quite understandable: firstly, they cannot "by their very nature" refrain from strangling every "liberty," even the most elementary; secondly, they are obliged to behave in this way because the oil industry, which provides the Treasury with a "revenue" of not less than 40,000,000 rubles per annum in the shape of royalties, quotas in money or in kind from government fields, excise duties and transportation charges, "needs" tranquillity and uninterrupted production. This is quite apart from the fact that every hitch in the oil industry has a depressing effect upon the Central Industrial region, and this, in turn, disturbs the government's "affairs." True, in the recent past the government considered it necessary to permit certain "liberties" in the oil districts and arranged "conferences" between the workers and the oil owners. But this was in the past, when the chances of the counter-revolution were not yet clear—then the policy of flirting with the workers was the most profitable one. Now, however, the situation is clear, the counter-revolution is "definitely" established—and the policy of brutal reprisals has taken the place of the flirting policy, the pogromist-Martynov has replaced the silver-tongued Junkovsky.

Meanwhile, the workers are becoming completely disillusioned about the expediency of partial strikes; they are more and more resolutely talking about a general economic strike. The fact that "business" is improving for the oil owners but that their acts of persecution are increasing for all that, greatly incenses the workers and puts them in a fighting mood. And the more resolutely their former gains are withdrawn the more the idea of a general strike matures in their minds, and the greater is the impatience with which they are "waiting" for the "declaration" of a strike.

The organization took into account the favourable situation for a strike in the oil industry and the strike mood among the workers and decided to start preparatory work for a general strike. At present the Baku Committee is engaged in canvassing the masses and in drawing up common demands that can rally the entire oil proletariat. In all probability the demands will include: an eight-hour day, higher wages, abolition of overtime and gang work, increased medical assistance, housing settlements and rent allowances, people's halls and schools, recognition of the commissions and the unions. The organization and its executive body, the Baku Committee, believe that, in spite of the intensification of the counter-revolution and the growing organization of the oil owners, the workers will succeed in gaining what they want if they oppose the enemy forces with their class organization by uniting the oil field and works commissions, by enlarging and strengthening the unions and by rallying around Social-Democracy. The choice of the moment to launch the struggle depends upon a variety of conditions which are difficult to foresee. So far, one thing is clear, namely, that a strike is inevitable and that it is necessary to prepare for it "without a moment's delay.". . .

LOCAL GOVERNMENT IN THE OIL FIELDS

The revival in the oil industry is not the only important event in the life of the Baku proletariat. A no less important event is the "Zemstvo campaign" that was launched here recently. We refer to local government in the Baku oil districts. After the Minister of the Interior's well-known "plan" for setting up Zemstvos for the border regions and the corresponding "circular" issued by the Viceroy of the Caucasus on the practical measures to be taken to introduce the Zemstvo in the Caucasus, the oil owners set to work to draw up a scheme of local government for the oil fields. The principles of the scheme, which the next (28th) oil owners' congress will undoubtedly endorse, are approximately as follows: The oil region (Balakhany, Romany, Sabunchi, Surakhany and Bibi-Eibat) is to form a Zemstvo unit separate from the city and the uyezd, to be called the oil field local government body. The functions of the oil field local government body are to cover: water supply, lighting, road building, tramways, medical assistance, people's halls, schools, erection of slaughter-houses and baths, workers' settlements, etc. In general the local government body is to be organized in conformity with the "regulations" of June 12, 1890,[84] with the difference, however, that according to these "regulations" half the seats in the Zemstvo are guaranteed to the nobility, whereas here, owing to the absence of members of the nobility (by separating the oil region from the uyezd the oil owners have insured themselves against the predominance of the landowners and have established their own predominance) this proportion of seats is guaranteed not even to all the oil owners, but to 23 of the biggest. Of the 46 seats in this local government body, 6 are allocated to representatives of government departments and public institutions, 4 to the working population numbering 100,000, 18 to the group paying two-thirds of all the taxes, i.e., to 23 of the biggest oil owners (the total budget is to amount to about 600,000 rubles per annum), 9 to the group paying one-sixth of the taxes, i.e., 140 to 150 medium oil owners who are in vassal dependence upon the big ones, and the remaining 9 seats are to go to the petty trading and industrial bourgeoisie (about 1,400 persons).

As you see, we have before us, first, the privileged capitalists, and second, a purely industrial Zemstvo, which is bound to become the arena of sharp conflicts between labour and capital.

By setting up a Zemstvo of precisely this character the oil owners want: firstly, to shift most of the cultural and municipal functions from their "congress" to the oil field local government body and thus convert the "congress" into a pure syndicate; secondly, to pass on some of the expenditure on the needs of the oil-field working population to the rest of the bourgeoisie, the owners of auxiliary enterprises, boring contractors, etc. As regards the allocation of four seats to the workers, who will elect "in conformity with the regulations governing the Third State Duma" (delegates to be elected by the workers' curia who are to elect four electors), this, far from being a sacrifice on the part of the oil owners, is very much to their advantage: four workers' representatives as window dressing for the local government body is so "liberal" and . . . so cheap, that the oil kings can readily concede this.

On the other hand, there can be no doubt that in so far as the oil field local government body will unite the oil bourgeoisie and the "auxiliary" bourgeoisie, so to speak, it must also unite the hitherto disunited oil industry workers and the workers in the auxiliary enterprises and give them the opportunity to voice their common demands through their four representatives.

Taking all this into account, the Baku Committee, in its resolution on oil field local government, decided to utilize the proposed scheme of local government *by participating in it* for the purpose of conducting agitation for the general economic needs of the workers and of strengthening the latter's organization.

Further, with a view to expanding the electoral system, and bearing in mind that the oil field local government body will, in general, deal with the same questions that excite the workers as those which the conferences hitherto called dealt with—and in the latter the workers always had equal representation with the oil owners—the organization is demanding in its resolution equal representation for the workers in the local government body, emphasizing in this resolution that the struggle inside the local government body will be effective only to the extent that it is backed by the struggle outside the local government body and serves the interests of that struggle.

Moreover, in view of the fact that the decision of the gubernia conference to exclude from the oil field local government area the villages of Balakhany, Sabunchi and Romany—which are actually workers' settlements—is disadvantageous to the workers, the organization is demanding that these villages be included in the oil field local government area.

Lastly, in the general part of the resolution, pointing to universal, equal, direct and secret suffrage as an essential condition for the free development of local government bodies and for the free manifestation of existing class antagonisms, the Baku Committee emphasizes the necessity of overthrowing the tsarist regime and of convening a popular Constituent Assembly as a preliminary condition for the creation of consistently democratic local government bodies. . . .

Oil field local government is still in the formative stage. The scheme proposed by the oil owners' commission has yet to be endorsed by the oil owners' congress, after which it must be submitted to the Ministry of the

Interior through the Viceroy's office, after that to the
State Duma, etc. Nevertheless, the organization decided
to launch a campaign forthwith, and to convene meetings
in the oil fields and at the works for the purpose of exposing the oil owners, of popularizing our platform among
the broad masses and of agitating for a popular Constituent
Assembly. With the same objects in view it will not reject either "participation" in the oil owners' congress
or utilization of the floor of the Duma, and will supply
our group in the Duma with the necessary materials.

THE STATE OF THE ORGANIZATION

In view of certain specifically Baku conditions prevailing in the oil fields (some possibility of holding meetings
not yet entirely destroyed by the authorities, the existence
of the oil field and works commissions), the state of the
organization in Baku differs favourably from the state of
the organizations in other parts of Russia. Furthermore,
the existence of so-called legal possibilities also facilitates our work. As a consequence, the organization has
fairly considerable connections. But these connections are
not being utilized owing to a shortage of forces and funds.
Oral, and more especially printed, agitation must be conducted in the Tatar, Armenian and Russian languages, but,
owing to the shortage of funds (and forces) we are obliged
to confine ourselves to the Russian language, although
the Moslem workers, for example, occupy the most important post in the industry (bailing) and they are relatively more numerous than the Russians or Armenians.
Bakinsky Proletary (the organ of the Baku Committee)[85]
which is published in Russian, has not come out for three

months owing, chiefly, to the absence of funds. At its last meeting the Baku Committee accepted the proposal of the Tiflis Committee to publish a joint organ, if possible in four, or three, languages (Russian, Tatar, Georgian and Armenian). The membership (in the strict sense of the term) of our organization does not exceed 300. Amalgamation with the Menshevik comrades (about 100 members) has not yet entered the phase of accomplishment—so far only wishes are observable, but the split cannot be liquidated by wishes alone. . . . Propaganda is being conducted only in the advanced study circles, which we here call "discussion groups." The system is one of lectures. A great shortage of serious propaganda literature is felt. . . . Isolation from the Party and complete lack of information about what the Party organizations in Russia are doing have a bad effect upon the Party membership. An all-Russian organ, regular general Party conferences, and systematic tours by members of the Central Committee could help matters. Of the decisions of a general organizational character adopted by the Baku Committee, the most important are the following two: on a general Party conference, and on an all-Russian organ.* On the first question, the Baku Committee considers that it is necessary to convene a conference at the earliest possible date to settle urgent, mainly organizational, questions. The Baku Committee also considers that it is necessary to convene, parallel with this conference, a conference of Bolsheviks to liquidate the abnormal situation that has existed within the group for the past few months. On the second question the Baku

---

* See pp. 202-05 in this volume.—*Ed*.

Committee, noting the isolation of the organizations from one another, and believing that only an *all-Russian organ* published in Russia can link up the Party organizations into a single whole, proposes that the Party should set to work to organize such a newspaper.

"LEGAL POSSIBILITIES"

The fact that our organization has coped with the crisis with relative ease, that it never suspended its activities and always responded to all the questions of the day in one way or another, is due to a large extent to the "legal possibilities" it enjoys, which continue to exist to this day. The "legal possibilities," in their turn, owe their existence, of course, to the special conditions prevailing in the oil industry, to the special role the latter plays in the national economy, but that is not the point just now. . . . Of the "legal possibilities" in Baku, of special interest are the oil field and works commissions. These commissions are elected by all the workers of a given firm without exception, irrespective of nationality and political convictions. Their function is to negotiate on behalf of the workers with the firm's management on questions affecting the oil fields and works. They are not yet legal organizations in the direct sense of the term, but indirectly, and actually, they are fully legal, for they exist on the basis of the "December agreement," the whole of which is published in the workers' "pay books" that have been issued with the permission of the authorities. The importance of the oil field and works commissions for our organization is clear; they enable our organization to exercise organized influence upon the entire mass of the oil workers; all that is necessary is that the commissions should uphold the decisions of our organization before the masses. True, the importance of the commissions is not so great now, for the oil owners no longer reckon with them, but the workers do "reckon" with them, and that is the most important for us. . . .

In addition to the commissions there are also the unions, actually two unions: that of the "oil industry workers" (about 900 members) and that of the "mechanical workers" (about 300 members). The union for "oil extraction" can be ignored, as its importance is extremely small. We shall not speak of the unions of other crafts which have no direct connection with the oil industry, or of the illegal seamen's union (about 200 members), which is under the influence of the Socialist-Revolutionaries, although this union is important for the oil industry. Of the two unions mentioned, the first (under Bolshevik influence) is especially popular among the workers. It is organized on the principle of industrial unionism and unites the workers of all categories of labour in the oil industry (extraction, boring, mechanical, refining, general labour). This type of organization is dictated by the conditions of the struggle, which make inexpedient strikes of mechanics, for example, independently of the oil producers, etc. This the workers realized* and they began to desert en masse the union of "mechanical workers." The point

---

* This has not yet been realized by Dmitriyev, who in his book *Practical Experience of the Trade Union Movement* "proves" the necessity of three unions on the basis of an "analysis" not of the conditions of the oil workers' struggle, but of . . . the technique of production: there are different crafts, therefore, there must be different unions, he argues.

is that this union (under Menshevik influence) is organized as a craft union, rejects the principle of industrial unionism and instead of one general union proposes three separate unions (mechanics, oil workers, and refiners). The craft union principle, however, was rejected by Baku practice long ago. This, incidentally, explains the steady decline of the "mechanical workers'" union. The leaders of the union themselves admit this by accepting as members workers other than mechanics, thereby violating their own principle. Had it not been for the false pride of the above-mentioned leaders, the union of "mechanical workers," after openly admitting its mistake, would long ago have merged with the union of the "oil industry workers."

Incidentally, about merging. "Negotiations" for merging the unions have been going on for two years already, but so far they have been fruitless because: 1) the Menshevik leaders are deliberately hindering the merger for fear that they will be submerged by the Bolshevik majority; 2) the groups under whose influence the unions are functioning have so far not yet united. And besides, with whom shall we unite? The 80 to 100 "members" that perhaps the Mensheviks have are themselves not yet united. At all events, during the past eight months we have not seen a single leaflet or heard a single pronouncement from the Menshevik "leading body," in spite of the fact that during this period the oil districts have witnessed important campaigns such as the general strike, the Zemstvo, the temperance, and other campaigns. The Menshevik organization is practically non-existent, liquidated. To put it plainly, there is nobody to unite with. And this state of affairs naturally hinders the merging of the unions. . . .

Both unions are non-party; but this does not prevent them from maintaining the closest connection with the Party organization.

The influence of the unions upon the masses is considerable, especially that of the union of the "oil industry workers," and this automatically facilitates the task of uniting the most active elements around our organization.

Of the other "legal possibilities," those worthy of attention are the clubs (under Social-Democratic influence) and the "Trud" consumers' co-operative society[86] (under Socialist-Revolutionary and Social-Democratic influence), both being centres where the most active elements of the Baku proletariat are concentrated. Concerning their attitude towards the organization, especially the attitude of the "Znanie—Sila" club,[87] which operates in all the oil districts (the "Nauka" club operates only in the town), the same may be said as about the unions. . . .

The past two weeks were taken up with the temperance campaign, which called for the activity of nearly all the legal organizations. The stand taken by the Baku Committee on this question is expressed in its resolution. In the latter, drunkenness is regarded as an inevitable evil under capitalism, which can be abolished only with the fall of capitalism and the triumph of socialism. By reducing the workers and peasants to the condition of rightless slaves and robbing them of the opportunity to satisfy their cultural requirements, the existing autocratic-feudal regime helps to spread drunkenness among the toiling population to the utmost degree. This is apart from the fact that representatives of the "authorities" deliberately encourage drunkenness as a source of revenue for the Treasury. In view of all this, the Baku Committee maintains that neither the sermons preached by the "liberals," who convene congresses to combat drunkenness and organize "temperance societies," nor the exhortations of priests can diminish, let alone abolish, drunkenness, which is engendered by the inequalities in society, and intensified by the autocratic regime. All that is possible and necessary within the framework of the capitalist system is a struggle with the object not of abolishing drunkenness, but of reducing it to a minimum. But for such a struggle to be successful it is first of all necessary to overthrow the tsarist regime and to win a democratic republic, which will create the possibility for the free development of the class struggle and for the organization of the proletariat in town and country, for raising its cultural level and for widely training its forces for the great struggle for socialism. The Baku Committee regards the forthcoming congress to combat drunkenness[88] as a means of agitating for the democratic and socialist demands of the Russian proletariat, and instructs our delegate to combat the opportunist delegates at the congress who obscure the class tasks of the proletariat. . . .

December 20

First published in
Sotsial-Demokrat, No. 11,
February 13 (26), 1910

Signed: *K. S.*

The section "Legal
Possibilities" was written on
December 20, 1909

Signed: *K. Stefin*

Reprinted from the newspaper.
The section "Legal Possibilities"
reprinted from the manuscript

II

TIFLIS

As regards industrial development, Tiflis is the very opposite of Baku. While Baku is interesting as the centre of the oil industry, Tiflis can be of interest only as the administrative-commercial and "cultural" centre of the Caucasus. The total number of industrial workers in Tiflis is about 20,000, i.e., less than the number of troops and police. The only large enterprise here is the railway workshops (employing about 3,500 workers). Other enterprises employ 200 or 100 workers each, but most employ from 40 to 20. On the other hand, Tiflis is literally crammed with commercial establishments and with a "commercial proletariat" connected with them. Its small dependence on the big markets of Russia, which are always animated and feverish, puts an impress of stagnation on Tiflis. The absence of the sharp class conflicts that are characteristic only of large industrial centres converts it into something in the nature of a marsh, waiting to be stirred from outside. It is this, in particular, that explains why Menshevism, real, "Right" Menshevism, has held on so long in Tiflis. How different from Baku, where the sharp class stand of the Bolsheviks finds a lively response among the workers!

What is "self-evident" in Baku becomes evident in Tiflis only after prolonged discussion—the uncompromising speeches of the Bolsheviks are assimilated with great difficulty. It is this, in particular, that explains the "exceptional propensity" of the Tiflis Bolsheviks for discussion and, on the contrary, the desire of the Mensheviks to "avoid" discussion as far as possible. But the only conclusion to be drawn from the above is that the work of the revolutionary Social-Democrats in promoting the socialist education of the Tiflis proletariat will very often and inevitably assume the form of an ideological struggle against Menshevism. In view of this, exceptional interest attaches to even a cursory analysis of the ideological atmosphere, which must first of all be combated, and which is created by the Tiflis Mensheviks who so far are predominant in Tiflis. This atmosphere may be described as liquidationist, liquidationist not only in the organizational sense, but also in the tactical and programmatic sense. It is with a description of this atmosphere that we shall begin our cursory sketch of the state of Party affairs in Tiflis.

PROGRAMMATIC LIQUIDATIONISM

The organ in which Menshevik "public opinion" finds expression is the Georgian Menshevik press. The credo of the Tiflis Mensheviks is expressed in the articles "Questions of the Day" (see issues of the *Azri* and *Dasatskisi*[89]). The author of these articles is the most influential of the Tiflis Mensheviks, Comrade *An.*[90]

Let us proceed to review these articles, which provided the ideological ground for Liquidationism in Tiflis.

In the above-mentioned articles the author undertakes a "revaluation of all values" and arrives at the conclusion that the Party (and the Bolsheviks in particular) has erred in certain theses of its programme, especially its tactical theses. In the author's opinion, it is necessary "radically to change the entire tactics of the Party" in order to make it possible "to unite the forces of the bourgeoisie and the proletariat"—the sole guarantee of victory for the revolution. But let the author himself speak.

"The Bolsheviks argued," says the author, "that it (the proletariat) must carry out (in the bourgeois revolution) its entire minimum programme. But the carrying out of the social section of this minimum would fetter bourgeois production, would rouse the protest of the entire bourgeoisie, and lay the basis for a gigantic counter-revolution. . . . Who will dare assert that the introduction of an eight-hour day harmonizes with the interests of the present-day undeveloped bourgeoisie?" Clearly, "the carrying out of the Bolshevik minimum programme is mere declamation" (see *Azri*, No. 17, February 1908).

Of course, the Bolsheviks were not the only ones to talk about carrying out the entire minimum programme, and history knows of no Bolshevik minimum programme, it knows only of the minimum programme of the whole Party—but that is not the point of interest just now. The important thing is that in view of "the undeveloped state of the bourgeoisie" and the danger of counter-revolution that follows from it, our author rises in arms against the "social section" of the programme as "mere declamation," which, evidently, ought to be liquidated.

No analysis of the actual state of industry (Comrade *An*, obviously, uses incorrect terms in describing the backwardness of industry as the "undeveloped state of

13*

the bourgeoisie"—*K. St.*), no figures, nothing like serious data, are to be found in Comrade *An's* articles. He simply starts out with the bare proposition that the bourgeoisie will not tolerate the introduction of an eight-hour day, and yet, without the "union of the forces of the proletariat and the bourgeoisie," the victory of the revolution is impossible—hence, down with the "social section" of the programme. . . .

We shall not attempt to prove the absurdity of the author's assertions, which the liberals of our times advance against Social-Democrats every now and again. In our opinion it is quite sufficient to quote them to be able at once to grasp the nature of the Tiflis Mensheviks. . . .

But our author rises in arms not only against the "social section" of the programme. He does not spare its political section either, although he does not attack it so bluntly and openly. Let us hear what he says:

"The struggle of the proletariat alone, or of the bourgeoisie* alone, will under no circumstances smash the reaction. . . . Clearly, the union of their forces, their combination in one form or another, and their direction towards one common goal is the *only path* (our italics) to victory over the reaction.". . . "The defeat of the reaction, the winning of a constitution and the putting of the latter into effect, depends upon the conscious union of the forces of the bourgeoisie and the proletariat and their direction towards a common goal.". . . Moreover, "the proletariat must march in such a way as not to weaken the general movement by its uncompromising attitude." But as "the immediate demand of the bourgeoisie can consist only of a moderate constitution," obviously it is the duty of the proletariat to cast

---

* By "bourgeoisie" the author everywhere means the "middle," liberal bourgeoisie, "whose ideologists are the Cadets."—*K. St.*

aside its "radical constitution" if it does not wish "to weaken the general movement by its uncompromising attitude" and prevent the "conscious direction of the forces of the bourgeoisie and the proletariat towards one common goal," in short, if it does not want to prepare the ground for the victory of the counter-revolution (see *Dasatskisi*, No. 4, 1908).

The conclusion is obvious: down with the democratic republic, long live the "general movement" and ... a "moderate constitution" "to promote the victory" of the revolution, of course. ...

Before us, as you see, is a poor paraphrasing of the well-known article by the ex-Social-Democrat Vasilyev, in *Tovarishch* of 1906, on "the union of classes," on temporarily forgetting the class tasks of the proletariat, on withdrawing the demand for a democratic republic, etc. The difference is that Vasilyev spoke out bluntly and clearly, whereas Comrade *An* is ashamed to talk with sufficient clarity.

We have neither the time nor the inclination at the present moment to analyze the whole of this liberal prattle which, in the main, was analyzed and appraised in the Russian Social-Democratic press long ago. We would only like to call things by their proper names: our author's programmatic exercises, which the Tiflis Mensheviks have accepted as a "new" group manifesto, are tantamount to the liquidation of the Party's minimum programme, a liquidation that calls for the adaptation of our programme to the programme of the Cadets.

Let us pass from the "new" programme of the Tiflis Mensheviks to their "new tactics."

TACTICAL LIQUIDATIONISM

Comrade *An* is particularly displeased with the Party's tactics, which, in his opinion, must be "radically changed" (see *Dasatskisi*, No. 4). He therefore devotes the greater part of his articles to a criticism of these tactics. He particularly attacks the well-known "Plekhanov formula" ("the revolution in Russia will be victorious as a workers' movement, or will not be victorious at all "[91]), identifies it with the proposition about the hegemony of the proletariat and decides that it does not stand criticism. He proposes that this "formula" be replaced by a "new" (old!) proposition about "uniting the forces of the bourgeoisie and the proletariat" in the interests of the "general movement" . . . "towards one common goal." Listen to this:

"The proposition concerning the leading role of the proletariat in the bourgeois revolution is justified neither by Marx's theory nor by historical facts."

The appeal to theory:

"The proletariat cannot with its own hands build up the system of its own enemies. Hence, the leadership of the bourgeois revolution by the proletariat is impossible."

The appeal to historical facts:

"Our revolution was at the same time our workers' movement, but in spite of that the revolution was not victorious. Clearly, Plekhanov's formula proved to be wrong" (see *Azri*, No. 17).

Short and clear. We can only feel sorry for German Social-Democracy which admitted (frivolously no doubt!) in its letter of greeting to the London Congress that the leading role of the proletariat in our revolution is fully proved both by "Marx's theory" and by "historical facts." We shall say nothing about our (unhappy!) Party. . . .

What does our author substitute for the leading role of the proletariat? What does he offer in its place?

"The struggle of the proletariat alone," says Comrade *An*, "or of the bourgeoisie alone, will under no circumstances smash the reaction. . . . Clearly, the union of their forces, their combination in one form or another, and their direction towards one common goal is the only path to victory over the reaction." Moreover, "the proletariat must march in such a way as not to weaken the general movement by its uncompromising attitude" . . . (see *Dasatskisi*, No. 4). For, the author assures us, "*the weaker* the class struggle between the proletariat and the bourgeoisie the *more victorious* (all italics ours—*K. St.*) is the bourgeois revolution, other conditions being equal, of course" (see *Azri*, No. 15).

What "other equal conditions" the author is referring to—Allah knows! Only one thing is clear, and that is, that he is advocating a weakening of the class struggle in the interests . . . of the revolution. The proposition, confirmed by the experience of our entire revolution, that the more this revolution rests on the class struggle of the proletariat, which leads the rural poor against the landlords and the liberal bourgeoisie, the more complete will the victory of the revolution be—this proposition has remained for our author a secret sealed with seven seals. The only guarantee of the triumph of the revolution that Comrade *An* can see is: "The union of the forces of the proletariat with the forces of the bourgeoisie."

But what is this bourgeoisie in whom our author reposes such great hopes? Listen:

"The reactionaries," says our author, "are exceptionally vigorous in fighting the Cadet Party . . . because . . . the future masters of Russia will spring from that very middle class whose ideology the Cadets express. Political power can be wrested from the reactionaries only by the middle bourgeoisie, which has matured for the function of ruling; this class is their direct competitor, and that is why the reactionaries fear it more than any other." In general, "in all revolutions the reactionary class did not fear the revolutionaries as much as it feared the *moderate* bourgeoisie. Why? Because only that class takes the reins of government out of the hands of the old regime, as we said above. Hence, thanks to its *moderate* constitution it is this class that is destined to make the new system acceptable to the overwhelming majority and thereby cut the ground from under the feet of the reaction" (see *Azri*, No. 24). But as "the bourgeoisie cannot establish the new system without the proletariat," "the proletariat will have to support the bourgeois opposition" (see *Dasatskisi*, No. 4).

And so, it appears, the "moderate" Cadet bourgeoisie with its "moderate" monarchist constitution will save our revolution.

And the peasantry, what is its role in the revolution?

"Of course," says our author, "the peasantry will intervene in the movement and will lend it a spontaneous character, but only the two modern classes will play a decisive role": the moderate bourgeoisie and the proletariat (see *Dasatskisi*, No. 4).

And so, it is no use counting much on the peasantry, it appears.

Now everything is clear. For the triumph of the revolution we need the moderate Cadet bourgeoisie with a moderate constitution. But it cannot achieve victory alone, it needs the assistance of the proletariat. The proletariat must assist it because it has nobody to rely on—not even on the peasantry—except the moderate bourgeoisie. But for this it must cast aside its own un-compromising attitude and, extending a hand to the moderate bourgeoisie, wage a common struggle for a moderate Cadet constitution. All the rest will come of its own accord. A party which regards the struggle of the workers and peasants against the moderate bourgeoisie and the feudal landlords as a guarantee of the triumph of the revolution—is making a mistake.

In short, instead of the leading role of the proletariat which leads the peasants, we have the leading role of the Cadet bourgeoisie which leads the proletariat by the nose.

Such are the "new" tactics of the Tiflis Mensheviks.

There is no need, in our opinion, to analyze all this vile liberal rubbish. We need only observe that the "new" tactics of the Tiflis Mensheviks mean the liqui-dation of the Party's tactics, the correctness of which has been confirmed by the revolution, a liquidation which calls for the conversion of the proletariat into an ap-pendage of the moderate Cadet bourgeoisie.

First published in *Diskus-sionny Listok* (Supplement to *Sotsial-Demokrat*), No. 2, May 25 (June 7), 1910

Signed: *K. St.*

RESOLUTIONS ADOPTED
BY THE BAKU COMMITTEE
ON JANUARY 22, 1910

(*For the Forthcoming General Party Conference*)

I
POLITICAL AGITATION
AND THE ACTUAL CONSOLIDATION
OF THE PARTY

The state of depression and torpor into which the driving forces of the Russian revolution had fallen at one time is beginning to pass off.

The failure of the tsarist government's policy in the Balkans, in Persia, and in the Far East, the ridiculous efforts of the government to pacify the peasants with the aid of the law of November 9,[92] by which the poor are being driven from the land and the rich are being made richer; the utterly unsatisfactory nature of the government's "labour policy," which is depriving the workers of elementary liberties and putting them at the mercy of the capitalist robbers; the growing indebtedness of the Treasury and the selling of Russia piecemeal to foreign capital; the utter collapse of the administrative departments expressed in thieving by quartermasters and railway magnates, in the blackmail practised by criminal investigation departments, in the swindles practised by the secret police, etc.—all this is revealing to the masses the incapacity of the counter-revolution to cope with the latent forces of the revolution and is thereby facilitating the revival observed among the workers during the past months, rousing among them an interest in the political life of the country, and giving rise to the questions: What is to be done? Where shall we go? And so on.

The Party is faced with the burning necessity of conducting extensive political Party agitation. The pseudo-liberal counter-revolutionaries, who enjoy freedom of the press, are attempting to tame the masses by means of legal "congresses" and "societies" and to undermine Social-Democratic influence among the masses; that makes the question of conducting Party political agitation a matter of life or death for the Party.

Meanwhile, the isolation of our organizations from one another and the absence of a (leading) practical centre regularly functioning in Russia and actually uniting the local organizations in a single Party, preclude the possibility of conducting genuinely Party (and not amateurish group) political agitation, make it impossible for the Party effectively to counteract the systematic campaign of slander conducted by the "liberals," and so discredit the Party in the eyes of the workers.

This is apart from the fact that, instead of leading to the utilization of "legal possibilities," such a state of affairs can lead to the scattered and therefore weak illegal organizations being actually utilized by the "legal possibilities," to the detriment of the interests of Social-Democracy, of course.

In view of all this, the Baku Committee regards as an immediate and urgent task the drafting of measures for the actual consolidation of the Party and, consequently, for the conduct of Party political agitation.

The Baku Committee is of the opinion that among the necessary measures, the following should occupy the principal place:

1) the transference of the (leading) practical centre to Russia;

2) the establishment of an all-Russian leading newspaper connected with the local organizations, to be published in Russia and edited by the above-mentioned practical centre;

3) the establishment of local organs of the press in the most important centres of the labour movement (the Urals, Donets Basin, St. Petersburg, Moscow, Baku, etc.).

The Baku Committee is firmly convinced that the adoption of these measures can unite in the Social-Democratic Party all the genuine Party elements, irrespective of group, can create the possibility of conducting extensive political agitation, and greatly facilitate the extensive utilization of "legal possibilities" for the purpose of enlarging and consolidating our Party.

The Baku Committee therefore proposes that the Central Committee of the Party should immediately convene a general Party conference, at which the Baku Committee will submit the above-mentioned questions for discussion.

II

REPRESENTATION AT THE FORTHCOMING GENERAL PARTY CONFERENCE

The Baku Committee, having examined the organizational plan ("The Immediate Task," *Proletary*, No. 50) for the convocation of a general Party conference, is of the opinion that to it should be invited (in addition to the regular representation) representatives of the actually existing and functioning illegal Party organizations, and that attention should be paid mainly to the big centres where large masses of the proletariat are concentrated.

The necessity of such a kind of representation requires no proof (see special resolution concerning the conference agenda).

While recognizing the necessity of enlarged representation at the conference, the Baku Committee, nevertheless, expresses its emphatic opposition to giving special representation to groups functioning in legal "organizations."

The Baku Committee is of the opinion that special representation for such groups will contribute nothing material to the conference proceedings, either in those cases where such groups belong to local Party organizations and submit to their guidance, or in those cases where such groups only regard themselves as Social-Democratic, but do not recognize the leadership of the respective local organizations. In the first case, the representation of the Party organizations renders superfluous every kind of special representation. In the second case, special representation would contradict the very character of the conference, which must be strictly Party.

Published in leaflet form   Reprinted from the leaflet

AUGUST BEBEL,
LEADER OF THE GERMAN WORKERS

Who does not know Bebel, the veteran leader of the German workers, once a "mere" turner, but now a famous political leader before whose criticism "crowned heads" and accredited savants have often retreated as from hammer blows, whose words are heeded by the millions of proletarians in Germany like the words of a prophet?

On February 22 of this year Bebel reached the age of seventy.

On that day the militant proletariat of the whole of Germany, the International Socialist Bureau, and the organized workers in all countries all over the globe celebrated old Bebel's seventieth birthday.

How has Bebel earned this veneration? What has he done for the proletariat?

How did Bebel rise from the mass of the workers, how did he, a "mere" turner, become the great champion of the world proletariat?

What is the story of his life?

Bebel spent his childhood amidst poverty and privation. At the age of three he lost his father, the breadwinner of his family, a poor, consumptive non-commissioned officer. To provide the children with another breadwinner Bebel's mother married a second time, this time a prison warder. The mother and children left the army barracks in which they had lived hitherto and moved to the prison building.

But three years later the second husband died. The family was left without a breadwinner, so the mother took the children to her birthplace in the remote provinces, and there they lived in semi-starvation. Bebel, as the child of a poor family, was taken into a "charity school," which he successfully finished at the age of thirteen. But a year before he finished school another misfortune befell him—he lost his mother, his last support. A complete orphan, left to his own devices, and unable to continue his education, Bebel became the apprentice of a turner of his acquaintance.

A life of monotonous and arduous toil began. From five in the morning until seven at night Bebel worked in the workshop. Some variety was introduced in his life by books, to the reading of which he devoted all his spare time. To obtain books he subscribed to the local library, sacrificing the few pence per week he earned by carrying water for his mistress every morning before starting work.

Evidently, far from breaking the spirit of young Bebel, far from killing in him his striving towards the light, poverty and privation still further strengthened his will, increased his thirst for knowledge, raised in his mind questions, the answers to which he zealously sought in books.

And so, in the struggle against poverty, the future tireless fighter for the emancipation of the proletariat was trained.

On reaching the age of seventeen Bebel finished his apprenticeship and started life as a journeyman turner.

At the age of nineteen he attended a meeting of workers
in Leipzig and heard the speeches of socialist working men. This was the first meeting at which Bebel
came face to face with working-men orators. He was
not yet a Socialist, he sympathized with the liberals,
but he was sincerely glad to hear the independent
speeches of the workers, he envied them—and he was filled
with the ambition to become a working-man orator like
them.

From that moment a new life opened for Bebel—
a definite road stretched before him. He joined workers'
organizations and became very active in them. Soon
he acquired influence, and he was elected to the committee of the workers' unions. In the course of his activities in the unions he fought the Socialists and went
hand in hand with the liberals, but while fighting
the Socialists he gradually became convinced that they
were right.

In his twenty-sixth year he was already a Social-
Democrat. His fame spread so rapidly that a year later
(1867) he was elected chairman of the committee of
the unions and the first workers' representative in parliament.

Thus, fighting and winning, step by step surmounting
the obstacles that surrounded him, Bebel at last rose
from the mass of the workers and became the leader of
the militant workers of Germany.

From that time onwards Bebel openly supported
Social-Democracy. His immediate aim was to wage war
against the liberals, to free the workers from their influence, and to unite the workers in their own workers'
Social-Democratic Party.

Bebel achieved his aim in the following year, 1868, at the Nuremberg Congress. The skilful and relentless attack he launched at this congress brought about the utter defeat of the liberals, and German Social-Democracy rose up on the ruins of liberalism.

The emancipation of the workers can be the act only of the workers themselves, said Bebel at the congress, and therefore, the workers must break away from the bourgeois liberals and unite in their own workers' party—and in spite of the opposition of the handful of liberals, the overwhelming majority at the congress repeated after him the great words of Karl Marx.

To achieve their complete emancipation the workers of all countries must unite, said Bebel, and therefore, it was necessary to affiliate to the International Workingmen's Association—and the majority at the congress unanimously repeated after him the words of the great teacher.

Thus, the Social-Democratic Labour Party of Germany was born, and Bebel was its midwife.

From that time onwards Bebel's life was merged with that of the Party, his sorrows and joys were merged with the Party's sorrows and joys. He became the German workers' beloved leader and inspirer, because, comrades, one cannot help loving a man who has done so much to put the workers on their own feet, to free them from the tutelage of the bourgeois liberals and to give them their own workers' party.

The year 1870 put the young party to its first test. The war against France began, the German government demanded money for the war from parliament, of which

Bebel was also a member, and a definite stand had to be taken for or against the war. Bebel realized, of course, that the war benefited only the enemies of the proletariat; but all classes of German society, from the bourgeoisie to the workers, had been swept off their feet by the fever of false patriotism and regarded refusal to vote the government the money it demanded as treachery to the fatherland. But Bebel paid no heed to "patriotic" prejudices and, not fearing to swim against the stream, loudly proclaimed from the floor of parliament: I, as a Socialist and a republican, am in favour not of war but of the fraternity of nations, not of enmity with the French workers but of our German workers' unity with them. Denunciation, ridicule and contempt —such was the response to Bebel's bold pronouncement even on the part of the workers. But, faithful to the principles of scientific socialism, Bebel did not for a moment haul down the flag to suit the prejudices of his fellow-workers; on the contrary, he did all in his power to raise them to the level of clearly understanding the fatal consequences of the war. Subsequently, the workers realized their mistake and loved their staunch and sturdy Bebel all the more. The government, however, rewarded him with two years' imprisonment, but he did not idle away his time in prison. It was in prison that he wrote his famous book *Woman and Socialism.*

The end of the 'seventies and the 'eighties put the party to further tests. Alarmed by the growth of Social-Democracy, the German government issued the Anti-Socialist Laws, broke up the party and trade union organizations, suppressed all the Social-Democratic newspapers without exception, annulled freedom of assembly and freedom of association, and the Social-Democratic Party, which had been legal only the day before, was driven underground. By these measures the government wanted to provoke Social-Democracy into unsuccessful and fatal actions, and to demoralize and crush it. Exceptional firmness and unexampled foresight were needed to avoid losing one's head, to change tactics in time, and wisely to adjust the movement to the new conditions. Many Social-Democrats yielded to these acts of provocation and swung towards anarchism. Others renounced all their ideals and sank to the level of the liberals. But Bebel staunchly remained at his post, encouraging some, cooling the excessive zeal of others and exposing the phrasemongering of still others, and skilfully guided the Party along the true path, forward, ever forward. Ten years later the government was obliged to yield to the growing strength of the labour movement and repealed the Anti-Socialist Laws. Bebel's line of policy proved to be the only correct line.

The end of the 'nineties and the 1900's put the Party to still another test. Encouraged by the industrial boom and the relatively easy economic victories, the moderate elements in the Social-Democratic movement began to deny the necessity of an uncompromising class struggle and a socialist revolution. We must not be uncompromising, we do not need a revolution, they said; what we need is class collaboration, we need agreements with the bourgeoisie and the government, so that we may jointly with them patch up the existing system. Let us therefore vote for the bourgeois government's budget, let us enter the present bourgeois government.

By these arguments the moderates undermined the principles of scientific socialism and the revolutionary tactics of Social-Democracy. Bebel realized how dangerous the situation was and, together with other leaders of the Party, he proclaimed uncompromising war upon the moderates. At the Dresden Congress (1903) he utterly defeated Bernstein and Vollmar, the German leaders of the moderates, and proclaimed the necessity of revolutionary methods of struggle. In the following year, in Amsterdam, in the presence of Socialists from all countries, he defeated Jean Jaurès, the international leader of the moderates, and once again proclaimed the necessity of an uncompromising struggle. From that time onwards he gave the "moderate enemies of the Party" no rest, inflicting defeat after defeat upon them in Jena (1905) and Nuremberg (1908). As a result, the Party emerged from the internal struggle united and strong, astonishingly consolidated and immensely grown, and for all this it was indebted mainly to August Bebel. . . .

But Bebel was not satisfied merely with activity within the Party. His thunderous speeches in the German parliament, in which he lashed out at the musty aristocracy, tore the mask from the liberals and pilloried the "imperial government," and his long years of activity in the trade unions—all show that Bebel, the faithful guardian of the interests of the proletariat, appeared wherever the fight was hottest, wherever his seething proletarian energy was needed.

That is why the German and international Socialists revere Bebel so much.

Of course, Bebel made mistakes—who does not? (Only the dead make no mistakes.) But all small mistakes pale into insignificance when contrasted with the tremendous services he has rendered the Party, which today, after forty-two years of leadership by Bebel, has over 600,000 members, about 2,000,000 workers organized in trade unions, enjoys the confidence of 3,000,000 to 4,000,000 voters, and by a wave of the hand can organize demonstrations of hundreds of thousands in Prussia.

It is noteworthy that the celebrations in honour of Bebel's birthday coincided with a striking demonstration of the might of German Social-Democracy, with huge and unprecedentedly well-organized demonstrations in favour of universal suffrage in Prussia.

Bebel has every right to claim that he has not worked in vain.

Such are the life and activities of old Bebel, yes, very old, but ever so young in spirit, standing, as of old, at his post in anticipation of fresh battles and fresh victories.

Only the militant proletariat could have produced a man like Bebel, virile, eternally young and eternally forward looking, as it is itself.

Only the theory of scientific socialism could have given wide scope for Bebel's ebullient nature, for his tireless efforts to destroy the old, decaying capitalist world.

Bebel's life and activities testify to the strength and invincibility of the proletariat, to the inevitable triumph of socialism. . . .

Let us, then, comrades, send greetings to our beloved teacher—the turner August Bebel!

Let him serve as an example to us Russian workers, who are particularly in need of Bebels in the labour movement.

Long Live Bebel!
Long Live International Social-Democracy!

The Baku Committee of the R.S.D.L.P.

Published in leaflet form
March 23, 1910

Reprinted from the leaflet

A LETTER TO THE CENTRAL COMMITTEE
OF THE PARTY FROM EXILE
IN SOLVYCHEGODSK

Comrade Semyon! Yesterday I received your letter from the comrades. First of all, hearty greetings to Lenin and the others. Next about your letter and, in general, about the "vexed questions."

In my opinion, the line of the bloc (Lenin-Plekhanov) is the only correct one: 1) this line, and it alone, answers to the real interests of the work in Russia, which demand that all real Party elements should rally together; 2) this line, and it alone, will expedite the process of emancipation of the legal organizations from the yoke of the Liquidators, by digging a gulf between the Menshevik workers and the Liquidators, and dispersing and disposing of the latter. A fight for influence in the legal organizations is the burning question of the day, a necessary stage on the road towards the regeneration of the Party; and a bloc is the only means by which these organizations can be cleansed of the garbage of Liquidationism.

The plan for a bloc reveals the hand of Lenin—he is a shrewd fellow, and knows a thing or two. But this does not mean that any kind of bloc is good. A Trotsky bloc (he would have said "synthesis") would be rank unprincipledness, a Manilov amalgam of heterogenous principles, the helpless longing of an unprincipled person for a "good" principle. The logic of things, by its nature, adheres strictly to principle and abhors an amalgam. A Lenin-Plekhanov bloc is practical because it is thoroughly based on principle, on unity of views on the question of how to regenerate the Party. But precisely because it is a bloc and not a merger—precisely for that reason, the Bolsheviks must have their own group. It is quite possible that in the course of their work the Bolsheviks will completely tame the Plekhanovites, but that is only a possibility. At all events, we must not go to sleep and wait for such a result, even if it is a very probable one. The more unitedly the Bolsheviks act, the more organized they are in their actions, the greater will be the chances of taming. We must, therefore, tirelessly hammer away on all anvils. I shall say nothing about the *Vperyod*-ists, because they are now of less interest than the Liquidators and the Plekhanovites. If they do wake up one of these days—all to the good, of course; but if not—well, never mind, let them stew in their own juice.

That is what I think about things abroad.

But that is not all, nor even the most important. The most important thing is to organize the work in Russia. The history of our Party shows that disagreements are ironed out not in debates, but mainly in the course of the work, in the course of applying principles. Hence, the task of the day is to organize work in Russia around a strictly defined principle. The Liquidators at once realized what was in the wind (their scent is highly developed) and have begun to penetrate (have already penetrated) the legal workers' organizations, and it appears that they already have their underground centre in Russia, which is directing, etc., the work. We, however, are still only "preparing," still in the stage of rehearsals. In my opinion, our immediate task, the one that brooks no delay, is to organize a central group (in Russia), to co-ordinate the illegal, semi-legal and legal work at first in the main centres (St. Petersburg, Moscow, the Urals, the South). Call it what you like—the "Russian section of the Central Committee" or auxiliary group of the Central Committee—it makes no difference, but such a group is as essential as air, as bread. At the present time lack of information, loneliness and isolation reign among the Party workers in the localities and they are all becoming discouraged. This group could give fresh stimulus to the work and introduce clarity. And that would clear the road for the actual utilization of legal possibilities. And that, in my opinion, will start the revival of the Party spirit. To begin with, it would do no harm to arrange a conference of the Party workers who accept the decisions of the plenum,[93] under the guidance of the Central Committee, of course. But all this after the "reform" of the central bodies,[94] and provided the Plekhanovites agree. It is quite possible that such a conference will produce the people suitable for the above-mentioned central group. I think that the benefits of such a conference are obvious in many other respects too. But we must act firmly and relentlessly and not fear reproaches from the Liquidators, Trotskyites and *Vperyod*-ists. If the Plekhanovites and Leninites unite on the basis of work in Russia, they can afford to ignore all reproaches, no matter from what quarter they come.

That is what I think about work in Russia.

Now about myself. I have another six months to go here.[95] When the term expires I shall be entirely at your service. If the need for Party workers is really acute, I could get away at once. I have read No. 1 of *Mysl*.[96] I can picture to myself how much clarity and encouragement the workers will gain even from the mere fact that yesterday's opponents are acting together, and how much confusion and chaos this will cause in the ranks of the Liquidators. And every honest person will say that this will not be bad.

There is a decent crowd here in exile, and it would be a very good thing if they could be supplied with the illegal periodicals. Send us *Sotsial-Demokrat* No. 17 and onwards, and also the "Supplement" to *Sotsial-Demokrat*. We have not received *Rabochaya Gazeta*,[97] neither No. 1 nor No. 2, nor have we received *Golos Sotsial-Demokrata*. I suppose we shall receive *Zvezda*.[98] Send to the following addresses: 1) Solvychegodsk, Vologda Gubernia, for Ivan Isaakovich Bogomolov; 2) Solvychegodsk, Vologda Gubernia, for Pyotr Mikhailovich Serafimov. The address for correspondence with me is: Solvychegodsk, Vologda Gubernia, the house of Grigorov, for Nikolai Alexandrovich Voznesensky.

With comradely greetings, *K. S.*

Don't send by registered mail. Write about how things are going on your side, I beg of you.

Written: December 31, 1910   Reprinted from a copy of the letter

FOR THE PARTY![99]

Interest in political life is reviving in the country and, simultaneously with it, the crisis in our Party is coming to an end. The dead point is past, the torpor is beginning to pass off. The general Party conference which took place recently[100] is a clear symptom of the Party's regeneration. Our Party gained strength with the growth of the Russian revolution and was shattered with its fall; it was therefore inevitable that the Party should rise to its feet with the political awakening of the country. The revival in the principal branches of industry and the growth of the capitalists' profits, along with the drop in the real wages of the workers; the free development of the economic and political organizations of the bourgeoisie along with the forcible suppression of the legal and illegal organizations of the proletariat; the rise in the prices of the necessities of life and the rise in landlords' profits, along with the ruination of peasant farming; the famine which has affected over 25,000,000 of the population and has demonstrated the helplessness of the "renovated" counter-revolutionary regime—all this was bound to affect the toiling strata, and primarily the proletariat, by awakening their interest in political life. One of the striking expressions of this awakening is the conference of the Russian Social-Democratic Labour Party held last January.

But the awakening of minds and hearts cannot be self-contained—under present political conditions it must inevitably develop into open mass action.

The conditions of life of the workers must be improved, wages must be raised, the working day must be shortened, the conditions of the workers in the mills, factories and mines must be radically changed. But how can all this be done if not by means of still prohibited partial and general economic actions?

We must win the right freely to wage a struggle against the employers, the right to strike, freedom of association, assembly, speech, press, etc.: otherwise the workers' struggle to improve their conditions of life will be hampered to the utmost degree. But how can all this be won if not by open political actions, by means of demonstrations, political strikes, etc.?

We must bring about the recovery of the country, which is suffering from chronic starvation; we must put a stop to the present state of affairs under which tens of millions of tillers of the soil are compelled periodically to suffer famine with all its horrors; it is impossible to look on with folded arms and see starving fathers and mothers, with tears in their eyes, "selling for a mere song" their daughters and sons! We must uproot the present rapacious financial policy which is ruining the poverty-stricken peasant farms and which with every crop failure inevitably pushes millions of peasants on to the path of devastating famine! The country must be saved from pauperization and demoralization! But can all this be done without overthrowing the entire edifice of tsarism from top to bottom? And how can the tsarist government, with all its feudal survivals, be overthrown, if not by a wide, popular revolutionary movement, led by its historically recognized leader, the socialist proletariat? . . .

But in order that the future actions shall not be isolated and sporadic, in order that the proletariat may honourably fulfil its lofty task of uniting and leading the future actions—for all this it is necessary to have— in addition to the revolutionary consciousness of broad strata of the people and the class consciousness of the proletariat—a strong and flexible proletarian party that will be able to unite the separate efforts of the local organizations in one common effort and thereby direct the mass revolutionary movement against the main fortifications of the enemy. To set to rights the party of the proletariat, the Russian Social-Democratic Labour Party—that is what is particularly necessary in order that the proletariat may worthily meet the coming revolutionary actions.

The imperative necessity of uniting the Party becomes still more strikingly evident in view of the approaching elections to the Fourth State Duma.

But how can the Party be set to rights?

First of all, the local party organizations must be strengthened. Broken up into small and tiny groups, surrounded by a slough of despondency and lack of confidence in the cause, destitute of intellectual forces and not infrequently disrupted by provocateurs—is not this dismal picture of the life of the local organizations familiar to all? This dispersion of forces can and must be brought to an end! The incipient awakening of the masses of the workers on the one hand, and the recent conference as an expression of this awakening on the other, greatly facilitate the task of putting an end to this dispersion. Let us, then, do all in our power to put an end to organizational dispersion! Let the Social-Democratic workers in every town and in every industrial centre, all those, irrespective of group, who believe that an illegal Russian Social-Democratic Labour Party is needed, join together in local Party organizations! Let the machines which unite the workers in a single army of exploited—let those very machines unite them in a single party of fighters against exploitation and violence! . . . There is no need to strive after a large membership: under present conditions of work this may even be dangerous. The whole point is the quality of the comrades, the whole point is that the influential comrades grouped in local organizations should appreciate the importance of the cause they are serving and steadfastly carry on their work on revolutionary Social-Democratic lines. And let the local organizations thus formed not shut themselves off in isolation, let them constantly intervene in all the affairs connected with the struggle of the proletariat, from the most "petty," ordinary affairs to the biggest and most "extraordinary"; let not a single clash between labour and capital, not a single protest of the masses of the workers against the brutalities of the tsarist government escape their influence. It must always be borne in mind that only in this way will it be possible to strengthen and bring about the recovery of the local organizations. That is why, among other things, they must maintain the most lively connections with the open mass organizations of the workers, with the unions and clubs, and facilitate their development in every way.

Let our comrades the workers not be daunted by the difficulties and complexity of the tasks that fall exclusively on them owing to the absence of intellectual forces; totally unnecessary modesty and fear of "unaccustomed" work must be cast aside once and for all; one must have the courage to undertake complex Party tasks! It does not matter if a few mistakes are discovered in the course of this; you will stumble once or twice, and then you will get accustomed to stepping out freely. Bebels do not drop from the skies, they grow up from the ranks in the course of Party activity in all its spheres. . . .

But the local organizations taken separately, even if they are strong and influential, do not constitute the Party. To constitute the Party they must be gathered together, linked up in a single whole that lives a common life. Scattered local organizations, not only isolated from one another, but not even aware of one another's existence, organizations left entirely to their own devices, acting entirely on their own initiative and not infrequently conducting their work on opposite lines— all this constitutes the familiar picture of amateurish methods in the Party. To link the local organizations together and rally them around the Central Committee of the Party means, precisely, putting an end to amateurish methods and preparing the ground for setting the proletarian party to rights. An influential Central Committee connected by living roots with the local organizations, systematically keeping the latter informed and linking them up together; a Central Committee which constantly intervenes in all matters concerning general proletarian actions; a Central Committee which possesses an illegal newspaper published in Russia for the purpose of conducting wide political agitation—such is the direction in which the renovation and consolidation of the Party must proceed.

Needless to say, the Central Committee will be unable to cope with this difficult task unaided: the comrades in the local organizations must bear in mind that unless it receives their systematic support from the localities, the Central Committee will inevitably be converted into a cipher, and the Party will be reduced to a fiction. Hence, joint work of the Central Committee and the local organizations—such is the essential condition for renovating the Party, that is what we call upon the comrades to do.

And so, for the Party, comrades, for a regenerated, underground, Russian Social-Democratic Labour Party!

Long Live the United Russian Social-Democratic Labour Party!

The Central Committee of the R.S.D.L.P.

Published in leaflet form   Reprinted from the manuscript
in March 1912

LONG LIVE THE FIRST OF MAY![101]

Comrades!

As far back as last century, the workers of all countries resolved to celebrate annually this day, the First of May. That was in 1889, when, at the Paris Congress of the Socialists of all countries, the workers resolved to proclaim, precisely on this day, the First of May, when nature is awakening from her winter sleep, when the woods and hills are donning their green mantles and the fields and meadows are adorning themselves with flowers, when the sun shines more warmly, the joy of revival fills the air and nature gives herself up to dancing and rejoicing—they resolved to proclaim loudly and openly to the whole world, precisely on this day, that the workers are bringing spring to mankind and deliverance from the shackles of capitalism, that it is the mission of the workers to renovate the world on the basis of freedom and socialism.

Every class has its own favourite festivals. The nobility introduced their festivals, and on them they proclaim their "right" to rob the peasants. The bourgeoisie have their festivals and on them they "justify" their "right" to exploit the workers. The clergy, too, have their festivals, and on them they eulogize the existing system under which the toilers die in poverty while the idlers wallow in luxury.

The workers, too, must have their festival, and on it

they must proclaim: universal labour, universal freedom, universal equality of all men. That festival is the festival of the First of May.

That is what the workers resolved as far back as 1889.

Since then the battle cry of workers' socialism has rung out louder and louder at meetings and demonstrations on the First of May. The ocean of the labour movement is expanding more and more, spreading to new countries and states, from Europe and America to Asia, Africa and Australia. In the course of only a few decades the formerly weak international workers' association has grown into a mighty international brotherhood, which holds regular congresses and unites millions of workers in all parts of the world. The sea of proletarian wrath is rising in towering waves, and is more and more menacingly advancing against the tottering citadels of capitalism. The great coal miners' strike which recently flared up in Great Britain, Germany, Belgium, America, etc., a strike which struck fear into the hearts of the exploiters and rulers all over the world, is a clear sign that the socialist revolution is not far off. . . .

"We do not worship the golden calf!" We do not want the kingdom of the bourgeoisie and the oppressors! Damnation and death to capitalism and its horrors of poverty and bloodshed! Long live the kingdom of labour, long live socialism!

That is what the class-conscious workers of all countries proclaim on this day.

And confident of victory, calm and strong, they are marching proudly along the road to the promised land, towards glorious socialism, step by step carrying out Karl Marx's great call: "Workers of all countries, unite!"

That is how the workers in free countries celebrate the First of May.

The Russian workers, ever since they began to realize their position, and not wishing to lag behind their comrades, have always joined the general chorus of their foreign comrades and, jointly with them, have celebrated the First of May in spite of everything, in spite of the brutal acts of repression of the tsarist government. True, for the past two or three years, during the period of counter-revolutionary bacchanalia and disorganization of the Party, industrial depression and the deadening political indifference of the broad masses, the Russian workers have been unable to celebrate their glorious workers' festival in the old way. But the revival that has started in the country recently; the economic strikes and the political protests of the workers in connection, say, with the re-hearing of the case of the Social-Democratic deputies in the Second Duma; the growing discontent among broad strata of the peasants because of the famine which has affected over twenty gubernias, and the protests of hundreds of thousands of shop assistants against the "renovated" system of the Russian diehards—all go to show that the deadening torpor is passing off, giving place to a political revival in the country, primarily among the proletariat. That is why this year the Russian workers can and must on this day extend a hand to their foreign comrades. That is why they must celebrate the First of May in one way or another together with them.

They must declare today that they are at one with their comrades in the free countries—they do not and will not worship the golden calf.

Moreover, to the general demand of the workers of all countries they must add their own Russian demand for the overthrow of tsarism and the establishment of a democratic republic.

"We detest the crowns of tyrants!" "We honour the chains of the martyred people!" Death to bloody tsarism! Death to landlordism! Death to the tyranny of the masters in factories, mills and mines! Land for the peasants! An eight-hour day for the workers! A democratic republic for all the citizens of Russia!

That is also what the Russian workers must proclaim on this day.

It is lies and grovelling before Nicholas the Last when the Russian liberals assure themselves and others that tsarism has consolidated itself in Russia and is capable of satisfying the principal needs of the people.

It is deception and hypocrisy when the Russian liberals sing in all keys that the revolution is dead and that we are living under a "renovated" system.

Look around! Does long-suffering Russia resemble a "renovated," "well-governed" country?

Instead of a democratic constitution—a regime of gallows and brutal tyranny!

Instead of a popular parliament—the black Duma of the black landlords!

Instead of the "unshakable foundations of civil liberty," instead of the freedom of speech, assembly, press, association and strike promised by the Manifesto of October 17—the dead hand of "discretion" and "prevention," the closing of newspapers, the deportation of editors, the suppression of unions and the breaking-up of meetings!

Instead of inviolability of the person—beating up in prisons, outrages against citizens, the bloody suppression of strikers in the Lena goldfields!

Instead of satisfaction of the peasants' needs—the policy of still further driving the peasant masses from the land!

Instead of a well-ordered administration—the thieving by quartermasters, thieving at railway Head Offices, thieving in the Forestry Department, thieving in the Naval Department!

Instead of order and discipline in the governmental machine—forgery in the courts, swindling and blackmail by criminal investigation departments, murder and provocation in the secret-police departments!

Instead of the international greatness of the Russian state—the ignominious failure of Russian "policy" in the Near and Far East and the role of butcher and despoiler in the affairs of bleeding Persia!

Instead of peace of mind and security for the inhabitants—suicides in the towns and horrible starvation among 30,000,000 peasants in the rural districts!

Instead of improvement and purification of morals —incredible dissoluteness in the monasteries, those citadels of official morality!

And to complete the picture—the brutal shooting of hundreds of toilers in the Lena goldfields! ...

Destroyers of already won liberties, worshippers of gallows and firing squads, inventors of "discretion" and "prevention," thieving quartermasters, thieving engineers, robber police, murdering secret police, dissolute Rasputins—these are the "renovators" of Russia!

And yet there are people in the world who have the

effrontery to say that all is well in Russia, that the revolution is dead!

No, comrades; where millions of peasants are starving and workers are shot down for going on strike the revolution will go on living until the disgrace to mankind— Russian tsarism—is swept from the face of the earth.

And on this day, the First of May, we must say in one way or another, at meetings, mass gatherings or at secret assemblies—whichever is the most expedient— that we pledge ourselves to fight for the complete over- throw of the tsarist monarchy, that we welcome the coming Russian revolution, the liberator of Russia!

Let us, then, extend our hands to our comrades abroad and together with them proclaim:

Down With Capitalism!

Long Live Socialism!

Let us hoist the flag of the Russian revolution bear- ing the inscriptions:

Down With the Tsarist Monarchy!

Long Live the Democratic Republic!

Comrades! Today we are celebrating the First of May! *Long Live the First of May!*

Long Live International Social-Democracy!

Long Live the Russian Social-Democratic Labour Party!

The Central Committee of the R.S.D.L.P.

Published in leaflet form in April 1912

Reprinted from the manuscript

A NEW PERIOD

The economic actions of the workers are being followed by their political actions.

The strikes over wages are being followed by protests, meetings, and political strikes in connection with the Lena shooting.

In St. Petersburg and Moscow, in Riga and Kiev, in Saratov and Yekaterinoslav, in Odessa and Kharkov, in Baku and Nikolayev—everywhere, in all parts of Russia, the workers are rising in vindication of their comrades who were murdered on the Lena.

"We live! Our scarlet blood seethes with the fire of unspent strength!". . .

In its increasing revival the labour movement is passing through a third stage. And this after the bacchanalia of the counter-revolution.

About two years ago the workers were still trying to resist the growing attacks of the insatiable employers. Defensive strikes and, in places, offensive strikes— thus the revival of the movement expressed itself. That was the first stage. The Moscow region was the pioneer.

About eighteen months ago the workers passed on to offensive strikes. They put forward new economic demands and strove to secure the restoration of the conditions of

1905-06, of which the workers were robbed when counter-revolution was rampant. That was the second stage. Here the western border regions were the pioneers.

Now the third stage has been reached, the period of the political movement.

From stage to stage!

And this was to be expected. The boom in the main branches of industry and the growth of capitalist profits simultaneously with the fall in real wages, the growth of the industrial and political organizations of the bourgeoisie simultaneously with the crushing of the workers' organizations, the rise in the prices of the necessities of life and growth of landlords' incomes simultaneously with starvation reigning among 30,000,000 peasants, when, driven by want, mothers and fathers are compelled to sell their daughters and sons—all this was bound to bring about a political revival in the ranks of the working class.

The Lena shooting merely served as a signal.

Obviously, "all is not quiet at the Shipka Pass." This is felt even by the representatives of the government, who are hastily preparing to "pacify" the country. Apparently, it is affecting even our foreign affairs. . . .

But news of political protest strikes continues to pour in.

There can be no doubt that the subterranean forces of the movement for emancipation have set to work. . . .

Greetings to you, first swallows!

The St. Petersburg *Zvezda*,   Reprinted from the newspaper
No. 30, April 15, 1912
Signed: *K. S.*

LIBERAL HYPOCRITES

Rech has "erred" again! It appears that it "did not expect" from "the government" "tactless" explanations of the Lena atrocities. You see, it had "hoped" that Minister Makarov would "take legal proceedings" against the Treshchenkos. But suddenly came Makarov's statement that Treshchenko was right and that in future too the workers would be shot down!

"We erred," observes the liberal *Rech* with false contrition, commenting on this matter (see *Rech* of April 12).

Poor Cadets! How many times they have "erred" in their expectations concerning the government!

Not so very long ago they "thought" that we had a constitution in Russia, and they assured Europe, in all languages, that "our united government" is "quite constitutional." That was in London, far away from Russia. But it was enough for them to return to Russia, to the land of "discretion" and "prevention," for them to admit their "error" and to "become disillusioned."

Only very recently they "believed" that Stolypin had succeeded in putting the country on the road to parliamentary "renovation." But it was enough for Stolypin to put the notorious 87 clause[102] into operation for the Cadets to start singing again about "errors" and "misunderstandings."

Was it so long ago that the Cadets drew a parallel between the Russian government (recall the dock workers' strike) and the British government in their attitude towards strikes? But it was enough for the Lena tragedy to be enacted for the Cadets to begin again to chant their hypocritical "we erred."

The remarkable thing is that while "errors" and "disillusionments" continue to multiply, the Cadet tactics of making advances to the government remain unchanged!

Poor, poor Cadets! Evidently they "count on" naive readers who believe in their sincerity.

They "think" that people do not notice their obsequious grovelling before the enemies of Russia's emancipation.

They do not yet realize that, while until now they have "erred" again and again in their expectations of the government, they are now going to be "disillusioned" with the masses of the people, who, at last, will discern their counter-revolutionary character and turn their backs on them.

Whom will Messrs. the Cadets deceive then?

Grovelling before the government and hypocrisy towards the country—why are they called the "Party of Popular Freedom"?

The St. Petersburg *Zvezda*,   Reprinted from the newspaper
No. 30, April 15, 1912
Signed: *S.*

NON-PARTY SIMPLETONS

Non-party progressivism has become the fashion. Such is the nature of the Russian intellectual—he must have a fashion. At one time Saninism was the fashion, then decadence became the rage—now it is the turn of non-partyism.

What is non-partyism?

In Russia there are landlords and peasants, their interests are antagonistic, a struggle between them is inevitable. But non-partyism ignores this fact, it is inclined to hush up the antagonism of interests.

In Russia there are bourgeois and proletarians; the victory of one of these classes means the defeat of the other. But non-partyism glosses over the antagonism of interests, it shuts its eyes to their struggle.

Every class has its own party, with a special programme and a special complexion. Parties direct the struggle of classes. Without parties there would be not a struggle but chaos, absence of clarity and confusion of interests. But non-partyism abhors clarity and definiteness, it prefers nebulousness and absence of programme.

Glossing over of class antagonisms, hushing up of the class struggle, absence of a definite complexion, hostility to all programme, gravitation towards chaos and the confusion of interests—such is non-partyism.

What is the aim of non-partyism?

To unite the ununitable, to bring about the impossible.

To unite bourgeois and proletarians in an alliance, to erect a bridge between the landlords and the peasants, to haul a wagon with the aid of a swan, a crab and a pike—this is what non-partyism aims at.

Non-partyism realizes that it is incapable of uniting the ununitable and therefore says with a sigh:

"If 'ifs' and 'ans'

Were pots and pans. . ."

But "ifs" and "ans" are not pots and pans and so non-partyism is always left in the cart, always remains the simpleton.

Non-partyism is like a man without a head on his shoulders, or—rather—like a man with a turnip instead of a head.

This is precisely the position of the "progressive" journal *Zaprosy Zhizni*.[103]

"The parties of the Right have already taken a decision," says *Zaprosy Zhizni*. "They are uniting in one reactionary mass to fight the entire progressive opposition. . . . Therefore, the bloc of the Rights must be opposed by a bloc of the Lefts, which must embrace all the progressive social elements" (see *Zaprosy Zhizni*, No. 6).

But who are these "progressive elements"?

They are the Party of Peaceful Renovation,[104] the Cadets, the Trudoviks and the Social-Democrats. That is to say, the "progressive" bourgeoisie, the pro-liberal landlords, the peasants who are thirsting for the landlords' land, and the proletarians who are fighting the bourgeoisie.

And *Zaprosy Zhizni* wants to unite these "elements"! Very original and . . . foolish, is it not?

And this organ of people without principles wants to lecture the Social-Democrats on the tactics they should pursue in the elections to the Fourth Duma!

Simpletons! . . .

The St. Petersburg *Zvezda*, No. 30, April 15, 1912

Signed: *K. S—n*

Reprinted from the newspaper

LIFE TRIUMPHS!

"The petitions which the workers sent demanding freedom . . . of association did not improve their conditions in the least. On the contrary, in answer to these demands the workers were shot down.". . .

Excerpt from the speech delivered by Deputy Kuznetsov

It was not so long ago, only a year back, that Messrs. the Liquidators, the zealous advocates of a "legal party," launched with a lot of noise and clamour the so-called petition campaign.

The well-known *Delo Zhizni*,[105] the "publicist" organ of the Liquidators, wrote that the immediate task of the labour movement was to fight for the right of association *by means of petitions.*

Nasha Zarya,[106] the "scientific" organ of the Liquidators, "substantiating" this task, assured the workers that petitions would organize around them the "broad masses."

But then the bloody tragedy in the Lena goldfields was enacted, real life with its implacable antagonisms came upon the scene and the Liquidators' petition tactics were scattered to the winds like dust. Lawful strikes, petitions, requests, were all simply swept overboard. The "renovated" system revealed its true features. And Minister Makarov, the representative of this system, stated, as if to introduce more clarity into the matter, that the shooting of 500 workers was not the end but only the beginning, and that, with God's help, the same thing would be repeated in future. . . .

That was a perfect bull's-eye! The petition tactics, so noisily proclaimed, were shattered by life! The petition policy proved to be impotent!

It is evident, therefore, that it is not petitions that are destined to settle the age-long contest between the old and the new Russia. . . .

And do not the innumerable meetings and strikes of the workers which have taken place throughout Russia in connection with the Lena massacre prove once again that the workers will not take the path of petitions?

Listen to the workers' deputy Kuznetsov:

"Actually, the petitions which the workers sent demanding freedom of association did not improve their conditions in the least. On the contrary, in answer to these demands the workers were shot down.". . .

That is what Deputy Kuznetsov says.

A workers' deputy who heeds the voice of the workers, from whose ranks he comes, could not say anything else.

No, the Liquidators are out of luck! . . .

Well, what about the petition tactics? Where are they to be put?

As far away from the workers as possible, of course. . . .

Yes, indeed, the lessons of life are evidently not being wasted, even on the Liquidators. It seems that the
petition intoxication is beginning to pass off. Well, we
congratulate them on becoming sober, congratulate them
from the bottom of our hearts!

We have been saying for a long time: life is all-
powerful, and it always triumphs. . . .

The St. Petersburg *Zvezda*,   Reprinted from the newspaper
No. 30, April 15, 1912

Signed: *K. Salin*

THEY ARE WORKING WELL....

After the Lena shooting—strikes and protests all over Russia.

After Minister Makarov's "explanations" in the Duma—a demonstration in the capital of Russia.

The government wanted to drive Russia into the clutches of sanguinary "orders."

But Russia proved to be stronger than the government and decided to go its own way....

Let us cast another glance at the history of the Lena events.

A strike of 6,000 workers was proceeding at the Lena goldfields. The strike was peaceful and organized. The mendacious *Rech* can, of course, speak of a "spontaneous riot" on the Lena (see No. 103). But we judge, not by what the mendacious *Rech* says, but by the "report" of the eyewitness Tulchinsky. And Mr. Tulchinsky asserts that on that day the workers behaved in an exemplary manner, that the workers had "no sticks or stones." And then the hellish conditions of labour in the goldfields, the very modest demands of the workers, their voluntary abandonment of the demand for an eight-hour day, the workers' readiness to make further concessions—all this is the familiar picture of the peaceful Lena strike.

Nevertheless, the government found it necessary to shoot down the workers, peaceful unarmed workers with their tobacco pouches in their hands and with petitions in their pockets for the release of their arrested comrades. . . .

Proceedings have not been taken against Treshchenko —is it not clear that he was acting on orders from above?

It has been decided to take proceedings against the workers and not against Treshchenko—is it not clear that somebody was thirsting for the proletariat's blood?

They wanted to kill two birds with one stone on the day of the shooting. First, to satisfy the voracious appetites of the Lena cannibals. Second, to intimidate the workers of other towns and localities, as much as to say— bear the yoke of capital uncomplainingly, otherwise we shall do to you what we did to the Lena workers.

The result was that neither of these objects was achieved.

The Lena cannibals have not been satisfied, for the strike in the goldfields is continuing.

As for the workers of other towns, far from being intimidated, they have risen in strike after strike in protest against the shooting.

More than that. St. Petersburg, the capital of Russia, responded to Makarov's "explanations" by a demonstration of thousands of students and workers.

The most sensitive section of Russian society, the students, extended a hand to the most revolutionary section of the Russian people, the proletariat, and hoisting the red flag they proclaimed: Yes, "so it was," but it must never be so again!

From a peaceful economic strike on the Lena to political strikes all over Russia, and from political strikes all over Russia to a demonstration of many thousands of students and workers in the very heart of Russia—that is what the representatives of the government have achieved in their struggle against the workers.

Yes, the "old mole" of the movement for emancipation, the far-sighted Russian government, is "grubbing well"!

Two or three more "feats" like this and it will be possible to say with certainty that nothing will remain of Minister Makarov's bluster except a miserable recollection.

Go on working, gentlemen, go on working!

The St. Petersburg *Zvezda*, Reprinted from the newspaper
No. 31, April 17, 1912
Signed: *K. Solin*

THE ICE HAS BROKEN!...

The country lay in chains at the feet of its enslavers.

It needed a popular constitution, but it received brutal tyranny, measures of "prevention" and "discretion."

It needed a popular parliament, but it was presented with the gentry's Duma, the Duma of Purishkevich and Guchkov.

It needed freedom of speech, press, assembly, strike and association, but it sees all around nothing but wrecked workers' organizations, suppressed newspapers, arrested editors, broken-up meetings and deported strikers.

It demanded land for the peasants, and it was offered agrarian laws which intensified the land hunger of the masses of the peasants in order to please a handful of the rural rich.

It was promised protection of "person" and "property," but the prisons and places of exile are overcrowded with "unreliables," and the chiefs of criminal investigation departments (remember Kiev and Tiflis!) enter into an alliance with bandits and thieves to tyrannize over persons and to plunder property.

It was promised "prosperity" and "abundance," but peasant farming is steadily declining, tens of millions of peasants are starving, scurvy and typhus are carrying away thousands of victims. . . .

And the country bore all this and went on bearing it. . . .

Those who could not bear it committed suicide.

But everything must come to an end—the patience of the country came to an end.

The Lena shooting has broken the ice of silence—and the river of the people's movement has begun to flow. The ice has broken!...

All that was evil and pernicious in the present regime, all the ills of much-suffering Russia were focused in the one fact, the Lena events.

That is why it was the Lena shooting that served as a signal for the strikes and demonstrations.

That, and that alone, explains the latest events.

And the bosses of the Duma—the Octobrists, Cadets and Progressives[107] are waiting for "explanations" from above, from the lips of the representatives of the government!

The Octobrists "make inquiries," the Progressives simply "inquire" and the Cadets "deem it opportune" to talk about certain Treshchenkos, miserable puppets in the hands of events!

And this at a time when Makarov had already hurled at them his boastful: "So it was, so it will be"!

In the capital, tens of thousands of workers are on strike, the troops are ready for action, internal "complications" are upsetting "our" foreign affairs in connection with the Dardanelles—but they are waiting for a reply from the "upper spheres"!

They are blind! They fail to see that today it is for the proletariat, and not the representatives of the government, to have its say....

The St. Petersburg *Zvezda*,   Reprinted from the newspaper
No. 32, April 19, 1912
Signed: *K. S.*

HOW THEY ARE PREPARING
FOR THE ELECTIONS

The elections to the Fourth Duma[108] are approaching and the enemies of the movement for emancipation are mobilizing their forces.

Before us are, first of all, the counter-revolutionary parties: the extreme Rights, the Nationalists, the Octobrists. All, in one way or another, support the government. What can they count on in the forthcoming election campaign? Not on the sympathy of broad strata of the population, of course; the parties which have bound their fate with the fate of the Lena massacre government cannot count on the sympathy of the masses! Their only hope is the government's "orders": and, as usual, of "orders" there will be no lack. The Ministry of the Interior has already issued a circular to the Provincial Governors recommending the adoption of "measures to ensure the election of delegates from the volosts who are fully reliable and do not belong to the Lefts." What all these "measures" amount to we know from practical experience: the erasure of Left candidates from the lists, the framing up of charges against them, their arrest and deportation—such are the "measures"! On the other hand, the Holy Synod is advising bishops to take a most active part in the forthcoming elections, to secure the election to the Duma of staunch champions of the interests of the church, and with that object in view to convene election congresses of the clergy in their respective sees, to proceed to publish special election newspapers, etc.

The affairs of the governmental parties must be in a very bad way indeed if even the fathers of the church are obliged to neglect "church affairs" for the sake of "mundane affairs"!

Elections under the pressure of the Provincial Governors, spiritual and temporal—these, consequently, are the measures upon which they can count.

True, there is one other method they can resort to, namely, to put on the non-party label, hoodwink the electors that way, get into the Duma somehow, and then throw off the mask. That is precisely the "idea" of the Kovno nationalists, who came out under the non-party mask the other day. But that method is a subtle one and will scarcely suit our clumsy diehards. . . .

It is different with the Russian liberals—the Cadets, the Peaceful Renovators, and the Progressives. That crowd is more agile and, perhaps, will be able to make the utmost use of the non-party label. . . . And the Cadets, whose colouring has faded, need this non-party label, need it in the extreme.

The point is that during the period in which the Third Duma was functioning, the man in the street learned to look with a critical eye upon the Octobrists and Cadets. On the other hand, the "First Curia" people, the big urban bourgeoisie, are "disappointed" with the Octobrists, who failed to "justify" their hopes. Consequently, an opportunity occurs to "knock out of the saddle" the Octobrists, the Cadets' competitors in Ministerial ante-rooms. But how can a bridge to the "First Curia" be erected if not through the progressive Peaceful Renovators? Therefore—long live the alliance with the Peaceful Renovators! True, it is necessary to go "just a little bit" to the right for this, but that does not matter: why not go to the right if it is so profitable?

And so—dress by the right!

On the other hand, the "small and medium urban people" of the "Second Curia"—the intellectuals, shop assistants and others—have swung considerably to the left, especially in connection with the developing Lena events. The Cadets are conscious of having committed grave political sins, they have tried too often to betray the cause of the "popular freedom," and—God knows—they would even now gladly rush into the Ministerial ante-rooms, if only they were sure that they would be admitted! But it is precisely for this reason that the urban democratic strata are beginning to look askance at the Cadets. Is it necessary to say also that to come before such voters without a mask, to expose their true features as liberal traitors, is somewhat dangerous? But what, under these circumstances, can be invented for the leftward-swinging urban people, who are already deserting the Cadets, but have not yet come over to the Social-Democrats? Of course, progressive fog . . . pardon me, I mean progressive non-partyism. Oh, don't think that the Progressives are Cadets! No, they are not Cadets at all; they will only vote for the Cadet candidates, they are only the "non-party" servants of the Cadets. . . . And the Cadets advertise the "non-party" Progressives: what else can they do? They must swing to the left, at least in words, in the direction of . . . non-partyism!

And so—dress by the left!

On the one hand . . . on the other hand . . . to the right . . . to the left. . . . Such is the policy of the party of the liberal deception of the people, the Cadet Party.

Hoodwinking the voters—such are the means the Russian liberals will count on.

And—this must be emphasized—non-party charlatanry may play an important role in the elections. It may play an important role if the Social-Democrats fail to tear the masks off the liberal gentry, if they fail to conduct a vigorous campaign in connection with the forthcoming elections, if they fail to exercise all the strength at their command to rally the urban democratic strata around the leader of the movement for emancipation, around the Russian proletariat.

The St. Petersburg *Zvezda*,
No. 32, April 19, 1912   Reprinted from the newspaper
Signed: *K. Solin*

DEDUCTIONS

The first wave of the political upsurge is beginning to recede. The "last" strikes are in progress. Here and there voices of protesting strikers are still heard, but these will be the "last" voices. For the time being, the country is beginning to assume its "normal" appearance. . . .

What lessons can the proletariat learn from the recent events?

Let us reconstruct the picture of the "days of the movement."

April 4. The Lena shooting. About 500 killed and wounded. Apparent calm reigns in the country. The government's mood is firm. Protest strikes begin in the South.

April 10. An interpellation in the Duma. Strikes increase in number. The situation becomes alarming.

April 11. Minister Makarov's answer: "So it was, so it will be." Timashov does "not quite" agree with Makarov. The first signs of confusion are observed in the ranks of the government representatives. Meetings and strikes in St. Petersburg. The movement grows in the provinces.

April 15. A demonstration of students and workers in St. Petersburg.

April 18. Over 100,000 workers strike in St. Petersburg. Workers' demonstrations are organized. The government are losing their heads. Makarov is afraid to appear in the Duma. Timashov apologizes. The government retreats. A concession to "public opinion."

The deduction to be drawn is clear: emancipation cannot be achieved by silence and patience. The more loudly the voices of the workers resound, the more the forces of reaction lose their heads and the sooner they retreat. . . .

The "days of the movement" are the best field for testing the political parties. Parties must be assessed not by what they say, but by the way they behave "in the days of the struggle." How did the parties which call themselves "popular" parties behave in those days?

The extreme Black-Hundred landlord group, headed by the Zamyslovskys and Markovs, had difficulty in concealing their joy over the Lena shooting. There! The government has displayed strength and sternness—let the "lazy" workers know whom they have to deal with! They applauded Makarov. They voted against the Social-Democratic group's interpellation in the Duma. Their newspaper *Zemshchina*[109] did all in its power to incite the government against the Lena "agitators," against the workers on strike all over Russia, and against the workers' newspaper *Zvezda*.

The moderate Black-Hundred landlord group, headed by the Balashovs and Krupenskys, had no real objection to the shooting—it merely regretted that the government had acted in too transparent a manner, too openly. Therefore, while shedding crocodile tears over the "killed," it at the same time expressed the wish that the government should be "tactful" in regard to shooting. It voted against the Social-Democratic group's interpellation, and its organ *Novoye Vremya*[110] urged the government "not to stand on ceremony" with "convinced strikers," to subject demonstrators "not to light fines or arrest, but to stern punishment" and, as regards the "agitators" under arrest, not to release them from prison.

The party of the conservative landlords and parasitical strata of the bourgeoisie, the Octobrist Party, headed by the Guchkovs and Gololobovs, mourned, not over the dead, but over the fact that the ministry which it supported had suffered "unpleasantness" (the strikes) as a consequence of the "improper resort to firearms" on the Lena. Describing Makarov's statement as being "not altogether tactful" it, in its organ *Golos Moskvy*,[111] expressed the conviction that the government was "not to blame for the bloodshed." It caused the defeat of the Social-Democrats' interpellation. It incited the authorities against the "instigators"; and when Timashov tried to rehabilitate Makarov, it applauded him and considered the "incident" closed.

The party of the liberal landlords and the middle strata of the bourgeoisie, the Cadet Party, headed by the Milyukovs and Maklakovs, hurled verbal thunderbolts against the Lena shooting, but expressed the view that it was not the principles of the regime, but individuals of the type of Treshchenko and Belozyorov who were to blame. Therefore, while chanting a hypocritical "we erred" in connection with Makarov's statement, it was quite satisfied with Timashov's "repentant" statement and quietened down. *On the one hand* it supported the

Social-Democratic group, which demanded that the representatives of the government should come before the court of the country. *On the other hand*, it welcomed the representatives of the industrial bourgeoisie, Messrs. the Peaceful Renovators, who appealed to the same representatives of the government to curb the striking workers by means of "civilized measures." And, to leave no doubt whatever about its, the Cadet Party's, loyalty, it came out and declared in its *Rech* that the Lena strike was a "spontaneous riot."

That is how all these "popular" parties behaved during the "days of the movement."

Let the workers remember it and give them their deserts during the "days of the election" to the Fourth Duma.

Social-Democracy alone defended the interests of the workers in the "days of struggle," it alone told the whole truth.

The deduction to be drawn is clear: Social-Democracy is the sole champion of the proletariat. All the other parties mentioned are enemies of the working class, the only difference between them being the different ways in which they fight the workers: one fights by means of "civilized measures," another by means of "not quite civilized measures" and a third by means of "quite uncivilized measures."

Now that the first wave of the upsurge is receding, the dark forces which have been hiding behind a screen of crocodile tears are beginning to come out into the open again. *Zemshchina* is calling for "measures" against the workers' press. *Novoye Vremya* urges that the "convinced" workers be shown no mercy. And the authorities are setting to "work," arresting more and more "unreliables." What can they count on in their "new campaign"? How are we to explain the boldness now displayed by the authorities, who had almost lost their wits.

They can count on only one thing: on the impossibility of rousing mass protests on every occasion, on the unorganized state of the workers, on their insufficient class consciousness.

The St. Petersburg *Zvezda*,   Reprinted from the newspaper
No. 33, April 22, 1912

Signed: *K. Solin*

OUR AIMS

Anyone who reads *Zvezda* and knows its contributors, who are also contributors to *Pravda*,[112] will not find it difficult to understand the line *Pravda* will pursue. To illuminate the path of the Russian labour movement with the light of international Social-Democracy, to spread the truth among the workers about the friends and enemies of the working class, to guard the interests of labour's cause—such are the aims *Pravda* will pursue.

In pursuing these aims we do not in the least intend to gloss over the disagreements that exist among the Social-Democratic workers. More than that: in our opinion, a powerful and virile movement is inconceivable without disagreements—"complete identity of views" can exist only in the graveyard! But that does not mean that points of disagreement outweigh points of agreement. Far from it! Much as the advanced workers may disagree among themselves, they cannot forget that all of them, irrespective of group, are equally exploited, that all of them, irrespective of group, are equally without rights. Hence, *Pravda* will call, firstly and mainly, for unity in the proletarian class struggle, for unity at all costs. Just as we must be uncompromising towards our enemies, so must we yield to one another. War upon the enemies of the labour movement, peace and co-operation within the movement—that is what *Pravda* will be guided by in its daily activities.

It is particularly necessary to emphasize this now, when the Lena events and the forthcoming elections to the Fourth Duma raise before the workers with exceptional persistence the necessity of uniting in a single class organization. . . .

In entering upon our task we are aware that our path is bestrewn with thorns. It is sufficient to recall *Zvezda*, which has experienced repeated confiscations and "prosecutions." But the thorns will not daunt us if the sympathy of the workers which *Pravda* now enjoys continues in the future. From this sympathy it will draw energy for the struggle! We would like this sympathy to grow. Moreover, we would like the workers not to confine themselves to sympathy alone, but to take an active part in the conduct of our newspaper. Let not the workers say that they are "not used to" writing. Working-class writers do not drop ready-made from the skies; they can be trained only gradually, in the course of literary activity. All that is needed is to start on the job boldly: you may stumble once or twice, but in the end you will learn to write. . . .

And so, all together let us set to work!

Pravda, No. 1,   Reprinted from the newspaper
April 22, 1912
Unsigned

MANDATE
OF THE ST. PETERSBURG WORKERS TO THEIR LABOUR DEPUTY[113]

The demands of the Russian people that were advanced by the movement of 1905 have remained unfulfilled.

The development of the reaction and of the "renovated system" did not merely leave these demands unsatisfied; it made them still more imperative.

The workers often lack the possibility not only of going on strike—because there is no guarantee that they will not be shot down for doing so; not only of organizing unions and holding meetings—because there is no guarantee that they will not be arrested for doing so; but even of taking part in the Duma elections, because if they do so they will be "interpreted"[114] or deported all the same. Were not the workers at the Putilov Works and at the Neva Shipbuilding Yard "interpreted" the other day?

That is apart from the tens of millions of starving peasants who have been put at the mercy of the landlords and the Zemstvo officials. . . .

All this points to the necessity of satisfying the demands of 1905.

And the state of economic life in Russia, the already visible signs of a coming industrial crisis, and the steadily growing pauperization of broad strata of the peasantry are making the fulfilment of the tasks of 1905 imperative.

Hence, we think that Russia is on the eve of impending mass movements, which will, perhaps, be more profound than in 1905. That is proved by the Lena actions, by the protest strikes against "interpretations," etc.

As in 1905, in the van of these movements will be the most advanced class in Russian society, the Russian proletariat.

Its only ally can be the much-suffering peasantry, which is vitally interested in the emancipation of Russia.

A fight on two fronts—against the feudal-bureaucratic order of things and against the liberal bourgeoisie, who are seeking an alliance with the old regime—that is the form the coming actions of the people must assume.

And that struggle will be victorious only to the extent that the working class comes out at the head of the popular movement.

But in order that the working class may honourably fulfil its role as leader of the popular movement, it must be equipped with consciousness of its interests and a high degree of organization.

Under the present conditions the floor of the Duma is one of the best means of enlightening and organizing the broad masses of the proletariat.

It is precisely for this reason that we are sending our deputy to the Duma and instructing him, and the entire Social-Democratic group in the Fourth Duma, widely to proclaim our demands from the floor of the Duma and not to indulge in the futile game of legislating in the Duma of the gentry.

We would like the Social-Democratic group in the Fourth Duma, and our deputy in particular, to hold high the banner of the working class in the hostile camp of the Black Duma.

We would like to hear from the floor of the Duma the voices of the members of the Social-Democratic group loudly proclaiming the ultimate aim of the proletariat, the full and uncurtailed demands of 1905, proclaiming the Russian working class as the leader of the popular movement, the peasantry as the most reliable ally of the working class and the liberal bourgeoisie as the betrayer of "popular freedom."

We would like the Social-Democratic group in the Fourth Duma to be united and solid in its activities on the basis of the above-mentioned slogans.

We would like it to obtain its strength from permanent contact with the broad masses.

We would like it to march in step with the political organization of the working class of Russia.

Published in leaflet form
in the first half
of October 1912

Reprinted from the leaflet

THE WILL
OF THE VOTERS' DELEGATES

The results of the elections in the workers' curia have now been finally established.[115] Of the six electors, three are Liquidators and three supporters of *Pravda*. Which one of them should be nominated for the Duma? Which one of them, indeed, ought to be nominated? Did the assembly of voters' delegates give any instructions on this matter?

The Liquidators got their supporters elected because they concealed their views from the voters' delegates, they glossed over disagreements and played at "unity." They were supported by the non-party voters' delegates, who dislike disagreements and who accepted the word of the Liquidators. But in spite of all the Liquidators' efforts to confuse the issue, in one thing—and the main thing at that—the will of the voters' delegates made itself felt. This was on the question of the mandate. By an overwhelming majority the assembly of voters' delegates adopted a definite mandate to the Duma deputy, the mandate of the supporters of *Pravda*.

In its report of the elections, *Luch*[116] hushes up this point, but it cannot conceal from its readers the truth which is known to all the voters' delegates. We shall not permit it to misrepresent the will of the voters' delegates.

The mandate is an instruction to the deputy. The mandate moulds the deputy. The deputy is the image of the mandate. What does the mandate proposed by the big plants in St. Petersburg, and adopted by the assembly of voters' delegates, speak of?

First of all the mandate speaks of the tasks of 1905 and says that these tasks have not been fulfilled, that the economic and political situation in the country makes the fulfilment of these tasks inevitable. According to the mandate, the emancipation of the country can be achieved by a struggle, a struggle on two fronts: against the feudal-bureaucratic survivals on the one hand, and against the treacherous liberal bourgeoisie on the other. In this the peasantry alone can be the reliable ally of the workers. But the struggle can be victorious only on the condition that hegemony (the leading role) is exercised by the proletariat. The more class conscious and organized the workers are, the better will they fulfil the role of leader of the people. In view of the fact that under present conditions the floor of the Duma is one of the best means of organizing and enlightening the masses, the workers are sending their deputy to the Duma in order that he, and the entire Social-Democratic group in the Fourth Duma, shall champion the fundamental tasks of the proletariat, the full and uncurtailed demands of the country. . . .

Such is the content of the mandate.

It is not difficult to perceive that this mandate differs fundamentally from the "platform" of the Liquidators—it is entirely anti-liquidationist.

The question then arises: if the Liquidators, after all, dare to nominate their candidate for Duma deputy, what is to happen to the mandate which the Duma

deputy is in duty bound to carry out, since the assembly
of voters' delegates passed a definite decision to that
effect?

An anti-liquidationist mandate carried out by a Liquidator—will our Liquidators sink to such a disgrace?

Do they realize that playing at "unity" has driven
them into an impasse?

Or perhaps they intend to violate the mandate, to
relegate it to oblivion?

But in that case what about the will of the voters'
delegates, which the workers of St. Petersburg will undoubtedly come out to defend?

Will the Liquidators dare to trample upon the will
of the voters' delegates?

They are still talking about victory, but do they
realize that the mandate has inflicted mortal defeat
upon them by emphasizing that only an anti-Liquidator
can be a Duma deputy?

Pravda, No. 147,   Reprinted from the newspaper
October 19, 1912

Signed: *K. St.*

THE RESULTS OF THE ELECTIONS
IN THE WORKERS' CURIA
OF ST. PETERSBURG

1. THE ELECTION OF THE VOTERS' DELEGATES

The most characteristic feature of the temper of the workers compared with 1907 is the great revival of interest in the elections. If we leave out of account the small groups scattered here and there among the enterprises, we may boldly assert that the boycott mood is entirely absent. Obukhov's[117] did not boycott the elections, it was deprived of the opportunity to take part in them by the works' administration. The Neva Shipbuilding Yard was the only place where the boycotters acted in an organized manner, but even there the overwhelming majority of the workers declared in favour of taking part in the elections. The broad masses of the workers were in favour of taking part in the elections. Moreover, they demanded elections and went to the polls with immense interest as long as no unsurmountable obstacles were put in their way. This is proved by the recent mass protests against the "interpretations.". . .

In almost every case Social-Democrats, or those associated with the Social-Democrats, were elected. Owing to circumstances beyond our control, it was possible only in a few factories to expound fully the platform of consistent workers' democracy, the more so because the Liquidators wisely hid their platform from the workers. But wherever such exposition was possible, the workers adopted the platform of the anti-Liquidators in the form of a "mandate." In these cases, the Liquidators—evidently having no respect for themselves or for their own views—declared that "in substance they too were in favour of such a mandate" (Neva Shipbuilding Yard), and they moved "amendments" about freedom of association, which were rejected on the grounds that they were superfluous. Thus, the voters' delegates were elected mainly on their "personal merits." The overwhelming majority of those elected proved to be Social-Democrats, or people associated with them.

Social-Democracy alone expresses the interests of the working class—that is what the election of the voters' delegates tells us.

2. THE ELECTION OF ELECTORS

Of the 82 voters' delegates who assembled, 26 were definite anti-Liquidators, 15 definite Liquidators, while the remaining 41 were "just Social-Democrats," people associated with the Social-Democrats, and non-party Lefts.

For whom would these 41 vote, what political line would they approve of?—that was the question that primarily interested the "factionalists."

By an overwhelming majority the assembly of voters' delegates declared in favour of the mandate proposed by the supporters of *Pravda*. By so doing it defined its complexion. The political line of the anti-Liquidators triumphed. The attempt of the Liquidators to prevent this failed.

Had the Liquidators been politically honest and respected their own views they would have withdrawn their candidates and would have left all the places for the supporters of *Pravda*, for it was self-evident that only supporters of the mandate could be nominated as candidates. *Opponents* of the mandate as *champions* of the mandate—only political bankrupts could go to such lengths. The Liquidators did go even to such lengths! Concealing their own views from the voters' delegates, pretending for the time being to be "our people" who "had no objection" to the mandate that had been adopted, playing at unity and complaining that the anti-Liquidators were splitters, they tried to soften the hearts of the non-factional voters' delegates and "smuggle" their men through somehow. And in fact they did smuggle them through by deceiving the voters' delegates.

It was evident that there would be no end to the trickery of the Liquidators.

It was no less evident that the political line of *Pravda*, and that line alone, enjoyed the sympathy of the St. Petersburg proletariat, that in conformity with the will of the voters' delegates only a supporter of *Pravda* could be a Duma deputy representing the workers.

A bigger victory we could not have desired. . . .

3. TWO UNITIES

Before coming to the election of the Duma deputy we must say a word or two about the "unity" which played a fatal role during the election of the electors, and at which the Liquidators are clutching like a drowning man at a straw.

Trotsky recently wrote in *Luch* that *Pravda* was once for unity, but is now against it. Is that true? It is true and yet not true. It is true that *Pravda* was for unity. It is not true that it is now against unity:

Pravda always calls for the unity of consistent workers' democracy.

What is the point then? The point is that *Pravda*, and *Luch* and Trotsky, look at unity in totally different ways. Evidently there are different kinds of unity.

Pravda is of the opinion that only Bolsheviks and pro-Party Mensheviks can be united into a single whole. Unity on the basis of dissociation from anti-Party elements, from Liquidators! *Pravda* has always stood and always will stand for such unity.

Trotsky, however, looks at the matter differently: he jumbles everybody together—opponents of the Party principle as well as its supporters. And of course he gets no unity whatever: for five years he has been conducting this childish propaganda in favour of uniting the un-unitable, and what he has achieved is that we have two newspapers, two platforms, two conferences, and not a scrap of unity between workers' democracy and the Liquidators!

And while the Bolsheviks and the pro-Party Mensheviks are uniting more and more into a single whole, the Liquidators are digging a chasm between themselves and this whole.

The practical experience of the movement confirms *Pravda's* plan of unity.

The practical experience of the movement smashes Trotsky's childish plan of uniting the ununitable.

More than that. From an advocate of a fantastic unity Trotsky is turning into an agent of the Liquidators, doing what suits the Liquidators.

Trotsky has done all in his power to ensure that we should have two rival newspapers, two rival platforms, two conferences which repudiate each other—and now this champion with fake muscles is singing us a song about unity!

This is not unity, it is a game worthy of a comedian.

And if this game enabled the Liquidators to secure the election of three of their men as electors it was only because it was impossible in the short period available to expose the unity comedians who concealed their flag from the workers. . . .

4. THE ELECTION OF THE DUMA DEPUTY

After that it is not difficult to understand what kind of "unity" the Liquidators talked about when they proposed to the supporters of *Pravda* the nomination of a joint candidate for the Duma. It was simply a proposal to vote for the Liquidators' candidate, in spite of the will expressed by the voters' delegates, and in spite of the mandate of the St. Petersburg proletariat. What other answer could the supporters of *Pravda* give except that the mandate of the voters' delegates was sacred, and that only a supporter of the mandate could be elected as Duma deputy? Should they have gone against the will of the voters' delegates to please the spineless Liquidators, or should they have disregarded the latter's caprices for the sake of the mandate of the St. Petersburg proletariat? *Luch* is howling about *Pravda's* splitting tactics and is spreading fairy tales about the electors, but why did not the Liquidators agree to draw lots among the six electors from the workers as recommended by *Pravda*? In the interests of a joint workers' candidate we were ready to make even this concession, but why, we ask, did the

Liquidators reject the proposal to draw lots? Why did the supporters of *Luch* prefer six candidates for the Duma instead of one? In the interests of "unity," perhaps?

Luch says that Gudkov nominated the *Pravda* supporter Badayev as a candidate, but, the Liquidator newspaper modestly adds, the proposal was rejected. But have the *Luch* Liquidators forgotten that it was their supporter Petrov, and not the "*Pravda*-ist," who refused to withdraw his candidature and so by his action exposed the Liquidators' urge for "unity." And yet they call this unity! Perhaps the fact that Gudkov, the other supporter of *Luch*, put up his candidature after Badayev, the supporter of *Pravda*, had already been elected, will also be claimed as unity? Who will believe it?

Luch hypocritically advertises that political nonentity Sudakov who, it alleges, withdrew his candidature in the interests of unity. But does not *Luch* know that Sudakov simply *could not* go to the ballot because he had received only two nominations? What should we call a newspaper which dares to lie in full view of everybody?

Is political spinelessness the only "merit" of the Liquidators?

The Liquidators tried to get their man into the Duma by the will of the Cadets and Octobrists in opposition to the will of the St. Petersburg workers. But does not *Luch*, which is divorced from the masses of the workers, realize that the St. Petersburg workers would have expressed their lack of confidence in such a deputy?

Pravda, No. 151,   Reprinted from the newspaper
October 24, 1912

Signed: *K. St.*

TODAY IS ELECTION DAY

Today is election day in St. Petersburg. Elections in the Second Curia. The fight is between two camps: the Social-Democrats and the Cadets. The voters must decide to whom they are going to entrust the fate of the country.

What do the Social-Democrats want?

What do the Cadets want?

The Social-Democrats, as the representatives of the working class, are striving to liberate mankind from all exploitation.

The Cadets, however, as the representatives of the liberal bourgeoisie, build their future on the exploitation of man by man, an embellished exploitation, it is true, but exploitation for all that.

The Social-Democrats are of the opinion that the question of renovating the country has remained unsettled, that it must be settled, and settled by the efforts of the country itself.

The Cadets, however, believe that it is superfluous to talk about renovation because, "thank God we have a Constitution.". . .

The Social-Democrats are of the opinion that on the road to the renovation of the country Russia has split up into two Russias: old, official Russia, and the new, future Russia.

The Cadets, however, believe that after "the granting of a Constitution" "this contrasting" of the two Russias is "no longer possible" because "Russia is now one."

The only deduction to be drawn is: the constitutional ideal of the Cadets has already been achieved. The framework of the June the Third regime is not irksome to them.

For example, the following is what Milyukov said at a banquet in London in 1909, at which he "represented" Russia in conjunction with the Octobrist Guchkov and the "moderate" Black-Hundred Bobrinsky:

"You have before you men of very diverse shades of political opinion, but these differences, supplementing each other, represent our great ideal of a constitutional Russia" (see I. Yefremov's book, *Russia's People's Representatives*, etc., p. 81).

Thus, the Black-Hundred Bobrinsky, "supplementing" the Cadet Milyukov in the interests of . . . "popular freedom"—such, it appears, is the "great ideal" of the Cadets.

Not a single representative of the workers, *not a single* representative of the peasants was present at the London banquet, but, it appears, the "great ideals" of the Cadets can do without workers, can do without peasants. . . .

A Constitution of the Bobrinskys, Guchkovs and Milyukovs *without* representatives of the workers, *without* representatives of the peasants—such are the "ideals" of the Cadets!

Is it surprising, after this, that the Cadets in the Third Duma voted for 1) the anti-popular budget,

2) indirect taxes, 3) grants for the maintenance of prisons, etc.?

Is it surprising, after this, that the Cadets oppose the demands of the workers, of the peasants and of the entire democracy?

Is it surprising, after this, that the Cadets, through the mouth of Maklakov, demanded "more vigour, sternness and severity" towards the student movement, and in *Rech* contemptuously described the peaceful strike of the Lena workers as a "spontaneous riot"?

No, this is not a party of "popular freedom," but a party of betrayers of "popular freedom."

Such people are only capable of striking a bargain with the bureaucracy behind the backs of the people. The "negotiations" with Witte, Stolypin and Trepov, and now with Sazonov, are by no means accidental.

Such people are only capable of entering into an alliance with the Black Hundreds to defeat the Social-Democrats in the elections in Kharkov, Kostroma, Yekaterinodar and Riga.

To entrust the fate of the country to such people would be tantamount to surrendering the country to the derision of the enemies.

We express the conviction that self-respecting voters will not link their honour with the fate of the Cadets.

Let the Cadets today bear well-merited punishment for the heinous sins they have committed against the Russian people!

Worker voters! Vote for those who represent your interests, for the Social-Democrats!

Shop assistant voters! Don't vote for the Cadets, who ignored your interests as regards leisure time—

vote for the Social-Democrats, the only consistent champions of your interests!

Polish voters! You are striving for the right to free national development—remember that freedom for nationalities is inconceivable without general freedom, and the Cadets are betraying freedom!

Jewish voters! You are striving for equal rights for the Jews, but remember that the Milyukovs who hobnob with the Bobrinskys, and the Cadets who enter into a bloc with the Rights, will not strive for equal rights!

For the betrayers of the popular freedom, or for its champions; for the Cadets or for the Social-Democrats! Choose, citizens!

Pravda, No. 152,   Reprinted from the newspaper
October 25, 1912
Signed: *K. St.*

TO ALL THE WORKING MEN
AND WORKING WOMEN OF RUSSIA![118]

January 9

Comrades!

We are again about to commemorate January 9 —the day that was sealed with the blood of hundreds of our fellow-workers who, on January 9, 1905, were shot down by tsar Nicholas Romanov because they had come to him, peaceful and unarmed, to petition for better conditions of life.

Eight years have elapsed since then. Eight long years, during which, except for a brief flash of freedom, our country has been harrowed and tortured by the tsar and the landlords!

And today, as in the past, workers in Russia are being shot down for peacefully going on strike—as was the case on the Lena. And today, as in the past, millions and millions of peasants are being reduced to starvation—as was the case in 1911. And today, as in the past, the finest sons of the people are being tortured and tormented in the tsar's prisons and being driven to wholesale suicide— as was the case recently in Kutomar, Algachi,[119] and elsewhere. And today, as in the past, the tsar's courts-martial sentence sailors and soldiers to be shot for demanding land for the peasants and freedom for all the people—as was the case recently with the seventeen sailors of the Black Sea Fleet.[120] That is the way Nicholas Romanov, Autocrat of All the Russias by the grace of the landlords, is exercising the power bestowed on him "by God" and blessed by the surpliced villains of the Synod and by the Black Hundreds—the Purishkeviches and Khvostovs.

Russia is still being strangled by the Romanov monarchy, which is preparing this year to celebrate the 300th anniversary of its bloody rule over our country.

But Russia is no longer the downtrodden and submissive Russia which suffered in silence under the yoke of the Romanovs for so many years. And above all, our Russian working class, now marching at the head of all the fighters for freedom, is not what it was. We shall commemorate January 9, 1913, not as crushed and downtrodden slaves, but with heads erect—a united army of fighters, who feel, who know, that the people's Russia is waking up again, that the ice of the counter-revolution has been broken, that the river of the people's movement has begun to flow again, and that "behind us fresh warriors march in serried ranks.". . .

Eight years! How little lived, how much endured. . . . In this period we have seen three State Dumas. The first two, in which the liberals had the majority, but in which the voices of the workers and peasants were loudly heard, the tsar dispersed in obedience to the will of the Black-Hundred landlords. The Third Duma was a Black-Hundred Duma, and for five years it co-operated with the tsarist gang in still further enslaving and oppressing the peasants, the workers—the whole of people's Russia.

During these years of dark counter-revolution it was

the working class that had to drain the bitterest cup. Since 1907, when the forces of the old order succeeded in temporarily crushing the revolutionary mass movement, the workers have been groaning under a double yoke. On them above all the tsarist gang took ruthless vengeance. And it is against them that the onslaught of the capitalist offensive was directed. Taking advantage of the political reaction, the factory and mill owners step by step robbed the workers of all the gains they had won with so much effort and sacrifice. By means of lockouts, and protected by the gendarmerie and the police, the employers lengthened the working day, cut wages and restored the old system in the factories and mills.

Clenching their teeth, the workers remained silent. In 1908 and 1909 the Black Hundreds' intoxication with their triumph reached its peak and the labour movement reached its lowest ebb. But already in the summer of 1910 a revival of workers' strikes began, and the end of 1911 brought with it the active protest of tens of thousands of workers against the retention in penal servitude of the Social-Democratic deputies of the Second Duma, who had been sentenced on false charges.[121]

The mass movement of the workers *ended* with the strike of November 22, 1907, against the sentences of penal servitude on the Social-Democratic deputies of the Second Duma; and the mass movement of the workers *revived* at the end of 1911, again in connection with the fate of the Social-Democratic deputies of the Second Duma, those front-rank fighters, those working-class heroes, whose work is now being continued by the workers' deputies in the Fourth Duma.

The revival of the political struggle is accompanied by the revival of the workers' economic struggle. The political strike fosters the economic strike and vice versa. Wave follows wave, and the workers' movement is surging forward in a mighty flood against the strongholds of the tsarist monarchy and of the autocracy of capital. More and more sections of the workers are awakening to new life. Larger and larger masses are being drawn into the new struggle. The strikes in connection with the Lena shooting, the May Day strikes, the strikes in protest against the disfranchisement of the workers, and the protest strike against the execution of the sailors of the Black Sea Fleet involved about a million participants. Those were revolutionary strikes, strikes which inscribed on their banners the slogan: "Down with the Romanov monarchy, down with the whole of the old and decaying landlord regime which is strangling Russia!"

The workers' revolutionary movement is expanding and growing. The working class is beginning to rouse other sections of the population for the new struggle. All honest men and women, all those who are pressing forward towards a better life, are beginning to protest against the violence of the hounds of tsarism. Even the bourgeoisie is grumbling, even it is displeased with the complete and undivided rule of the Purishkeviches.

The June the Third regime has pacified nobody. All the years of counter-revolution have shown that there can be no free life in Russia so long as the Romanov monarchy and landlord rule remain intact.

A new revolution is maturing, in which the working class will again play the honourable role of leader of the entire army of emancipation.

On the banner of the working class are still inscribed the three old demands for which so much sacrifice has been made and so much blood has been shed.

An eight-hour day—for the workers!

All the landlords', tsar's and monasterial lands without compensation—for the peasants!

A democratic republic—for the whole people!

It is around these demands that the fight in Russia has raged and is raging today. They were advanced by the workers during the recent Lena strikes. They will be advanced also by the working class on January 9.

In 1912, the workers in St. Petersburg, Riga and Nikolayev tried to commemorate January 9 by strikes and demonstrations. In 1913, we shall commemorate January 9 in this way everywhere—*all over Russia.* On January 9, 1905, the first Russian revolution was born in the blood of the workers. Let the beginning of 1913 serve as the threshold of the *second* revolution in Russia. The house of Romanov, in preparing to celebrate its 300th anniversary in 1913, contemplates remaining on the back of Russia for a long time to come. Let us, then, on January 9, 1913, say to this gang:

Enough! Down with the Romanov monarchy! Long live the democratic republic!

Comrades! Let not January 9, 1913, pass unobserved anywhere where Russian workers are living and fighting.

With meetings, resolutions, mass rallies and where possible with

*a one-day strike and
demonstrations*

let us everywhere commemorate this day.

Let us on this day remember the heroes who fell in the struggle! We shall pay the highest tribute to their memory if, on that day, our old demands ring out all over Russia:

A Democratic Republic!
Confiscation of the Landlords' Land!
An Eight-Hour Working Day!

The Central Committee of the Russian
Social-Democratic Labour Party

Comrades!
Prepare to protest on January 9.

Published in leaflet form   Reprinted from the leaflet
at the end of December 1912
and beginning of January 1913

THE ELECTIONS IN ST. PETERSBURG

(A Letter From St. Petersburg)

Unlike the elections of 1907, the elections in 1912 coincided with a revolutionary revival among the workers. In 1907 the tide of revolution was receding and the counter-revolution triumphed, but in 1912 the first wave of a new revolution rose. This explains why the workers *then* went to the polls listlessly and in some places even boycotted the elections, boycotted them *passively*, of course, thereby showing that passive boycott is an undoubted symptom of listlessness and decline of strength. And it explains why *now*, in the atmosphere of a rising revolutionary tide, the workers went to the polls eagerly, casting aside flabby political indifference. More than that: the workers fought for the right to elections, strove for that right and secured it by means of immense strikes against the "interpretations," despite all the cunning devices and obstacles employed by the police. It is undoubtedly a sign that the political torpor has passed off, that the revolution has got past the dead point. True, the wave of the new revolution is not *yet* so strong as to enable us to raise the question, say, of a general political strike. But it is *already* strong enough to make it possible, in places, to break through the web of "interpretations" with the object of animating the elections, organizing the forces of the proletariat, and politically enlightening the masses.

I

THE WORKERS' CURIA

1. THE FIGHT FOR ELECTIONS

It will not be superfluous to note that the initiative in the strike campaign was taken by the representative of the Central Committee and the St. Petersburg Committee of our Party. Late in the evening of October 4, on the eve of the election of the electors, we learned that the Uyezd Commission had "interpreted" the voters' delegates of the largest plants (Putilov's and others). An hour later the Executive Commission of the St. Petersburg Committee met, together with the representative of the Central Committee,[122] and after drawing up a new list of electors decided to call for a one-day protest strike. That same night the Social-Democratic group at the Putilov Works met and accepted the decision of the St. Petersburg Committee. On the 5th, the Putilov strike began. The whole plant went on strike. On the 7th (Sunday) the Social-Democratic group at the Neva Shipbuilding Yard met and associated itself with the decision of the St. Petersburg Committee. On the 8th, the entire shipyard went on strike. Their example was followed by other factories and works. Not only did the "interpreted" factories go on strike, but so also did those which had not been "interpreted" (Pal's), and also those which, according to the "regulations governing the elections," had no right to vote in the workers' curia. They struck in solidarity. Of revolutionary songs and demonstrations there was no lack. . . . Late at night on October 8 it was learned that the Gubernia Election Commission had annulled the election of electors, had countermanded the "interpretations" of the Uyezd Commission, had "restored the rights" of the Putilov workers, and had extended the elections to a larger number of factories. The workers triumphed; they had won a victory.

Of interest is the resolution adopted by the workers at the Neva Shipbuilding Yard and at the Putilov Works in declaring their strikes:

"Protesting against the violation of our electoral rights, we declare that only the overthrow of tsarism and the winning of a democratic republic can ensure for the workers the right and real freedom to vote."

A resolution moved by the Liquidators to the effect that ". . . only universal suffrage *in the election of the State Duma* can guarantee the right to vote" was rejected. These resolutions were first discussed by the Social-Democratic groups in the respective plants, and when it was ascertained, at the meeting of the group at the Neva Shipbuilding Yard, for example, that the Liquidators' resolution met with no sympathy, its supporters pledged themselves not to move it at the meeting of the non-party masses, but to support the resolution adopted by the group. It must be said to their honour that they kept their word. On the other hand, the anti-Liquidators displayed equal loyalty by securing the election of Gudkov as a voters' delegate, whom they could have "dished" as they had the majority at the shipyard behind them.

It would not be amiss if at least a particle of the same sense of responsibility had been displayed by *Luch*, which is able to write so well about what *did not happen* at the various plants, but which hushed up the above-mentioned resolution that was adopted at the Neva Shipbuilding Yard and, on top of that, garbled the resolution that was adopted at the Putilov Works.

Thus, the workers fought for elections and secured elections. Let the St. Petersburg Socialist-Revolutionaries, who at the Neva Shipbuilding Yard so unsuccessfully opposed participation in the elections, learn a lesson from this.

The workers fought for elections under the watchword of a democratic republic. Let the Liquidators of *Luch*, who make a fetish of "partial reforms," learn a lesson from this.

2. THE DEPUTY'S MANDATE

The "interpretation" strikes were not yet over when the assembly of voters' delegates met. It was a foregone conclusion that the delegates would adopt the mandate which had been drawn up by the St. Petersburg Committee and approved by the big plants in St. Petersburg (Putilov's, the Neva Shipbuilding Yard and Pal's). And indeed the mandate was adopted by an overwhelming majority, only an insignificant group of Liquidators abstaining. The latter's attempts to prevent a vote from being taken were met with cries of "don't obstruct!"

In their mandate to the Duma deputy the voters' delegates referred to the "tasks of 1905" and said that these tasks had "remained unfulfilled," that the economic and political development of Russia "makes their fulfilment inevitable." A struggle of the workers and the revolutionary peasants for the overthrow of tsarism in spite of the compromising policy of the Cadet bourgeoisie, a struggle of which only the proletariat can be the leader—this, according to the mandate, could fulfil the tasks of 1905 (see "The Mandate" in *Sotsial-Demokrat*, No. 28-29).

As you see, this is very far from the liberal-liquidationist "revision of the agrarian decisions of the Third Duma," or "universal suffrage in the election of the State Duma" (see the Liquidators' platform).[123]

The St. Petersburg workers remained loyal to the revolutionary traditions of our Party. The slogans of revolutionary Social-Democracy, and these slogans alone, received recognition at the assembly of voters' delegates. At the assembly the question was decided by the non-party people (of the 82 delegates, 41 were "just Social-Democrats" and non-party), and the fact that the mandate drawn up by the St. Petersburg Committee was adopted at even such an assembly shows that the slogans of the St. Petersburg Committee are deeply rooted in the heart and mind of the working class.

What was the Liquidators' attitude towards all this? Had they really believed in their own views and not been shaky in the matter of political honesty, they would have launched an open struggle against the mandate, they would have proposed their own mandate or, if defeated, would have withdrawn their candidates from the lists. Did they not put up their own list of candidates for electors in opposition to the list put up by the anti-Liquidators? Why, then, could they not also openly put forward their own views, their own mandate? And when the mandate of the anti-Liquidators was adopted, why did they not honestly and openly declare that as opponents of this mandate they could not stand for election as future champions of the mandate, that they would withdraw their candidates and leave the place open for the supporters of the mandate? After all, this is an elementary rule of political honesty. Or perhaps the Liquidators avoided the question of the mandate because the question had not been sufficiently debated and because at the assembly the question was settled by the votes of the *non-party* people? But if that was the case, why did they not submit to the decision of the 26 *Social-Democratic* voters' delegates who met secretly several days before the assembly of voters' delegates and after a discussion adopted the platform of the anti-Liquidators (by a majority of 16 to 9, with one abstaining), at which meeting the Liquidators' leaders as well as their voters' delegates were present? By what lofty considerations were the Liquidators guided when they trampled upon the mandate of the entire assembly and upon the will of the 26 Social-Democratic voters' delegates? Obviously, there could be only one consideration: To spite the anti-Liquidators and smuggle through their own people "somehow." But the whole point is that if the Liquidators had dared to launch an open struggle, not one of their supporters would have been elected, because it was obvious to everybody that the Liquidators' proposal for a "revision of the agrarian decisions of the Third Duma" would find no support among the voters' delegates. There remained only one thing for them to do: to hide their flag, to pretend to be supporters of the mandate by declaring that "strictly speaking we, too, are in favour of some such mandate" and thereby get their people elected "somehow." And that is what they did; but by behaving in that way the Liquidators admitted their defeat and registered themselves as political bankrupts.

But compelling the enemy to furl his flag, i.e., compelling him to admit that his own flag is *worthless*, i.e., compelling him to admit the ideological superiority of his enemy—means, precisely, gaining a moral victory.

And so we have the following "strange situation": the Liquidators have a "broad workers' party," the anti-Liquidators, however, have only an "ossified circle," and yet the "narrow circle" vanquishes the "broad party"!

What miracles happen in this world! . . .

3. UNITY AS A MASK, AND THE ELECTION OF THE DUMA DEPUTY

When bourgeois diplomats prepare for war they begin to shout very loudly about "peace" and "friendly relations." When a Minister of Foreign Affairs begins to wax eloquent in favour of a "peace conference," you can take it for granted that "his government" has already issued contracts for the construction of new dreadnoughts and monoplanes. A diplomat's words *must* contradict his deeds—otherwise, what sort of a diplomat is he? Words are one thing—deeds something entirely different. Fine words are a mask to cover shady deeds. A sincere diplomat is like dry water, or wooden iron.

The same must be said about the Liquidators and their mendacious clamour about unity. Recently, Comrade Plekhanov, who is in favour of unity in the Party, wrote concerning the resolutions passed by the Liquidators' conference[124] that "they smell of diplomacy ten versts away." And the same Comrade Plekhanov went on to describe their conference as a "splitters' conference." To put it more bluntly, the Liquidators are deceiving the workers by their diplomatic clamour about unity, for while they talk about unity they are engineering a split. Indeed, the Liquidators are diplomats in the Social-Democratic movement; with fine words about unity they cover up their shady deeds in engineering a split. When a Liquidator waxes eloquent in favour of unity, you can take it for granted that he has already trampled upon unity for the sake of a split.

The elections in St. Petersburg are direct proof of this.

Unity means first of all unity of action by the Social-Democratically organized workers within the working class, which is as yet unorganized, as yet unenlightened by the light of socialism. The Social-Democratically organized workers raise questions at their meetings, discuss them, adopt decisions and then, as a single whole, bring these decisions, which are absolutely binding upon the minority, before the non-party workers. *Without this there can be no unity of Social-Democracy!* Was there such a decision adopted in St. Petersburg? Yes, there was. It was the decision adopted by the 26 Social-Democratic voters' delegates (of both trends) who accepted the anti-Liquidators' platform. Why did not the Liquidators submit to this decision? Why did they thwart the will of the majority of the Social-Democratic voters' delegates? *Why did they trample upon the unity of Social-Democracy* in St. Petersburg? Because the Liquidators are diplomats in the Social-Democratic movement, engineering a split under the mask of unity.

Further, unity means unity of action of the proletariat in face of the entire bourgeois world. The representatives of the proletariat adopt decisions and carry them out acting as a single whole, the condition being that the minority submits to the majority. *Without this there can be no unity of the proletariat!* Was there such a decision of the St. Petersburg proletariat? Yes, there was. It was the anti-liquidationist mandate adopted by the majority at the assembly of voters' delegates. Why did not the Liquidators submit to the mandate of the voters' delegates? Why did they thwart the will of the majority of the voters' delegates? *Why did they trample upon working-class unity in St. Petersburg?* Because liquidationist unity is a diplomatic *phrase* which covers up a *policy* of disrupting unity. . . .

When, after thwarting the will of the majority, nominating waverers (Sudakov) and making promises of a most diplomatic nature, the Liquidators at last managed to secure the election of three of their electors, the question arose—what is to be done now?

The only *honest* way out was to draw lots. The anti-Liquidators *proposed* to the Liquidators that lots should be drawn, but the Liquidators *rejected* this proposal!!

After discussing the proposal with the Bolshevik X, the Liquidator Y (we can, if necessary, give the names of the persons who discussed the matter on behalf of the

respective sides, provided the necessary secrecy is maintained),[125] consulted his like-minded friends and then
replied that "drawing lots is unacceptable, as our electors are bound by the decision of our leading body."

Let Messrs. the Liquidators try to refute this statement of ours!

Thwarting the will of the majority of the Social-
Democratic voters' delegates, thwarting the will of the
majority at the assembly of voters' delegates, rejecting
the proposal to draw lots, refusing to put up a joint candidate for the Duma,—all this in the interests of unity.
You have a very queer idea of "unity," Messrs. Liquidators!

Incidentally, the Liquidators' splitting policy is not
new. They have been agitating against the underground
Party ever since 1908. The Liquidators' outrageous conduct during the elections in St. Petersburg was a continuation of their old splitting policy.

It is said that by his "unity" campaign Trotsky introduced a "new current" into the Liquidators' old "affairs." But that is not true. In spite of Trotsky's "heroic"
efforts and "terrible threats" he, in the end, has proved
to be merely a vociferous champion with fake muscles,
for after five years of "work" he has succeeded in uniting
nobody but the Liquidators. New noise—old actions!

But let us return to the elections. The Liquidators
could have counted only on one thing when they rejected
the proposal to draw lots, namely, that the bourgeoisie
(the Cadets and Octobrists) *would prefer a Liquidator*!
To thwart this neat little scheme the St. Petersburg
Committee had no alternative but to instruct all the
electors to stand for election, for among the Liquidators

there was a "waverer" (Sudakov), and in general they had no solid group. In conformity with the instructions of the St. Petersburg Committee all the anti-liquidationist electors stood for election. And the Liquidators' neat little scheme was frustrated! Demoralization set in not among the anti-Liquidators, but among the liquidationist electors, who rushed to stand for election in spite of the decision of their "body." The surprising thing is not that Gudkov agreed to Badayev's nomination (hanging over Gudkov's head was the anti-liquidationist mandate that was adopted at his plant), but the fact that the Liquidator Petrov, followed by Gudkov himself, stood for election *after the election* of Badayev.

There is only one deduction to be drawn from the foregoing: for the Liquidators, unity is a mask to cover up their splitting policy, a means to get into the Duma in spite of the will expressed by the Social-Democrats and the proletariat of St. Petersburg.

II

THE CITY CURIA

The Lena events, and the revival among the workers generally, did not fail to affect the voters in the Second Curia. The democratic strata of the city population swung considerably to the left. Five years ago, after the revolution was defeated, they "buried" the ideals of 1905, but now, after the mass strikes, the old ideals began to revive. There was a definite mood of dissatisfaction with the dual policy of the Cadets, which the Cadets could not help noticing.

On the other hand, the Octobrists had "failed to justify" the hopes reposed in them by the big merchants and manufacturers. Vacancies occurred, which, too, the Cadets could not help noticing.

And already in May of this year the Cadets resolved to play on two fronts. Not to fight, but to play.

And that explains the dual character of the Cadets' election campaign in the two different curiae, which could not fail to astonish the voters.

The Social-Democrats' election campaign centred around their struggle with the Cadets for influence on the democratic strata. The hegemony of the counter-revolutionary bourgeoisie, or the hegemony of the revolutionary proletariat—such was the "formula" of the Bolsheviks, against which the Liquidators had been fighting hopelessly for many years, and which they were now obliged to accept as an obvious and inevitable vital necessity.

Victory in the Second Curia depended on the conduct of the democratic strata, who were democratic by virtue of their conditions, but were not yet conscious of their interests. Whom would these strata support, Social-Democracy or the Cadets? There was also a third camp, the Rights and the Octobrists, but there were no grounds for talking seriously about a "Black-Hundred danger," because it was evident that the Rights could poll only a small number of votes. Although there was some talk about "not frightening the bourgeoisie" (see F. D.'s article in *Nevsky Golos*[126]), it only raised a smile, because it was obvious that the task that confronted Social-Democracy was not only to "frighten" this bourgeoisie, but, in the shape of its advocates the Cadets, to dislodge it from its positions.

The hegemony of Social-Democracy, or the hegemony of the Cadets—that is how life itself presented the question.

From that it was clear that the utmost solidarity was needed in the ranks of Social-Democracy throughout the campaign.

It was precisely for that reason that the Election Commission of the St. Petersburg Committee concluded an agreement with the other Commission, which consisted of Mensheviks and solitary Liquidators. It was an agreement about persons, which allowed complete freedom for conducting election propaganda, on the definite understanding that the list of candidates for the Duma "must not include any person whose name or activities are associated with the struggle against the Party principle" (excerpt from the "minutes" of the negotiations). The well-known Social-Democratic list for the Second Curia was arrived at merely as a result of the anti-Liquidators' rejection of Ab. . . and L. . ., notorious St. Petersburg Liquidators "whose name and activities are associated," etc. It will not be superfluous to point out here, in order to characterize the "advocates of unity," that after Chkheidze was nominated in Tiflis they emphatically refused to withdraw his nomination in favour of the Social-Democrat Pokrovsky, ex-member of the Third Duma, and threatened to put up a parallel list and disrupt the campaign.

However, the reservation concerning "freedom of election propaganda" was perhaps superfluous, for the course of the campaign had clearly demonstrated that no campaign was possible in the fight against the Cadets other than a revolutionary Social-Democratic, i.e., a Bolshevik, campaign. Who does not remember the speeches delivered by the St. Petersburg speakers and Social-Democratic candidates about the "hegemony of the proletariat" and about the "old methods of struggle" as against the "new parliamentary methods," about the "second movement" and the "uselessness of the slogan of a responsible Cadet Ministry"? What became of the Liquidators' lamentations about "not splitting the opposition," about the "Cadet bourgeoisie swinging to the left," and about "bringing pressure to bear" on this bourgeoisie? And what about the anti-Cadet agitation of the Liquidators of *Luch* who "nagged" and "frightened" the Cadets, sometimes even too much? Does not all this show that life itself uttered the truth even "out of the mouths of babes and sucklings."

What became of the conscientious principles of Dan, Martov and the other opponents of "Cadetophobia"?

The Liquidators' "broad workers' party" again sustained defeat in its struggle against the "underground circle." Just think: the "broad workers'(?) party" a captive in the hands of the tiny, very tiny, "circle"! What a miracle! . . .

III

SUMMARY

The first thing that is clear from the foregoing is that all talk about two camps, the camp of the supporters of the June the Third regime and the camp of its opponents, is groundless. Actually, three and not two camps appeared in the elections: the revolutionary camp (the Social-Democrats), the counter-revolutionary camp (the Rights), and the camp of the compromisers, who are undermining the revolution and bringing grist to the mill of the counter-revolution (the Cadets). Of a "united opposition" against the reaction there was not a sign.

Further, the elections show that the line of demarcation between the two extreme camps will become more distinct, that, as a consequence, the middle camp will melt away, free the democratically minded to the advantage of Social-Democracy, and itself gradually shift to the side of the counter-revolution.

Hence, talk about "reforms" from above, about "upheavals" being impossible, and about Russia's "organic development" under the aegis of a "Constitution," becomes utterly baseless. The course of events is inevitably leading to a new revolution, and despite the assurances of the Larins and other Liquidators, we shall live through "another 1905."

Lastly, the elections show that the proletariat, and the proletariat alone, is destined to lead the impending revolution, step by step rallying around itself all that is honest and democratic in Russia, all those who are thirsting for the liberation of their country from bondage. To become convinced of that, it is sufficient to note the course of the elections in the workers' curia, to note the sympathies of the St. Petersburg workers that were so clearly expressed in the mandate of the voters' delegates, and to note their revolutionary struggle for elections.

All this gives us grounds for asserting that the elections in St. Petersburg have fully confirmed the correctness of the slogans of revolutionary Social-Democracy.

Revolutionary Social-Democracy is virile and strong—such is the first deduction to be drawn.

The Liquidators are politically bankrupt—such is the second deduction.

Sotsial-Demokrat, No. 30,
January 12 (25), 1913

Reprinted from the newspaper

Signed: *K. Stalin*

ON THE ROAD TO NATIONALISM

(A Letter From the Caucasus)

Among the decisions which will perpetuate the glory of the Liquidators' conference, the decision on "cultural-national autonomy" occupies by no means the last place.

Here it is:

"Having heard the communication of the Caucasian delegation to the effect that at the last conference of the Caucasian organizations of the R.S.D.L.P., as well as in the literary organs of these organizations, the Caucasian comrades expressed the opinion that it is necessary to demand national-cultural autonomy, this conference, while expressing no opinion on the merits of this demand, declares that such an interpretation of the clause of the Party programme which recognizes the right of every nationality to self-determination does not contradict the precise meaning of the programme, and it expresses the wish that the national question be put on the agenda of the next congress of the R.S.D.L.P."

This resolution is important not only because it expresses the Liquidators' opportunist shuffling in face of the rising nationalist tide. It is also important because every phrase in it is a gem.

For example, what a pearl is the statement that the conference, "while expressing no opinion on the merits of this demand, " nevertheless "declares" and decides? Things are "decided" in this way only in comic opera!

Or the phrase stating that "such an interpretation of the clause of the Party programme which recognizes the right of every nationality to self-determination does not contradict the precise meaning of the programme." Just think! The clause in the programme referred to (Clause 9), speaks of freedom of nationalities, of the *right* of nationalities to develop freely, of the Party's duty to combat all violence against them. Speaking generally, the *right* of nationalities, within the meaning of that clause, must not be restricted, it may be extended to autonomy and federation, as well as to secession. But does this mean that it is a matter of indifference to the Party, that it is all the same to it, how a given nationality decides its destiny, whether in favour of centralism or of secession? Does it mean that on the basis of the abstract right of nationalities alone it is possible "while expressing no opinion on the merits of this demand, " to recommend, even indirectly, autonomy for some, federation for others, and secession for still others? A nationality decides its destiny, but does that mean that the Party must not influence the will of a nationality towards a decision most in accordance with the interests of the proletariat? The Party stands for freedom of conscience, for the right of people to practise any religion they please. Does this mean that the Party will stand for Catholicism in Poland, for the Orthodox Church in Georgia and for the Gregorian Church in Armenia? That it will not combat these forms of world outlook? ... And is it not self-evident that Clause 9 of the Party programme and cultural-national autonomy are on two entirely different planes that are as capable of "contradicting" each other as, say, Cheops' pyramid and the notorious Liquidators' conference?

But it is by means of such equilibristics that the conference "decides" the question.

The most important thing in the above-mentioned decision of the Liquidators is the ideological collapse of the Caucasian Liquidators, who betrayed the old banner of internationalism in the Caucasus and succeeded in obtaining this decision from the conference.

The Caucasian Liquidators' turn towards nationalism is no accident. They began to liquidate the traditions of the Party long ago. The deletion of the "social section" from the minimum programme, the repudiation of the "hegemony of the proletariat" (see *Diskussionny Listok*, No. 2[127]), the declaration that the illegal Party is an auxiliary organization of the legal organizations (see *Dnevnik*, No. 9[128])—all these are commonly known facts. Now the turn has come for the national question.

From their very first appearance (in the beginning of the 'nineties) the organizations in the Caucasus bore a strictly international character. A united organization of Georgian, Russian, Armenian and Moslem workers fighting solidly against the foe—such was the picture of Party life. . . . In 1903, at the first, inaugural congress of the Caucasian (strictly speaking Transcaucasian) Social-Democratic organizations, which laid the foundation for the Caucasian Union, the international principle of building up the organization was re-affirmed as the only correct principle. From that time onwards Caucasian Social-Democracy grew in the struggle against nationalism. The Georgian Social-Democrats fought "their" nationalists, the National-Democrats and Federalists; the Armenian Social-Democrats fought "their" Dashnaktsakans; the Moslem Social-Democrats fought the Pan-Islamists.[129] And in this fight Caucasian Social-Democracy expanded and strengthened its organizations irrespective of groups. . . . The question of cultural-national autonomy came up for the first time in 1906, at the Caucasian Regional Conference. It was introduced by a small group from Kutais, which demanded a decision in its favour. The question "was a resounding failure," as it was said at the time, because, among other things, it was opposed with equal vigour by both groups, represented respectively by Kostrov and the writer of these lines. It was decided that what was called "regional self-government for the Caucasus" was the best solution for the national question, a solution most in accordance with the interests of the Caucasian proletariat which was united in the struggle. Yes, that is how it was in 1906. And this decision was re-affirmed at subsequent conferences; it was advocated and popularized in the Menshevik and Bolshevik press in the Caucasus, legal and illegal. . . .

But 1912 arrived, and it "turned out" that "we" need cultural-national autonomy, of course (of course!) in the interests of the proletariat! What had happened? What had changed? Perhaps the Caucasian proletariat had become less socialistic? But in that case, to erect national organizational and "cultural" barriers between the workers would have been the most unwise thing to do! Perhaps it had become more socialistic? In that case, what can we call these "Socialists," save the mark, who artificially erect and reinforce barriers which are breaking down, and which nobody needs? . . . What had happened then? What had happened was that peasant Kutais had dragged in its wake the "Social-Democratic Octobrists" of Tiflis. Henceforth, the affairs of the Caucasian Liquidators will be decided by the Kutais peasants who have been intimidated by militant nationalism. The Caucasian Liquidators were unable to stand up against the nationalist tide, they dropped the tried banner of internationalism and . . . they began to drift "on the waves" of nationalism, throwing their last thing of value overboard: "a useless thing, who wants it?". . .

But he who takes the first step must take the next: there is logic in everything. The Georgian, Armenian, Moslem (and Russian?) national-cultural autonomy advocated by the Caucasian Liquidators will be followed by Georgian, Armenian, Moslem and other Liquidationist parties. Instead of a common organization we shall have separate national organizations, Georgian, Armenian and other "Bunds," so to speak.

Is this what Messrs. the Caucasian Liquidators are driving at with their "solution" of the national question?

Well, we can wish them more courage. Do what you want to do!

At all events, we can assure them that the other section of the Caucasian organizations, the Georgian, Russian, Armenian and Moslem pro-Party Social-Democrats, will resolutely break away from Messrs. the National-Liquidators, from these traitors to the glorious banner of internationalism in the Caucasus.

Sotsial-Demokrat, No. 30, January 12 (25), 1913
Signed: *K. St.*

Reprinted from the newspaper

MARXISM
AND THE NATIONAL QUESTION[130]

The period of counter-revolution in Russia brought
not only "thunder and lightning" in its train, but also
disillusionment in the movement and lack of faith in
common forces. As long as people believed in "a bright
future," they fought side by side irrespective of nationality—common questions first and foremost! But when
doubt crept into people's hearts, they began to depart,
each to his own national tent—let every man count only
upon himself! The "national question" first and foremost!

At the same time a profound upheaval was taking
place in the economic life of the country. The year 1905
had not been in vain: one more blow had been struck
at the survivals of serfdom in the countryside. The
series of good harvests which succeeded the famine years,
and the industrial boom which followed, furthered the
progress of capitalism. Class differentiation in the countryside, the growth of the towns, the development of
trade and means of communication all took a big stride
forward. This applied particularly to the border regions.
And it could not but hasten the process of economic

consolidation of the nationalities of Russia. They were bound to be stirred into movement. . . .

The "constitutional regime" established at that time also acted in the same direction of awakening the nationalities. The spread of newspapers and of literature generally, a certain freedom of the press and cultural institutions, an increase in the number of national theatres, and so forth, all unquestionably helped to strengthen "national sentiments." The Duma, with its election campaign and political groups, gave fresh opportunities for greater activity of the nations and provided a new and wide arena for their mobilization.

And the mounting wave of militant nationalism above and the series of repressive measures taken by the "powers that be" in vengeance on the border regions for their "love of freedom," evoked an answering wave of nationalism below, which at times took the form of crude chauvinism. The spread of Zionism[131] among the Jews, the increase of chauvinism in Poland, Pan-Islamism among the Tatars, the spread of nationalism among the Armenians, Georgians and Ukrainians, the general swing of the philistine towards anti-Semitism—all these are generally known facts.

The wave of nationalism swept onwards with increasing force, threatening to engulf the mass of the workers. And the more the movement for emancipation declined, the more plentifully nationalism pushed forth its blossoms.

At this difficult time Social-Democracy had a high mission—to resist nationalism and to protect the masses from the general "epidemic." For Social-Democracy, and Social-Democracy alone, could do this, by

countering nationalism with the tried weapon of internationalism, with the unity and indivisibility of the class
struggle. And the more powerfully the wave of nationalism advanced, the louder had to be the call of Social-Democracy for fraternity and unity among the
proletarians of all the nationalities of Russia. And
in this connection particular firmness was demanded of
the Social-Democrats of the border regions, who came
into direct contact with the nationalist movement.

But not all Social-Democrats proved equal to
the task—and this applies particularly to the Social-
Democrats of the border regions. The Bund, which had
previously laid stress on the common tasks, now began
to give prominence to its own specific, purely nationalist
aims: it went to the length of declaring "observance
of the Sabbath" and "recognition of Yiddish" a fighting issue in its election campaign.* The Bund was followed by the Caucasus; one section of the Caucasian
Social-Democrats, which, like the rest of the Caucasian
Social-Democrats, had formerly rejected "cultural-national
autonomy," are now making it an immediate demand.**
This is without mentioning the conference of the Liquidators, which in a diplomatic way gave its sanction to
nationalist vacillations.***

But from this it follows that the views of Russian
Social-Democracy on the national question are not yet
clear to all Social-Democrats.

It is evident that a serious and comprehensive dis-

---

* See "Report of the Ninth Conference of the Bund."
** See "Announcement of the August Conference."
*** *Ibid.*

cussion of the national question is required. Consistent Social-Democrats must work solidly and indefatigably against the fog of nationalism, no matter from what quarter it proceeds.

I

THE NATION

What is a nation?

A nation is primarily a community, a definite community of people.

This community is not racial, nor is it tribal. The modern Italian nation was formed from Romans, Teutons, Etruscans, Greeks, Arabs, and so forth. The French nation was formed from Gauls, Romans, Britons, Teutons, and so on. The same must be said of the British, the Germans and others, who were formed into nations from people of diverse races and tribes.

Thus, a nation is not a racial or tribal, but a historically constituted community of people.

On the other hand, it is unquestionable that the great empires of Cyrus and Alexander could not be called nations, although they came to be constituted historically and were formed out of different tribes and races. They were not nations, but casual and loosely-connected conglomerations of groups, which fell apart or joined together according to the victories or defeats of this or that conqueror.

Thus, a nation is not a casual or ephemeral conglomeration, but a stable community of people.

But not every stable community constitutes a nation. Austria and Russia are also stable communities, but nobody calls them nations. What distinguishes a national community from a state community? The fact, among others, that a national community is inconceivable without a common language, while a state need not have a common language. The Czech nation in Austria and the Polish in Russia would be impossible if each did not have a common language, whereas the integrity of Russia and Austria is not affected by the fact that there are a number of different languages within their borders. We are referring, of course, to the spoken languages of the people and not to the official governmental languages.

Thus, *a common language* is one of the characteristic features of a nation.

This, of course, does not mean that different nations always and everywhere speak different languages, or that all who speak one language necessarily constitute one nation. A *common* language for every nation, but not necessarily different languages for different nations! There is no nation which at one and the same time speaks several languages, but this does not mean that there cannot be two nations speaking the same language! Englishmen and Americans speak one language, but they do not constitute one nation. The same is true of the Norwegians and the Danes, the English and the Irish.

But why, for instance, do the English and the Americans not constitute one nation in spite of their common language?

Firstly, because they do not live together, but inhabit different territories. A nation is formed only as a result of lengthy and systematic intercourse, as a result of people living together generation after generation.

But people cannot live together for lengthy periods unless they have a common territory. Englishmen and Americans originally inhabited the same territory, England, and constituted one nation. Later, one section of the English emigrated from England to a new territory, America, and there, in the new territory, in the course of time, came to form the new American nation. Difference of territory led to the formation of different nations.

Thus, *a common territory* is one of the characteristic features of a nation.

But this is not all. Common territory does not by itself create a nation. This requires, in addition, an internal economic bond to weld the various parts of the nation into a single whole. There is no such bond between England and America, and so they constitute two different nations. But the Americans themselves would not deserve to be called a nation were not the different parts of America bound together into an economic whole, as a result of division of labour between them, the development of means of communication, and so forth.

Take the Georgians, for instance. The Georgians before the Reform inhabited a common territory and spoke one language. Nevertheless, they did not, strictly speaking, constitute one nation, for, being split up into a number of disconnected principalities, they could not share a common economic life; for centuries they waged war against each other and pillaged each other, each inciting the Persians and Turks against the other. The ephemeral and casual union of the principalities which some successful king sometimes managed to bring about embraced at best a superficial administrative sphere, and rapidly disintegrated owing to the caprices of the princes and the indifference of the peasants. Nor could it be otherwise in economically disunited Georgia. . . . Georgia came on the scene as a nation only in the latter half of the nineteenth century, when the fall of serfdom and the growth of the economic life of the country, the development of means of communication and the rise of capitalism, introduced division of labour between the various districts of Georgia, completely shattered the economic isolation of the principalities and bound them together into a single whole.

The same must be said of the other nations which have passed through the stage of feudalism and have developed capitalism.

Thus, *a common economic life, economic cohesion*, is one of the characteristic features of a nation.

But even this is not all. Apart from the foregoing, one must take into consideration the specific spiritual complexion of the people constituting a nation. Nations differ not only in their conditions of life, but also in spiritual complexion, which manifests itself in peculiarities of national culture. If England, America and Ireland, which speak one language, nevertheless constitute three distinct nations, it is in no small measure due to the peculiar psychological make-up which they developed from generation to generation as a result of dissimilar conditions of existence.

Of course, by itself, psychological make-up or, as it is otherwise called, "national character," is something intangible for the observer, but in so far as it manifests itself in a distinctive culture common to the nation it is something tangible and cannot be ignored.

Needless to say, "national character" is not a thing that is fixed once and for all, but is modified by changes in the conditions of life; but since it exists at every given moment, it leaves its impress on the physiognomy of the nation.

Thus, *a common psychological make-up*, which manifests itself in a common culture, is one of the characteristic features of a nation.

We have now exhausted the characteristic features of a nation.

A nation is a historically constituted, stable community of people, formed on the basis of a common language, territory, economic life, and psychological make-up manifested in a common culture.

It goes without saying that a nation, like every historical phenomenon, is subject to the law of change, has its history, its beginning and end.

It must be emphasized that none of the above characteristics taken separately is sufficient to define a nation. More than that, it is sufficient for a single one of these characteristics to be lacking and the nation ceases to be a nation.

It is possible to conceive of people possessing a common "national character" who, nevertheless, cannot be said to constitute a single nation if they are economically disunited, inhabit different territories, speak different languages, and so forth. Such, for instance, are the Russian, Galician, American, Georgian and Caucasian Highland *Jews*, who, in our opinion, do not constitute a single nation.

It is possible to conceive of people with a common territory and economic life who nevertheless would not constitute a single nation because they have no common language and no common "national character." Such, for instance, are the Germans and Letts in the Baltic region.

Finally, the Norwegians and the Danes speak one language, but they do not constitute a single nation owing to the absence of the other characteristics.

It is only when all these characteristics are present together that we have a nation.

It might appear that "national character" is not one of the characteristics but the *sole* essential characteristic of a nation, and that all the other characteristics are, properly speaking, only *conditions* for the development of a nation, rather than its characteristics. Such, for instance, is the view held by R. Springer, and more particularly by O. Bauer, who are Social-Democratic theoreticians on the national question well known in Austria.

Let us examine their theory of the nation.

According to Springer, "a nation is a union of similarly thinking and similarly speaking persons." It is "a cultural community of modern people *no longer tied to the 'soil'* "* (our italics).

Thus, a "union" of similarly thinking and similarly speaking people, no matter how disconnected they may be, no matter where they live, is a nation.

Bauer goes even further.

"What is a nation?" he asks. "Is it a common language which makes people a nation? But the English and the Irish . . . speak

---

* See R. Springer, *The National Problem*, Obshchestvennaya Polza Publishing House, 1909, p. 43.

the same language without, however, being one people; the Jews have no common language and yet are a nation."*

What, then, is a nation?

"A nation is a relative community of character."**

But what is character, in this case national character?

National character is "the sum total of characteristics which distinguish the people of one nationality from the people of another nationality—the complex of physical and spiritual characteristics which distinguish one nation from another."***

Bauer knows, of course, that national character does not drop from the skies, and he therefore adds:

"The character of people is determined by nothing so much as by their destiny. . . . A nation is nothing but a community with a common destiny" which, in turn, is determined "by the conditions under which people produce their means of subsistence and distribute the products of their labour."****

We thus arrive at the most "complete," as Bauer calls it, definition of a nation:

"*A nation is an aggregate of people bound into a community of character by a common destiny.*"*****

We thus have common national character based on a common destiny, but not necessarily connected with a common territory, language or economic life.

But what in that case remains of the nation? What common nationality can there be among people who are

---

* See O. Bauer, *The National Question and Social-Democracy*, Serp Publishing House, 1909, pp. 1-2.

** *Ibid.*, p. 6.

*** *Ibid.*, p. 2.

**** *Ibid.*, pp. 24-25.

***** *Ibid.*, p. 139.

economically disconnected, inhabit different territories and from generation to generation speak different languages?

Bauer speaks of the Jews as a nation, although they "have no common language";* but what "common destiny" and national cohesion is there, for instance, between the Georgian, Daghestanian, Russian and American Jews, who are completely separated from one another, inhabit different territories and speak different languages?

The above-mentioned Jews undoubtedly lead their economic and political life in common with the Georgians, Daghestanians, Russians and Americans respectively, and they live in the same cultural atmosphere as these; this is bound to leave a definite impress on their national character; if there is anything common to them left, it is their religion, their common origin and certain relics of the national character. All this is beyond question. But how can it be seriously maintained that petrified religious rites and fading psychological relics affect the "destiny" of these Jews more powerfully than the living social, economic and cultural environment that surrounds them? And it is only on this assumption that it is possible to speak of the Jews as a single nation at all.

What, then, distinguishes Bauer's nation from the mystical and self-sufficient "national spirit" of the spiritualists?

Bauer sets up an impassable barrier between the "distinctive feature" of nations (national character) and the "conditions" of their life, divorcing the one from the other. But what is national character if not a reflection of the conditions of life, a coagulation of impressions derived

---

* *Ibid.*, p. 2.

from environment? How can one limit the matter to national character alone, isolating and divorcing it from the soil that gave rise to it?

Further, what indeed distinguished the English nation from the American nation at the end of the eighteenth and the beginning of the nineteenth centuries, when America was still known as New England? Not national character, of course; for the Americans had originated from England and had brought with them to America not only the English language, but also the English national character, which, of course, they could not lose so soon; although, under the influence of the new conditions, they would naturally be developing their own specific character. Yet, despite their more or less common character, they at that time already constituted a nation distinct from England! Obviously, New England as a nation differed then from England as a nation not by its specific national character, or not so much by its national character, as by its environment and conditions of life, which were distinct from those of England.

It is therefore clear that there is in fact no *single* distinguishing characteristic of a nation. There is only a sum total of characteristics, of which, when nations are compared, sometimes one characteristic (national character), sometimes another (language), or sometimes a third (territory, economic conditions), stands out in sharper relief. A nation constitutes the combination of all these characteristics taken together.

Bauer's point of view, which identifies a nation with its national character, divorces the nation from its soil and converts it into an invisible, self-contained force. The result is not a living and active nation, but something mystical, intangible and supernatural. For, I repeat, what sort of nation, for instance, is a Jewish nation which consists of Georgian, Daghestanian, Russian, American and other Jews, the members of which do not understand each other (since they speak different languages), inhabit different parts of the globe, will never see each other, and will never act together, whether in time of peace or in time of war?!

No, it is not for such paper "nations" that Social-Democracy draws up its national programme. It can reckon only with real nations, which act and move, and therefore insist on being reckoned with.

Bauer is obviously confusing *nation*, which is a historical category, with *tribe*, which is an ethnographical category.

However, Bauer himself apparently feels the weakness of his position. While in the beginning of his book he definitely declares the Jews to be a nation,* he corrects himself at the end of the book and states that "in general capitalist society makes it impossible for them (the Jews) to continue as a nation,"** by causing them to assimilate with other nations. The reason, it appears, is that "the Jews have no closed territory of settlement,"*** whereas the Czechs, for instance, have such a territory and, according to Bauer, will survive as a nation. In short, the reason lies in the absence of a territory.

By arguing thus, Bauer wanted to prove that the Jewish workers cannot demand national autonomy,****

---

* See p. 2 of his book.
** *Ibid.*, p. 389.
*** *Ibid.*, p. 388.
**** *Ibid.*, p. 396.

but he thereby inadvertently refuted his own theory, which denies that a common territory is one of the characteristics of a nation.

But Bauer goes further. In the beginning of his book he definitely declares that "the Jews have no *common* language, and yet are a nation."* But hardly has he reached p. 130 than he effects a change of front and just as definitely declares that *"unquestionably, no nation is possible without a common language"*** (our italics).

Bauer wanted to prove that "language is the most important instrument of human intercourse,"*** but at the same time he inadvertently proved something he did not mean to prove, namely, the unsoundness of his own theory of nations, which denies the significance of a common language.

Thus this theory, stitched together by idealistic threads, refutes itself.

II

THE NATIONAL MOVEMENT

A nation is not merely a historical category but a historical category belonging to a definite epoch, the epoch of rising capitalism. The process of elimination of feudalism and development of capitalism is at the same time a process of the constitution of people into nations. Such, for instance, was the case in Western Europe. The

---

* *Ibid.*, p. 2.
** *Ibid.*, p. 130.
*** *Ibid.*

British, French, Germans, Italians and others were formed into nations at the time of the victorious advance of capitalism and its triumph over feudal disunity.

But the formation of nations in those instances at the same time signified their conversion into independent national states. The British, French and other nations are at the same time British, etc., states. Ireland, which did not participate in this process, does not alter the general picture.

Matters proceeded somewhat differently in Eastern Europe. Whereas in the West nations developed into states, in the East multi-national states were formed, states consisting of several nationalities. Such are Austria-Hungary and Russia. In Austria, the Germans proved to be politically the most developed, and they took it upon themselves to unite the Austrian nationalities into a state. In Hungary, the most adapted for state organization were the Magyars—the core of the Hungarian nationalities—and it was they who united Hungary. In Russia, the uniting of the nationalities was undertaken by the Great Russians, who were headed by a historically formed, powerful and well-organized aristocratic military bureaucracy.

That was how matters proceeded in the East.

This special method of formation of states could take place only where feudalism had not yet been eliminated, where capitalism was feebly developed, where the nationalities which had been forced into the background had not yet been able to consolidate themselves economically into integral nations.

But capitalism also began to develop in the Eastern states. Trade and means of communication were developing. Large towns were springing up. The nations were becoming economically consolidated. Capitalism, erupting into the tranquil life of the nationalities which had been pushed into the background, was arousing them and stirring them into action. The development of the press and the theatre, the activity of the Reichsrat (Austria) and of the Duma (Russia) were helping to strengthen "national sentiments." The intelligentsia that had arisen was being imbued with "the national idea" and was acting in the same direction. . . .

But the nations which had been pushed into the background and had now awakened to independent life, could no longer form themselves into independent national states; they encountered on their path the very powerful resistance of the ruling strata of the dominant nations, which had long ago assumed the control of the state. They were too late! . . .

In this way the Czechs, Poles, etc., formed themselves into nations in Austria; the Croats, etc., in Hungary; the Letts, Lithuanians, Ukrainians, Georgians, Armenians, etc., in Russia. What had been an exception in Western Europe (Ireland) became the rule in the East.

In the West, Ireland responded to its exceptional position by a national movement. In the East, the awakened nations were bound to respond in the same fashion.

Thus arose the circumstances which impelled the young nations of Eastern Europe on to the path of struggle.

The struggle began and flared up, to be sure, not between nations as a whole, but between the ruling classes of the dominant nations and of those that had been pushed into the background. The struggle is usually

conducted by the urban petty bourgeoisie of the oppressed nation against the big bourgeoisie of the dominant nation (Czechs and Germans), or by the rural
bourgeoisie of the oppressed nation against the landlords of the dominant nation (Ukrainians in Poland),
or by the whole "national" bourgeoisie of the oppressed
nations against the ruling nobility of the dominant nation (Poland, Lithuania and the Ukraine in Russia).

The bourgeoisie plays the leading role.

The chief problem for the young bourgeoisie is the
problem of the market. Its aim is to sell its goods and to
emerge victorious from competition with the bourgeoisie
of a different nationality. Hence its desire to secure its
"own," its "home" market. The market is the first school
in which the bourgeoisie learns its nationalism.

But matters are usually not confined to the market.
The semi-feudal, semi-bourgeois bureaucracy of the dominant nation intervenes in the struggle with its own
methods of "arresting and preventing." The bourgeoisie—
whether big or small—of the dominant nation is able
to deal more "swiftly" and "decisively" with its competitor. "Forces" are united and a series of restrictive
measures is put into operation against the "alien" bourgeoisie, measures passing into acts of repression. The
struggle spreads from the economic sphere to the political
sphere. Restriction of freedom of movement, repression
of language, restriction of franchise, closing of schools,
religious restrictions, and so on, are piled upon the head
of the "competitor." Of course, such measures are designed not only in the interest of the bourgeois classes of
the dominant nation, but also in furtherance of the specifically caste aims, so to speak, of the ruling bureaucracy.

But from the point of view of the results achieved this is quite immaterial; the bourgeois classes and the bureaucracy in this matter go hand in hand—whether it be in Austria-Hungary or in Russia.

The bourgeoisie of the oppressed nation, repressed on every hand, is naturally stirred into movement. It appeals to its "native folk" and begins to shout about the "fatherland," claiming that its own cause is the cause of the nation as a whole. It recruits itself an army from among its "countrymen" in the interests of . . . the "fatherland." Nor do the "folk" always remain unresponsive to its appeals; they rally around its banner: the repression from above affects them too and provokes their discontent.

Thus the national movement begins.

The strength of the national movement is determined by the degree to which the wide strata of the nation, the proletariat and peasantry, participate in it.

Whether the proletariat rallies to the banner of bourgeois nationalism depends on the degree of development of class antagonisms, on the class consciousness and degree of organization of the proletariat. The class-conscious proletariat has its own tried banner, and has no need to rally to the banner of the bourgeoisie.

As far as the peasants are concerned, their participation in the national movement depends primarily on the character of the repressions. If the repressions affect the "land," as was the case in Ireland, then the mass of the peasants immediately rally to the banner of the national movement.

On the other hand, if, for example, there is no serious *anti-Russian* nationalism in Georgia, it is primarily because there are neither Russian landlords nor a Russian big bourgeoisie there to supply the fuel for such nationalism among the masses. In Georgia there is *anti-Armenian* nationalism; but this is because there is still an Armenian big bourgeoisie there which, by getting the better of the small and still unconsolidated Georgian bourgeoisie, drives the latter to anti-Armenian nationalism.

Depending on these factors, the national movement either assumes a mass character and steadily grows (as in Ireland and Galicia), or is converted into a series of petty collisions, degenerating into squabbles and "fights" over signboards (as in some of the small towns of Bohemia).

The content of the national movement, of course, cannot everywhere be the same: it is wholly determined by the diverse demands made by the movement. In Ireland the movement bears an agrarian character; in Bohemia it bears a "language" character; in one place the demand is for civil equality and religious freedom, in another for the nation's "own" officials, or its own Diet. The diversity of demands not infrequently reveals the diverse features which characterize a nation in general (language, territory, etc.). It is worthy of note that we never meet with a demand based on Bauer's all-embracing "national character." And this is natural: "national character" *in itself* is something intangible, and, as was correctly remarked by J. Strasser, "a politician can't do anything with it."*

Such, in general, are the forms and character of the national movement.

* See his *Der Arbeiter und die Nation*, 1912, p. 33.

From what has been said it will be clear that the national struggle under the conditions of *rising* capitalism is a struggle of the bourgeois classes among themselves. Sometimes the bourgeoisie succeeds in drawing the proletariat into the national movement, and then the national struggle *externally* assumes a "nation-wide" character. But this is so only externally. *In its essence* it is always a bourgeois struggle, one that is to the advantage and profit mainly of the bourgeoisie.

But it does not by any means follow that the proletariat should not put up a fight against the policy of national oppression.

Restriction of freedom of movement, disfranchisement, repression of language, closing of schools, and other forms of persecution affect the workers no less, if not more, than the bourgeoisie. Such a state of affairs can only serve to retard the free development of the intellectual forces of the proletariat of subject nations. One cannot speak seriously of a full development of the intellectual faculties of the Tatar or Jewish worker if he is not allowed to use his native language at meetings and lectures, and if his schools are closed down.

But the policy of nationalist persecution is dangerous to the cause of the proletariat also on another account. It diverts the attention of large strata from social questions, questions of the class struggle, to national questions, questions "common" to the proletariat and the bourgeoisie. And this creates a favourable soil for lying propaganda about "harmony of interests," for glossing over the class interests of the proletariat and for the intellectual enslavement of the workers.

This creates a serious obstacle to the cause of uniting
the workers of all nationalities. If a considerable proportion of the Polish workers are still in intellectual bondage
to the bourgeois nationalists, if they still stand aloof
from the international labour movement, it is chiefly
because the age-old anti-Polish policy of the "powers
that be" creates the soil for this bondage and hinders the
emancipation of the workers from it.

But the policy of persecution does not stop there.
It not infrequently passes from a "system" of *oppression*
to a "system" of *inciting* nations against each other, to a
"system" of massacres and pogroms. Of course, the latter
system is not everywhere and always possible, but where
it is possible—in the absence of elementary civil rights—
it frequently assumes horrifying proportions and threat-
ens to drown the cause of unity of the workers in blood
and tears. The Caucasus and south Russia furnish numerous examples. "Divide and rule"—such is the purpose
of the policy of incitement. And where such a policy
succeeds, it is a tremendous evil for the proletariat and a
serious obstacle to the cause of uniting the workers of
all the nationalities in the state.

But the workers are interested in the complete
amalgamation of all their fellow-workers into a single
international army, in their speedy and final emancipation from intellectual bondage to the bourgeoisie, and
in the full and free development of the intellectual
forces of their brothers, whatever nation they may
belong to.

The workers therefore combat and will continue to
combat the policy of national oppression in all its forms,
from the most subtle to the most crude, as well as the

policy of inciting nations against each other in all its forms.

Social-Democracy in all countries therefore proclaims the right of nations to self-determination.

The right of self-determination means that only the nation itself has the right to determine its destiny, that no one has the right *forcibly* to interfere in the life of the nation, to *destroy* its schools and other institutions, to *violate* its habits and customs, to *repress* its language, or *curtail* its rights.

This, of course, does not mean that Social-Democracy will support every custom and institution of a nation. While combating the coercion of any nation, it will uphold only the right of the *nation* itself to determine its own destiny, at the same time agitating against harmful customs and institutions of that nation in order to enable the toiling strata of the nation to emancipate themselves from them.

The right of self-determination means that a nation may arrange its life in the way it wishes. It has the right to arrange its life on the basis of autonomy. It has the right to enter into federal relations with other nations. It has the right to complete secession. Nations are sovereign, and all nations have equal rights.

This, of course, does not mean that Social-Democracy will support every demand of a nation. A nation has the right even to return to the old order of things; but this does not mean that Social-Democracy will subscribe to such a decision if taken by some institution of a particular nation. The obligations of Social-Democracy, which defends the interests of the proletariat, and the rights of a nation, which consists of various classes, are two different things.

In fighting for the right of nations to self-determination, the aim of Social-Democracy is to put an end to the policy of national oppression, to render it impossible, and thereby to remove the grounds of strife between nations, to take the edge off that strife and reduce it to a minimum.

This is what essentially distinguishes the policy of the class-conscious proletariat from the policy of the bourgeoisie, which attempts to aggravate and fan the national struggle and to prolong and sharpen the national movement.

And that is why the class-conscious proletariat cannot rally under the "national" flag of the bourgeoisie.

That is why the so-called "evolutionary national" policy advocated by Bauer cannot become the policy of the proletariat. Bauer's attempt to identify his "evolutionary national" policy with the policy of the "modern working class"* is an attempt to adapt the class struggle of the workers to the struggle of the nations.

The fate of a national movement, which is essentially a bourgeois movement, is naturally bound up with the fate of the bourgeoisie. The final disappearance of a national movement is possible only with the downfall of the bourgeoisie. Only under the reign of socialism can peace be fully established. But even within the framework of capitalism it is possible to reduce the national struggle to a minimum, to undermine it at the root, to render it as

---

* See Bauer's book, p. 166.

harmless as possible to the proletariat. This is borne out, for example, by Switzerland and America. It requires that the country should be democratized and the nations be given the opportunity of free development.

III
PRESENTATION OF THE QUESTION

A nation has the right freely to determine its own destiny. It has the right to arrange its life as it sees fit, without, of course, trampling on the rights of other nations. That is beyond dispute.

But *how* exactly should it arrange its own life, *what forms* should its future constitution take, if the interests of the majority of the nation and, above all, of the proletariat are to be borne in mind?

A nation has the right to arrange its life on autonomous lines. It even has the right to secede. But this does not mean that it should do so under all circumstances, that autonomy, or separation, will everywhere and always be advantageous for a nation, i.e., for its majority, i.e., for the toiling strata. The Transcaucasian Tatars as a nation may assemble, let us say, in their Diet and, succumbing to the influence of their beys and mullahs, decide to restore the old order of things and to secede from the state. According to the meaning of the clause on self-determination they are fully entitled to do so. But will this be in the interest of the toiling strata of the Tatar nation? Can Social-Democracy look on indifferently when the beys and mullahs assume the leadership of the masses in the solution of the national question?

Should not Social-Democracy interfere in the matter
and influence the will of the nation in a definite way?
Should it not come forward with a definite plan for the
solution of the question, a plan which would be most
advantageous for the Tatar masses?

But what solution would be most compatible with
the interests of the toiling masses? Autonomy, federation or separation?

All these are problems the solution of which will
depend on the concrete historical conditions in which
the given nation finds itself.

More than that; conditions, like everything else,
change, and a decision which is correct at one particular
time may prove to be entirely unsuitable at another.

In the middle of the nineteenth century Marx was
in favour of the secession of Russian Poland; and he was
right, for it was then a question of emancipating a higher
culture from a lower culture that was destroying it. And
the question at that time was not only a theoretical
one, an academic question, but a practical one, a question
of actual reality. . . .

At the end of the nineteenth century the Polish
Marxists were already declaring against the secession
of Poland; and they too were right, for during the fifty
years that had elapsed profound changes had taken place,
bringing Russia and Poland closer economically and
culturally. Moreover, during that period the question
of secession had been converted from a practical matter into a matter of academic dispute, which excited
nobody except perhaps intellectuals abroad.

This, of course, by no means precludes the possibility
that certain internal and external conditions may arise

in which the question of the secession of Poland may again come on the order of the day.

The solution of the national question is possible only in connection with the historical conditions taken in their development.

The economic, political and cultural conditions of a given nation constitute the only key to the question *how* a particular nation ought to arrange its life and *what forms* its future constitution ought to take. It is possible that a specific solution of the question will be required for each nation. If the dialectical approach to a question is required anywhere it is required here, in the national question.

In view of this we must declare our decided opposition to a certain very widespread, but very summary manner of "solving" the national question, which owes its inception to the Bund. We have in mind the easy method of referring to Austrian and South-Slav* Social-Democracy, which has supposedly already solved the national question and whose solution the Russian Social-Democrats should simply borrow. It is assumed that whatever, say, is right for Austria is also right for Russia. The most important and decisive factor is lost sight of here, namely, the concrete historical conditions in Russia as a whole and in the life of each of the nations inhabiting Russia in particular.

Listen, for example, to what the well-known Bundist, V. Kossovsky, says:

"When at the Fourth Congress of the Bund the principles of the question (i.e., the national question—*J. St.*) were discussed,

---

* South-Slav Social-Democracy operates in the Southern part of Austria.

the proposal made by one of the members of the congress to settle the question in the spirit of the resolution of the South-Slav Social-Democratic Party met with general approval."*

And the result was that "the congress unanimously adopted" . . . national autonomy.

And that was all! No analysis of the actual conditions in Russia, no investigation of the condition of the Jews in Russia. They first borrowed the solution of the South-Slav Social-Democratic Party, then they "approved" it, and finally they "unanimously adopted" it! This is the way the Bundists present and "solve" the national question in Russia. . . .

As a matter of fact, Austria and Russia represent entirely different conditions. This explains why the Social-Democrats in Austria, when they adopted their national programme at Brünn (1899)[132] in the spirit of the resolution of the South-Slav Social-Democratic Party (with certain insignificant amendments, it is true), approached the question in an entirely non-Russian way, so to speak, and, of course, solved it in a non-Russian way.

First, as to the presentation of the question. How is the question presented by the Austrian theoreticians of cultural-national autonomy, the interpreters of the Brünn national programme and the resolution of the South-Slav Social-Democratic Party, Springer and Bauer?

"Whether a multi-national state is possible," says Springer, "and whether, in particular, the Austrian nationalities are obliged to form a single political entity, is a question we shall not answer here but shall assume to be settled. For anyone who will not concede this possibility and necessity, our investigation will, of course, be purposeless. Our theme is as follows: inasmuch as these

* See V. Kossovsky, *Problems of Nationality*, 1907, pp. 16-17.

nations are *obliged* to live together, what *legal forms* will enable them *to live together in the best possible way*?" (Springer's italics).*

Thus, the starting point is the state integrity of Austria.

Bauer says the same thing:

"We therefore start from the assumption that the Austrian nations will remain in the same state union in which they exist at present and inquire how the nations within this union will arrange their relations among themselves and to the state."**

Here again the first thing is the integrity of Austria.

Can Russian Social-Democracy present the question *in this way*? No, it cannot. And it cannot because from the very outset it holds the view of the right of nations to self-determination, by virtue of which a nation has the right of secession.

Even the Bundist Goldblatt admitted at the Second Congress of Russian Social-Democracy that the latter could not abandon the standpoint of self-determination. Here is what Goldblatt said on that occasion:

"Nothing can be said against the right of self-determination. If any nation is striving for independence, we must not oppose it. If Poland does not wish to enter into 'lawful wedlock' with Russia, it is not for us to interfere with her."

All this is true. But it follows that the starting points of the Austrian and Russian Social-Democrats, far from being identical, are diametrically opposite. After this, can there be any question of borrowing the national programme of the Austrians?

---

* See Springer, *The National Problem*, p. 14.
** See Bauer, *The National Question and Social-Democracy*, p. 399.

Furthermore, the Austrians hope to achieve the "freedom of nationalities" by means of petty reforms, by slow steps. While they propose cultural-national autonomy as a practical measure, they do not count on any radical change, on a democratic movement for liberation, which they do not even contemplate. The Russian Marxists, on the other hand, associate the "freedom of nationalities" with a probable radical change, with a democratic movement for liberation, having no grounds for counting on reforms. And this essentially alters matters in regard to the probable fate of the nations of Russia.

"Of course," says Bauer, "there is little probability that national autonomy will be the result of a great decision, of a bold action. Austria will develop towards national autonomy step by step, by a slow process of development, in the course of a severe struggle, as a consequence of which legislation and administration will be in a state of chronic paralysis. The new constitution will not be created by a great legislative act, but by a multitude of separate enactments for individual provinces and individual communities."*

Springer says the same thing.

"I am very well aware," he writes, "that institutions of this kind (i.e., organs of national autonomy—*J. St.*) are not created in a single year or a single decade. The reorganization of the Prussian administration alone took considerable time. . . . It took the Prussians two decades finally to establish their basic administrative institutions. Let nobody think that I harbour any illusions as to the time required and the difficulties to be overcome in Austria."**

---

* See Bauer, *The National Question*, p. 422.
** See Springer, *The National Problem*, pp. 281-82.

All this is very definite. But can the Russian Marxists avoid associating the national question with "bold actions"? Can they count on partial reforms, on "a multitude of separate enactments" as a means for achieving the "freedom of nationalities"? But if they cannot and must not do so, is it not clear that the methods of struggle of the Austrians and the Russians and their prospects must be entirely different? How in such a state of affairs can they confine themselves to the one-sided, milk-and-water cultural-national autonomy of the Austrians? One or the other: either those who are in favour of borrowing do not count on "bold actions" in Russia, or they do count on such actions but "know not what they do."

Finally, the immediate tasks facing Russia and Austria are entirely different and consequently dictate different methods of solving the national question. In Austria parliamentarism prevails, and under present conditions no development in Austria is possible without parliament. But parliamentary life and legislation in Austria are frequently brought to a complete standstill by severe conflicts between the national parties. That explains the chronic political crisis from which Austria has for a long time been suffering. Hence, in Austria the national question is the very hub of political life; it is the vital question. It is therefore not surprising that the Austrian Social-Democratic politicians should first of all try in one way or another to find a solution for the national conflicts—of course on the basis of the existing parliamentary system, by parliamentary methods. . . .

Not so with Russia. In the first place, in Russia "there is no parliament, thank God."[133] In the second place—and this is the main point—the hub of the political life of Russia is not the national but the agrarian question. Consequently, the fate of the Russian problem, and, accordingly, the "liberation" of the nations too, is bound up in Russia with the solution of the agrarian question, i.e., with the destruction of the relics of feudalism, i.e., with the democratization of the country. That explains why in Russia the national question is not an independent and decisive one, but a part of the general and more important question of the emancipation of the country.

"The barrenness of the Austrian parliament," writes Springer, "is due precisely to the fact that every reform gives rise to antagonisms within the national parties which may affect their unity. The leaders of the parties, therefore, avoid everything that smacks of reform. Progress in Austria is generally conceivable only if the nations are granted indefeasible legal rights which will relieve them of the necessity of constantly maintaining national militant groups in parliament and will enable them to turn their attention to the solution of economic and social problems."*

Bauer says the same thing.

"National peace is indispensable first of all for the state. The state cannot permit legislation to be brought to a standstill by the very stupid question of language or by every quarrel between excited people on a linguistic frontier, or over every new school."**

All this is clear. But it is no less clear that the national question in Russia is on an entirely different plane. It is not the national, but the agrarian question that decides the fate of progress in Russia. The national question is a subordinate one.

---

* See Springer, *The National Problem*, p. 36.
** See Bauer, *The National Question*, p. 401.

And so we have different presentations of the question, different prospects and methods of struggle, different immediate tasks. Is it not clear that, such being the state of affairs, only pedants who "solve" the national question without reference to space and time can think of adopting examples from Austria and of borrowing a programme?

To repeat: the concrete historical conditions as the starting point, and the dialectical presentation of the question as the only correct way of presenting it—such is the key to solving the national question.

IV

CULTURAL-NATIONAL AUTONOMY

We spoke above of the formal aspect of the Austrian national programme and of the methodological grounds which make it impossible for the Russian Marxists simply to adopt the example of Austrian Social-Democracy and make the latter's programme their own.

Let us now examine the essence of the programme itself.

What then is the national programme of the Austrian Social-Democrats?

It is expressed in two words: cultural-national autonomy.

This means, firstly, that autonomy would be granted, let us say, not to Bohemia or Poland, which are inhabited mainly by Czechs and Poles, but to Czechs and Poles generally, irrespective of territory, no matter what part of Austria they inhabit.

That is why this autonomy is called *national* and not territorial.

It means, secondly, that the Czechs, Poles, Germans, and so on, scattered over the various parts of Austria, taken personally, as individuals, are to be organized into integral nations, and are as such to form part of the Austrian state. In this way Austria would represent not a union of autonomous regions, but a union of autonomous nationalities, constituted irrespective of territory.

It means, thirdly, that the national institutions which are to be created for this purpose for the Poles, Czechs, and so forth, are to have jurisdiction only over "cultural," not "political" questions. Specifically political questions would be reserved for the Austrian parliament (the Reichsrat).

That is why this autonomy is also called *cultural*, cultural-national autonomy.

And here is the text of the programme adopted by the Austrian Social-Democratic Party at the Brünn Congress in 1899.*

Having referred to the fact that "national dissension in Austria is hindering political progress," that "the final solution of the national question . . . is primarily a cultural necessity," and that "the solution is possible only in a genuinely democratic society, constructed on the basis of universal, direct and equal suffrage," the programme goes on to say:

_____

* The representatives of the South-Slav Social-Democratic Party also voted for it. See *Discussion of the National Question at the Brünn Congress*, 1906, p. 72.

"*The preservation and development of the national peculiarities** of the peoples of Austria is possible only on the basis of equal rights and by avoiding all oppression. Hence, all bureaucratic state centralism and the feudal privileges of individual provinces must first of all be rejected.

"Under these conditions, and only under these conditions, will it be possible to establish national order in Austria in place of national dissension, namely, on the following principles:

"1. Austria must be transformed into a democratic state federation of nationalities.

"2. The historical crown provinces must be replaced by nationally delimited self-governing corporations, in each of which legislation and administration shall be entrusted to national parliaments elected on the basis of universal, direct and equal suffrage.

"3. All the self-governing regions of one and the same nation must jointly form a single national union, which shall manage its national affairs on an absolutely autonomous basis.

"4. The rights of national minorities must be guaranteed by a special law passed by the Imperial Parliament."

The programme ends with an appeal for the solidarity of all the nations of Austria.**

It is not difficult to see that this programme retains certain traces of "territorialism," but that in general it gives a formulation of national autonomy. It is not without good reason that Springer, the first agitator on behalf of cultural-national autonomy, greets it with

---

* In M. Panin's Russian translation (see his translation of Bauer's book), "national individualities" is given in place of "national peculiarities." Panin translated this passage incorrectly. The word "individuality" is not in the German text, which speaks of *nationalen Eigenart*, i.e., *peculiarities*, which is far from being the same thing.

** *Verhandlungen des Gesamtparteitages* in Brünn, 1899.

enthusiasm;* Bauer also supports this programme, calling it a "theoretical victory"** for national autonomy;
only, in the interests of greater clarity, he proposes that
Point 4 be replaced by a more definite formulation, which
would declare the necessity of "constituting the national
minority within each self-governing region into a public
corporation" for the management of educational and
other cultural affairs.***

Such is the national programme of Austrian Social-
Democracy.

Let us examine its scientific foundations.

Let us see how the Austrian Social-Democratic Party
justifies the cultural-national autonomy it advocates.

Let us turn to the theoreticians of cultural-national
autonomy, Springer and Bauer.

The starting point of national autonomy is the conception of a nation as a union of individuals without regard
to a definite territory.

"Nationality," according to Springer, "is not essentially
connected with territory"; nations are "autonomous unions of
persons."****

Bauer also speaks of a nation as a "community of
persons" which does not enjoy "exclusive sovereignty in
any particular region."*****

But the persons constituting a nation do not always
live in one compact mass; they are frequently divided

---

     * See Springer, *The National Problem*, p. 286.
    ** See *The National Question*, p. 549.
   *** *Ibid.*, p. 555.
  **** See Springer, *The National Problem*, p. 19.
***** See *The National Question*, p. 286.

into groups, and in that form are interspersed among alien national organisms. It is capitalism which drives them into various regions and cities in search of a livelihood. But when they enter foreign national territories and there form minorities, these groups are made to suffer by the local national majorities in the way of restrictions on their language, schools, etc. Hence national conflicts. Hence the "unsuitability" of territorial autonomy. The only solution to such a situation, according to Springer and Bauer, is to organize the minorities of the given nationality dispersed over various parts of the state into a single, general, inter-class national union. Such a union alone, in their opinion, can protect the cultural interests of national minorities, and it alone is capable of putting an end to national discord.

"Hence the necessity," says Springer, "to organize the nationalities, to invest them with rights and responsibilities. . . ."* Of course, "a law is easily drafted, but will it be effective?". . . "If one wants to make a law for nations, one must first create the nations. . . ."** "Unless the nationalities are constituted it is impossible to create national rights and eliminate national dissension."***

Bauer expressed himself in the same spirit when he proposed, as "a demand of the working class," that "the minorities should be constituted into public corporations based on the personal principle."****

But how is a nation to be organized? How is one to determine to what nation any given individual belongs?

---

* See *The National Problem*, p. 74.
** *Ibid.*, pp. 88-89.
*** *Ibid.*, p. 89.
**** See *The National Question*, p. 552.

"Nationality," says Springer, "will be determined by cer-
tificates; every individual domiciled in a given region must declare
his affiliation to one of the nationalities of that region."*

"The personal principle," says Bauer, "presumes that the
population will be divided into nationalities. . . . On the basis
of the free declaration of the adult citizens national registers
must be drawn up."**

Further.

"All the Germans in nationally homogeneous districts," says
Bauer, "and all the Germans entered in the national registers in
the dual districts will constitute the German nation and elect a
National Council."***

The same applies to the Czechs, Poles, and so on.

"The *National Council*," according to Springer, "is the
cultural parliament of the nation, empowered to establish the
principles and to grant funds, thereby assuming guardianship
over national education, national literature, art and science,
the formation of academies, museums, galleries, theatres,"
etc.****

Such will be the organization of a nation and its
central institution.

According to Bauer, the Austrian Social-Democratic Party is striving, by the creation of these inter-class
institutions "to make national culture . . . the possession
of the whole people and thereby *unite all the members
of the nation into a national-cultural community*"*****
(our italics).

---

* See *The National Problem*, p. 226.
** See *The National Question*, p. 368.
*** *Ibid.*, p. 375.
**** See *The National Problem*, p. 234.
***** See *The National Question*, p. 553.

One might think that all this concerns Austria alone. But Bauer does not agree. He emphatically declares that national autonomy is essential also for other states which, like Austria, consist of several nationalities.

"In the multi-national state," according to Bauer, "the working class of all the nations opposes the national power policy of the propertied classes with the demand for national autonomy."*

Then, imperceptibly substituting national autonomy for the self-determination of nations, he continues:

"Thus, national autonomy, the self-determination of nations, will necessarily become the constitutional programme of the proletariat of all the nations in a multi-national state."**

But he goes still further. He profoundly believes that the inter-class "national unions" "constituted" by him and Springer will serve as a sort of prototype of the future socialist society. For he knows that "the socialist system of society . . . will divide humanity into nationally delimited communities";*** that under socialism there will take place "a grouping of humanity into autonomous national communities,"**** that thus, "socialist society will undoubtedly present a checkered picture of national unions of persons and territorial corporations,"***** and that accordingly "the socialist principle of nationality is a higher synthesis of the national principle and national autonomy."******

---

     * *Ibid.*, p. 337.
     ** See *The National Question*, p. 333.
   *** *Ibid.*, p. 555.
 **** *Ibid.*, p. 556.
 ***** *Ibid.*, p. 543.
****** *Ibid.*, p. 542.

Enough, it would seem. . . .

These are the arguments for cultural-national autonomy as given in the works of Bauer and Springer.

The first thing that strikes the eye is the entirely inexplicable and absolutely unjustifiable substitution of national autonomy for self-determination of nations. One or the other: either Bauer failed to understand the meaning of self-determination, or he did understand it but for some reason or other deliberately narrowed its meaning. For there is no doubt a) that cultural-national autonomy presupposes the integrity of the multi-national state, whereas self-determination goes outside the framework of this integrity, and b) that self-determination endows a nation with complete rights, whereas national autonomy endows it only with "cultural" rights. That in the first place.

In the second place, a combination of internal and external conditions is fully possible at some future time by virtue of which one or another of the nationalities may decide to secede from a multi-national state, say from Austria. Did not the Ruthenian Social-Democrats at the Brünn Party Congress announce their readiness to unite the "two parts" of their people into one whole?* What, in such a case, becomes of national autonomy, which is *inevitable for the proletariat of all the nations*? What sort of "solution" of the problem is it that mechanically squeezes nations into the Procrustean bed of an integral state?

Further: National autonomy is contrary to the whole

---

* See *Proceedings of the Brünn Social-Democratic Party Congress,* p. 48.

course of development of nations. It calls for the organization of nations; but can they be artificially welded together if life, if economic development tears whole groups from them and disperses these groups over various regions? There is no doubt that in the early stages of capitalism nations become welded together. But there is also no doubt that in the higher stages of capitalism a process of dispersion of nations sets in, a process whereby a whole number of groups separate off from the nations, going off in search of a livelihood and subsequently settling permanently in other regions of the state; in the course of this these settlers lose their old connections and acquire new ones in their new domicile, and from generation to generation acquire new habits and new tastes, and possibly a new language. The question arises: is it possible to unite into a single national union groups that have grown so distinct? Where are the magic links to unite what cannot be united? Is it conceivable that, for instance, the Germans of the Baltic Provinces and the Germans of Transcaucasia can be "united into a single nation"? But if it is not conceivable and not possible, wherein does national autonomy differ from the utopia of the old nationalists, who endeavoured to turn back the wheel of history?

But the unity of a nation diminishes not only as a result of migration. It diminishes also from internal causes, owing to the growing acuteness of the class struggle. In the early stages of capitalism one can still speak of a "common culture" of the proletariat and the bourgeoisie. But as large-scale industry develops and the class struggle becomes more and more acute, this "common culture" begins to melt away. One cannot seriously speak of the "common culture" of a nation when employers and workers of one and the same nation cease to understand each other. What "common destiny" can there be when the bourgeoisie thirsts for war, and the proletariat declares "war on war"? Can a single inter-class national union be formed from such opposed elements? And, after this, can one speak of the "union of all the members of the nation into a national-cultural community"?* Is it not obvious that national autonomy is contrary to the whole course of the class struggle?

But let us assume for a moment that the slogan "organize the nation" is practicable. One might understand bourgeois-nationalist parliamentarians endeavouring to "organize" a nation for the purpose of securing additional votes. But since when have Social-Democrats begun to occupy themselves with "organizing" nations, "constituting" nations, "creating" nations?

What sort of Social-Democrats are they who in the epoch of extreme intensification of the class struggle organize inter-class national unions? Until now the Austrian, as well as every other, Social-Democratic party, had one task before it: namely, to organize the proletariat. That task has apparently become "antiquated." Springer and Bauer are now setting a "new" task, a more absorbing task, namely, to "create," to "organize" a nation.

However, logic has its obligations: he who adopts national autonomy must also adopt this "new" task; but to adopt the latter means to abandon the class position and to take the path of nationalism.

---

* Bauer, *The National Question*, p. 553.

Springer's and Bauer's cultural-national autonomy is a subtle form of nationalism.

And it is by no means fortuitous that the national programme of the Austrian Social-Democrats enjoins a concern for the "*preservation* and *development* of the national peculiarities of the peoples.*"* Just think: to "preserve" such "national peculiarities" of the Trans-caucasian Tatars as self-flagellation at the festival of *Shakhsei-Vakhsei*; or to "develop" such "national peculiarities" of the Georgians as the vendetta! . . .

A demand of this character is in place in an outright bourgeois nationalist programme; and if it appears in the programme of the Austrian Social-Democrats it is because national autonomy tolerates such demands, it does not contradict them.

But if national autonomy is unsuitable now, it will be still more unsuitable in the future, socialist society.

Bauer's prophecy regarding the "division of humanity into nationally delimited communities"* is refuted by the whole course of development of modern human society. National barriers are being demolished and are falling, rather than becoming firmer. As early as the 'forties Marx declared that "national differences and antagonisms between peoples are daily more and more vanishing" and that "the supremacy of the proletariat will cause them to vanish still faster."[134] The subsequent development of mankind, accompanied as it was by the colossal growth of capitalist production, the re-shuffling of nationalities and the union of people

---

* See the beginning of this chapter.

within ever larger territories, emphatically confirms Marx's thought.

Bauer's desire to represent socialist society as a "checkered picture of national unions of persons and territorial corporations" is a timid attempt to substitute for Marx's conception of socialism a revised version of Bakunin's conception. The history of socialism proves that every such attempt contains the elements of inevitable failure.

There is no need to mention the kind of "socialist principle of nationality" glorified by Bauer, which, in our opinion, substitutes for the socialist principle of the *class struggle* the bourgeois *"principle of nationality."* If national autonomy is based on such a dubious principle, it must be admitted that it can only cause harm to the working-class movement.

True, such nationalism is not so transparent, for it is skilfully masked by socialist phrases, but it is all the more harmful to the proletariat for that reason. We can always cope with open nationalism, for it can easily be discerned. It is much more difficult to combat nationalism when it is masked and unrecognizable beneath its mask. Protected by the armour of socialism, it is less vulnerable and more tenacious. Implanted among the workers, it poisons the atmosphere and spreads harmful ideas of mutual distrust and segregation among the workers of the different nationalities.

But this does not exhaust the harm caused by national autonomy. It prepares the ground not only for the segregation of nations, but also for breaking up the united labour movement. The idea of national autonomy creates the psychological conditions for the division of the united workers' party into separate parties built on national lines. The breakup of the party is followed by the breakup of the trade unions, and complete segregation is the result. In this way the united class movement is broken up into separate national rivulets.

Austria, the home of "national autonomy," provides the most deplorable examples of this. As early as 1897 (the Wimberg Party Congress[135]) the once united Austrian Social-Democratic Party began to break up into separate parties. The breakup became still more marked after the Brünn Party Congress (1899), which adopted national autonomy. Matters have finally come to such a pass that in place of a united international party there are now six national parties, of which the Czech Social-Democratic Party will not even have anything to do with the German Social-Democratic Party.

But with the parties are associated the trade unions. In Austria, both in the parties and in the trade unions, the main brunt of the work is borne by the same Social-Democratic workers. There was therefore reason to fear that separatism in the party would lead to separatism in the trade unions and that the trade unions would also break up. That, in fact, is what happened: the trade unions have also divided according to nationality. Now things frequently go so far that the Czech workers will even break a strike of German workers, or will unite at municipal elections with the Czech bourgeois against the German workers.

It will be seen from the foregoing that cultural-national autonomy is no solution of the national question. Not only that, it serves to aggravate and confuse the question by creating a situation which favours the destruction of the unity of the labour movement, fosters the segregation of the workers according to nationality and intensifies friction among them.

Such is the harvest of national autonomy.

V

THE BUND, ITS NATIONALISM, ITS SEPARATISM

We said above that Bauer, while granting the necessity of national autonomy for the Czechs, Poles, and so on, nevertheless opposes similar autonomy for the Jews. In answer to the question, "Should the working class demand autonomy for the Jewish people?" Bauer says that "national autonomy cannot be demanded by the Jewish workers."* According to Bauer, the reason is that "capitalist society makes it impossible for them (the Jews—*J. St.*) to continue as a nation."**

In brief, the Jewish nation is coming to an end, and hence there is nobody to demand national autonomy for. The Jews are being assimilated.

This view of the fate of the Jews as a nation is not a new one. It was expressed by Marx as early as the 'forties,***[136] in reference chiefly to the German Jews. It was repeated by Kautsky in 1903,**** in reference to the Russian Jews. It is now being repeated by Bauer in reference to the Austrian Jews, with the difference,

---

* See *The National Question*, pp. 381, 396.

** *Ibid.*, p. 389.

*** See K. Marx, "The Jewish Question," 1906.

**** See K. Kautsky, "The Kishinev Pogrom and the Jewish Question," 1903.

however, that he denies not the present but the future of the Jewish nation.

Bauer explains the impossibility of preserving the existence of the Jews as a nation by the fact that "the Jews have no closed territory of settlement."* This explanation, in the main a correct one, does not however express the whole truth. The fact of the matter is primarily that among the Jews there is no large and stable stratum connected with the land, which would naturally rivet the nation together, serving not only as its framework but also as a "national" market. Of the five or six million Russian Jews, only three to four per cent are connected with agriculture in any way. The remaining ninety-six per cent are employed in trade, industry, in urban institutions, and in general are town dwellers; moreover, they are spread all over Russia and do not constitute a majority in a single gubernia.

Thus, interspersed as national minorities in areas inhabited by other nationalities, the Jews as a rule serve "foreign" nations as manufacturers and traders and as members of the liberal professions, naturally adapting themselves to the "foreign nations" in respect to language and so forth. All this, taken together with the increasing re-shuffling of nationalities characteristic of developed forms of capitalism, leads to the assimilation of the Jews. The abolition of the "Pale of Settlement" would only serve to hasten this process of assimilation.

The question of national autonomy for the Russian Jews consequently assumes a somewhat curious character: autonomy is being proposed for a nation whose

* See *The National Question*, p. 388.

future is denied and whose existence has still to be proved!

Nevertheless, this was the curious and shaky position taken up by the Bund when at its Sixth Congress (1905) it adopted a "national programme" on the lines of national autonomy.

Two circumstances impelled the Bund to take this step.

The first circumstance is the existence of the Bund as an organization of Jewish, and only Jewish, Social-Democratic workers. Even before 1897 the Social-Democratic groups active among the Jewish workers set themselves the aim of creating "a special Jewish workers' organization."* They founded such an organization in 1897 by uniting to form the Bund. That was at a time when Russian Social-Democracy as an integral body virtually did not yet exist. The Bund steadily grew and spread, and stood out more and more vividly against the background of the bleak days of Russian Social-Democracy. . . . Then came the 1900's. A *mass* labour movement came into being. Polish Social-Democracy grew and drew the Jewish workers into the mass struggle. Russian Social-Democracy grew and attracted the "Bund" workers. Lacking a territorial basis, the national framework of the Bund became too restrictive. The Bund was faced with the problem of either merging with the general international tide, or of upholding its independent existence as an extra-territorial organization. The Bund chose the latter course.

---

* See *Forms of the National Movement*, etc., edited by Kastelyansky, p. 772.

Thus grew up the "theory" that the Bund is "the sole representative of the Jewish proletariat."

But to justify this strange "theory" in any "simple" way became impossible. Some kind of foundation "on principle," some justification "on principle," was needed. Cultural-national autonomy provided such a foundation. The Bund seized upon it, borrowing it from the Austrian Social-Democrats. If the Austrians had not had such a programme the Bund would have invented it in order to justify its independent existence "on principle."

Thus, after a timid attempt in 1901 (the Fourth Congress), the Bund definitely adopted a "national programme" in 1905 (the Sixth Congress).

The second circumstance is the peculiar position of the Jews as separate national minorities within compact majorities of other nationalities in integral regions. We have already said that this position is undermining the existence of the Jews as a nation and puts them on the road to assimilation. But this is an objective process. Subjectively, in the minds of the Jews, it provokes a reaction and gives rise to the demand for a guarantee of the rights of a national minority, for a guarantee against assimilation. Preaching as it does the vitality of the Jewish "nationality," the Bund could not avoid being in favour of a "guarantee." And, having taken up this position, it could not but accept national autonomy. For if the Bund could seize upon any autonomy at all, it could only be national autonomy, i.e., *cultural-national* autonomy; there could be no question of territorial-political autonomy for the Jews, since the Jews have no definite integral territory.

It is noteworthy that the Bund from the outset

stressed the character of national autonomy as a guarantee of the rights of national minorities, as a guarantee of the "free development" of nations. Nor was it fortuitous that the representative of the Bund at the Second Congress of the Russian Social-Democratic Party, Goldblatt, defined national autonomy as "institutions which *guarantee* them (i.e., nations—*J. St.*) complete freedom of cultural development."* A similar proposal was made by supporters of the ideas of the Bund to the Social-Democratic group in the Fourth Duma. . . .

In this way the Bund adopted the curious position of national autonomy for the Jews.

We have examined above national autonomy in general. The examination showed that national autonomy leads to nationalism. We shall see later that the Bund has arrived at the same end point. But the Bund also regards national autonomy from a special aspect, namely, from the aspect of *guarantees* of the rights of national minorities. Let us also examine the question from this special aspect. It is all the more necessary since the problem of national minorities—and not of the Jewish minorities alone—is one of serious moment for Social-Democracy.

And so, it is a question of *"institutions which guarantee"* nations "complete freedom of cultural development" (our italics—*J. St.*).

But what are these "institutions which guarantee," etc.?

They are primarily the "National Council" of Springer and Bauer, something in the nature of a Diet for cultural affairs.

---

* See *Minutes of the Second Congress*, p. 176.

But can these institutions guarantee a nation "complete freedom of cultural development"? Can a Diet for cultural affairs guarantee a nation against nationalist persecution?

The Bund believes it can.

But history proves the contrary.

At one time a Diet existed in Russian Poland. It was a political Diet and, of course, endeavoured to guarantee freedom of "cultural development" for the Poles. But, far from succeeding in doing so, it itself succumbed in the unequal struggle against the political conditions generally prevailing in Russia.

A Diet has been in existence for a long time in Finland, and it too endeavours to protect the Finnish nationality from "encroachments," but how far it succeeds in doing so everybody can see.

Of course, there are Diets and Diets, and it is not so easy to cope with the democratically organized Finnish Diet as it was with the aristocratic Polish Diet. But the *decisive* factor, nevertheless, is not the Diet, but the general regime in Russia. If such a grossly Asiatic social and political regime existed in Russia now as in the past, at the time the Polish Diet was abolished, things would go much harder with the Finnish Diet. Moreover, the policy of "encroachments" upon Finland is growing, and it cannot be said that it has met with defeat. . . .

If such is the case with old, historically evolved institutions—political Diets—still less will young Diets, young institutions, especially such feeble institutions as "cultural" Diets, be able to guarantee the free development of nations.

Obviously, it is not a question of "institutions," but of the general regime prevailing in the country. If there is no democracy in the country there can be no guarantees of "complete freedom for cultural development" of nationalities. One may say with certainty that the more democratic a country is the fewer are the "encroachments" made on the "freedom of nationalities," and the greater are the guarantees against such "encroachments."

Russia is a semi-Asiatic country, and therefore in Russia the policy of "encroachments" not infrequently assumes the grossest form, the form of pogroms. It need hardly be said that in Russia "guarantees" have been reduced to the very minimum.

Germany is, however, European, and she enjoys a measure of political freedom. It is not surprising that the policy of "encroachments" there never takes the form of pogroms.

In France, of course, there are still more "guarantees," for France is more democratic than Germany.

There is no need to mention Switzerland, where, thanks to her highly developed, although bourgeois democracy, nationalities live in freedom, whether they are a minority or a majority.

Thus the Bund adopts a false position when it asserts that "institutions" by themselves are able to guarantee complete cultural development for nationalities.

It may be said that the Bund itself regards the establishment of democracy in Russia as a *preliminary* condition for the "creation of institutions" and guarantees of freedom. But this is not the case. From the report of the Eighth Conference of the Bund[137] it will be seen that the Bund thinks it can secure "institutions" *on the basis of* the present system in Russia, by "reforming" the *Jewish community.*

"The community," one of the leaders of the Bund said at this conference, "may become the nucleus of future cultural-national autonomy. Cultural-national autonomy is a form of self-service on the part of nations, a form of satisfying national needs. The community form conceals within itself a similar content. They are links in the same chain, stages in the same evolution."*

On this basis, the conference decided that it was necessary to strive "for *reforming* the Jewish community and transforming it by *legislative means* into a secular institution," democratically organized** (our italics— *J. St.*).

It is evident that the Bund considers as the condition and guarantee not the democratization of Russia, but some future "secular institution" of the Jews, obtained by "reforming the Jewish community," so to speak, by "legislative" means, through the Duma.

But we have already seen that "institutions" in themselves cannot serve as "guarantees" if the regime in the state generally is not a democratic one.

But what, it may be asked, will be the position under a future democratic system? Will not special "cultural institutions which guarantee," etc., be required even under democracy? What is the position in this respect in democratic Switzerland, for example? Are there special cultural institutions in Switzerland

---

* *Report of the Eighth Conference of the Bund*, 1911, p. 62.
** *Ibid.*, pp. 83-84.

on the pattern of Springer's "National Council"? No, there are *not*. But do not the cultural interests of, for instance, the Italians, who constitute a minority there, suffer for that reason? One does not seem to hear that they do. And that is quite natural: in Switzerland all special cultural "institutions," which supposedly "guarantee," etc., are rendered superfluous by democracy.

And so, impotent in the present and superfluous in the future—such are the *institutions* of cultural-national autonomy, and such is national autonomy.

But it becomes still more harmful when it is thrust upon a "nation" whose existence and future are open to doubt. In such cases the advocates of national autonomy are obliged to protect and preserve all the peculiar features of the "nation," the bad as well as the good, just for the sake of "saving the nation" from assimilation, just for the sake of "preserving" it.

That the Bund should take this dangerous path was inevitable. And it did take it. We are referring to the resolutions of recent conferences of the Bund on the question of the "Sabbath," "Yiddish," etc.

Social-Democracy strives to secure *for all nations* the right to use their own language. But that does not satisfy the Bund; it demands that "the rights of the *Jewish* language" (our italics—*J. St.*) be championed with "exceptional persistence,"* and the Bund itself in the elections to the Fourth Duma declared that it would give "preference to those of them (i.e., electors) who undertake to defend the rights of the Jewish language."**

---

* See *Report of the Eighth Conference of the Bund*, p. 85.
** See *Report of the Ninth Conference of the Bund*, 1912, p. 42.

Not the *general* right of all nations to use their own language, but the *particular* right of the Jewish language, Yiddish! Let the workers of the various nationalities fight *primarily* for their own language: the Jews for Jewish, the Georgians for Georgian, and so forth. The struggle for the general right of all nations is a secondary matter. You do not have to recognize the right of all oppressed nationalities to use their own language; but if you have recognized the right of Yiddish, know that the Bund will vote for you, the Bund will "prefer" you.

But in what way then does the Bund differ from the bourgeois nationalists?

Social-Democracy strives to secure the establishment of a compulsory weekly rest day. But that does not satisfy the Bund; it demands that "by legislative means" "the Jewish proletariat should be guaranteed the right to observe their Sabbath and be relieved of the obligation to observe another day."*

It is to be expected that the Bund will take another "step forward" and demand the right to observe all the ancient Hebrew holidays. And if, to the misfortune of the Bund, the Jewish workers have discarded religious prejudices and do not want to observe these holidays, the Bund with its agitation for "the right to the Sabbath," will remind them of the Sabbath, it will, so to speak, cultivate among them "the Sabbatarian spirit.". . .

Quite comprehensible, therefore, are the "passionate speeches" delivered at the Eighth Conference of the

---

* See *Report of the Eighth Conference of the Bund*, p. 83.

Bund demanding "Jewish hospitals," a demand that was based on the argument that "a patient feels more at home among his own people," that "the Jewish worker will not feel at ease among Polish workers, but will feel at ease among Jewish shopkeepers."*

Preservation of everything Jewish, conservation of *all* the national peculiarities of the Jews, even those that are patently harmful to the proletariat, isolation of the Jews from everything non-Jewish, even the establishment of special hospitals—that is the level to which the Bund has sunk!

Comrade Plekbanov was right a thousand times over when he said that the Bund "is adapting socialism to nationalism." Of course, V. Kossovsky and Bundists like him may denounce Plekhanov as a "demagogue"**[138]—paper will put up with anything that is written on it—but those who are familiar with the activities of the Bund will easily realize that these brave fellows are simply afraid to tell the truth about themselves and are hiding behind strong language about "demagogy.". . .

But since it holds such a position on the national question, the Bund was naturally obliged, in the matter of organization also, to take the path of segregating the Jewish workers, the path of formation of national curiae within Social-Democracy. Such is the logic of national autonomy!

And, in fact, the Bund did pass from the theory of "sole representation" to the theory of "national demar-

* *Ibid.*, p. 68.
** See *Nasha Zarya*, No. 9-10, 1912, p. 120.

cation" of workers. The Bund demands that Russian Social-Democracy should "in its organizational structure introduce demarcation according to nationalities."* From "demarcation" it made a "step forward" to the theory of "segregation." It is not for nothing that speeches were made at the Eighth Conference of the Bund declaring that "national existence lies in segregation."**

Organizational federalism harbours the elements of disintegration and separatism. The Bund is heading for separatism.

And, indeed, there is nothing else it can head for. Its very existence as an extra-territorial organization drives it to separatism. The Bund does not possess a definite integral territory; it operates on "foreign" territories, whereas the neighbouring Polish, Lettish and Russian Social-Democracies are international territorial collective bodies. But the result is that every extension of these collective bodies means a "loss" to the Bund and a restriction of its field of action. There are two alternatives: either Russian Social-Democracy as a whole must be reconstructed on the basis of national federalism—which will enable the Bund to "secure" the Jewish proletariat for itself; or the territorial-international principle of these collective bodies remains in force—in which case the Bund must be reconstructed on the basis of internationalism, as is the case with the Polish and Lettish Social-Democracies.

---

* See *An Announcement on the Seventh Congress of the Bund*,[139] p. 7.

** See *Report of the Eighth Conference of the Bund*, p. 72.

This explains why the Bund from the very beginning demanded "the reorganization of Russian Social-Democracy on a federal basis."*

In 1906, yielding to the pressure from below in favour of unity, the Bund chose a middle path and joined Russian Social-Democracy. But how did it join? Whereas the Polish and Lettish Social-Democracies joined for the purpose of peaceable joint action, the Bund joined for the purpose of waging war for a federation. That is exactly what Medem, the leader of the Bundists, said at the time:

"We are joining not for the sake of an idyll, but in order to fight. There is no idyll, and only Manilovs could hope for one in the near future. The Bund must join the Party armed from head to foot."**

It would be wrong to regard this as an expression of evil intent on Medem's part. It is not a matter of evil intent, but of the peculiar position of the Bund, which compels it to fight Russian Social-Democracy, which is built on the basis of internationalism. And in fighting it the Bund naturally violated the interests of unity. Finally, matters went so far that the Bund formally broke with Russian Social-Democracy, violating its statutes, and in the elections to the Fourth Duma joining forces with the Polish nationalists against the Polish Social-Democrats.

The Bund has apparently found that a rupture is the best guarantee for independent activity.

---

* See *Concerning National Autonomy and the Reorganization of Russian Social-Democracy on a Federal Basis*, 1902, published by the Bund.

** *Nashe Slovo*, No. 3, Vilno, 1906, p. 24.

And so the "principle" of organizational "demarcation" led to separatism and to a complete rupture.

In a controversy with the old *Iskra*[140] on the question of federalism, the Bund once wrote:

"*Iskra* wants to assure us that federal relations between the Bund and Russian Social-Democracy are bound to weaken the ties between them. We cannot refute this opinion by referring to practice in Russia, for the simple reason that Russian Social-Democracy does not exist as a federal body. But we can refer to the extremely instructive experience of Social-Democracy in Austria, which assumed a federal character by virtue of the decision of the Party Congress of 1897."*

That was written in 1902.

But we are now in the year 1913. We now have both Russian "practice" and the "experience of Social-Democracy in Austria."

What do they tell us?

Let us begin with "the extremely instructive experience of Social-Democracy in Austria." Up to 1896 there was a united Social-Democratic Party in Austria. In that year the Czechs at the International Congress in London for the first time demanded separate representation, and were given it. In 1897, at the Vienna (Wimberg) Party Congress, the united party was formally liquidated and in its place a federal league of six national "Social-Democratic groups" was set up. Subsequently these "groups" were converted into independent parties, which gradually severed contact with one another. Following the parties, the parliamentary group broke up—national "clubs" were

---

* *National Autonomy*, etc., 1902, p. 17, published by the Bund.

formed. Next came the trade unions, which also split
according to nationalities. Even the co-operative societies
were affected, the Czech separatists calling upon the
workers to split them up.* We will not dwell on the
fact that separatist agitation weakens the workers' sense
of solidarity and frequently drives them to strike-breaking.

Thus "the extremely instructive experience of Social-
Democracy in Austria" speaks *against* the Bund and for
the old *Iskra*. Federalism in the Austrian party has led
to the most outrageous separatism, to the destruction of
the unity of the labour movement.

We have seen above that "practical experience in Russia"
also bears this out. Like the Czech separatists, the Bundist
separatists have broken with the general Russian Social-
Democratic Party. As for the trade unions, the Bundist
trade unions, from the outset they were organized on
national lines, that is to say, they were cut off from the
workers of other nationalities.

Complete segregation and complete rupture—that is
what is revealed by the "Russian practical experience"
of federalism.

It is not surprising that the effect of this state of
affairs upon the workers is to weaken their sense of solidarity and to demoralize them; and the latter process
is also penetrating the Bund. We are referring to the
increasing collisions between Jewish and Polish workers in connection with unemployment. Here is the
kind of speech that was made on this subject at the Ninth
Conference of the Bund:

---

* See the words quoted from a brochure by Vaněk[141] in *Doku-
mente des Separatismus*, p. 29.

" . . . We regard the Polish workers, who are ousting us, as pogromists, as scabs; we do not support their strikes, we break them. Secondly, we reply to being ousted by ousting in our turn: we reply to Jewish workers not being allowed into the factories by not allowing Polish workers near the benches. . . . *If we do not take this matter into our own hands the workers will follow others*"* (our italics—*J. St.*).

That is the way they talk about solidarity at a Bundist conference.

You cannot go further than that in the way of "demarcation" and "segregation." The Bund has achieved its aim: it is carrying its demarcation between the workers of different nationalities to the point of conflicts and strike-breaking. And there is no other course: "If we do not take this matter into our own hands *the workers will follow others*. . . ."

Disorganization of the labour movement, demoralization of the Social-Democratic ranks—that is what the federalism of the Bund leads to.

Thus the idea of cultural-national autonomy, the atmosphere it creates, has proved to be even more harmful in Russia than in Austria.

VI

THE CAUCASIANS, THE CONFERENCE OF THE LIQUIDATORS

We spoke above of the waverings of one section of the Caucasian Social-Democrats who were unable to withstand the nationalist "epidemic." These waverings were revealed in the fact that, strange as it may seem,

---

* See *Report of the Ninth Conference of the Bund*, p. 19.

the above-mentioned Social-Democrats followed in the footsteps of the Bund and proclaimed cultural-national autonomy.

Regional autonomy for the Caucasus as a whole and cultural-national autonomy for the nations forming the Caucasus—that is the way these Social-Democrats, who, incidentally, are linked with the Russian Liquidators, formulate their demand.

Listen to their acknowledged leader, the not unknown *N.*

"Everybody knows that the Caucasus differs profoundly from the central gubernias, both as regards the racial composition of its population and as regards its territory and agricultural development. The exploitation and material development of such a region require local workers acquainted with local peculiarities and accustomed to the local climate and culture. All laws designed to further the exploitation of the local territory should be issued locally and put into effect by local forces. Consequently, the jurisdiction of the central organ of Caucasian self-government should extend to legislation on local questions. . . . Hence, the functions of the Caucasian centre should consist in the passing of laws designed to further the economic exploitation of the local territory and the material prosperity of the region."*

Thus—regional autonomy for the Caucasus.

If we abstract ourselves from the rather confused and incoherent arguments of *N.*, it must be admitted that his conclusion is correct. Regional autonomy for the Caucasus, within the framework of a general state constitution, which *N.* does not deny, is indeed essential because of the peculiarities of its composition and its conditions of life. This was also acknowledged by the

---

* See the Georgian newspaper *Chveni Tskhovreba (Our Life)*,[142] No. 12, 1912.

Russian Social-Democratic Party, which at its Second Congress proclaimed "regional self-government for those border regions which in respect of their conditions of life and the composition of their population differ from the regions of Russia proper."

When Martov submitted this point for discussion at the Second Congress, he justified it on the grounds that "the vast extent of Russia and the experience of our centralized administration point to the necessity and expediency of regional self-government for such large units as Finland, Poland, Lithuania and the Caucasus."

But it follows that regional *self-government* is to be interpreted as regional *autonomy*.

But *N*. goes further. According to him, regional autonomy for the Caucasus covers "only one aspect of the question."

"So far we have spoken only of the material development of local life. But the economic development of a region is facilitated not only by economic activity but also by spiritual, cultural activity.". . . "A culturally strong nation is strong also in the economic sphere.". . . "But the cultural development of nations is possible only in the national languages.". . . "Consequently, all questions connected with the native language are questions of national culture. Such are the questions of education, the judicature, the church, literature, art, science, the theatre, etc. If the material development of a region unites nations, matters of national culture disunite them and place each in a separate sphere. Activities of the former kind are associated with a definite territory.". . . "This is not the case with matters of national culture. These are associated not with a definite territory but with the existence of a definite nation. The fate of the Georgian language interests a Georgian, no matter where he lives. It would be a sign of profound ignorance to say that Georgian culture concerns only the Georgians who live in Georgia. Take, for instance, the Armenian church. Armenians of various localities and states take part in the administration of its affairs. Territory plays no part here. Or, for instance, the creation of a Georgian museum interests not only the Georgians of Tiflis, but also the Georgians of Baku, Kutais, St. Petersburg, etc. Hence, the administration and control of all affairs of national culture must be left to the nations concerned. We proclaim in favour of cultural-national autonomy for the Caucasian nationalities."*

In short, since culture is not territory, and territory is not culture, cultural-national autonomy is required. That is all *N.* can say in the latter's favour.

We shall not stop to discuss again national-cultural autonomy in general; we have already spoken of its objectionable character. We should like to point out only that, while being unsuitable in general, cultural-national autonomy is also meaningless and nonsensical in relation to Caucasian conditions.

And for the following reason:

Cultural-national autonomy presumes more or less developed nationalities, with a developed culture and literature. Failing these conditions, autonomy loses all sense and becomes an absurdity. But in the Caucasus there are a number of nationalities each possessing a primitive culture, a separate language, but without its own literature; nationalities, moreover, which are in a state of transition, partly becoming assimilated and partly continuing to develop. How is cultural-national autonomy to be applied to them? What is to be done with such nationalities? How are they to be "organized" into separate cultural-national unions, as is undoubtedly implied by cultural-national autonomy?

---

* See the Georgian newspaper *Ohveni Tskhovreba*, No. 12, 1912.

What is to be done with the Mingrelians, the Abkhasians, the Adjarians, the Svanetians, the Lesghians, and so on, who speak different languages but do not possess a literature of their own? To what nations are they to be attached? Can they be "organized" into national unions? Around what "cultural affairs" are they to be "organized"?

What is to be done with the Ossetians, of whom the Transcaucasian Ossetians are becoming assimilated (but are as yet by no means wholly assimilated) by the Georgians, while the Cis-Caucasian Ossetians are partly being assimilated by the Russians and partly continuing to develop and are creating their own literature? How are they to be "organized" into a single national union?

To what national union should one attach the Adjarians, who speak the Georgian language, but whose culture is Turkish and who profess the religion of Islam? Shall they be "organized" separately from the Georgians *with regard to religious affairs* and together with the Georgians *with regard to other cultural affairs*? And what about the Kobuletians, the Ingushes, the Inghilois?

What kind of autonomy is that which excludes a whole number of nationalities from the list?

No, that is not a solution of the national question, but the fruit of idle fancy.

But let us grant the impossible and assume that our *N.*'s national-cultural autonomy has been put into effect. Where would it lead to, what would be its results? Take, for instance, the Transcaucasian Tatars, with their minimum percentage of literates, their schools controlled by the omnipotent mullahs and their culture permeated by the religious spirit. . . . It is not difficult to understand that to "organize" them into a cultural-national union would mean to place them under the control of the mullahs, to deliver them over to the tender mercies of the reactionary mullahs, to create a new stronghold of spiritual enslavement of the Tatar masses to their worst enemy.

But since when have Social-Democrats made it a practice to bring grist to the mill of the reactionaries?

Could the Caucasian Liquidators really find nothing better to "proclaim" than the isolation of the Transcaucasian Tatars within a cultural-national union which would place the masses under the thraldom of vicious reactionaries?

No, that is no solution of the national question.

The national question in the Caucasus can be solved only *by drawing the belated nations and nationalities into the common stream of a higher culture.* It is the only progressive solution and the only solution acceptable to Social-Democracy. Regional autonomy in the Caucasus is acceptable because it would draw the belated nations into the common cultural development; it would help them to cast off the shell of small-nation insularity; it would impel them forward and facilitate access to the benefits of higher culture. Cultural-national autonomy, however, acts in a diametrically opposite direction, because it shuts up the nations within their old shells, binds them to the lower stages of cultural development and prevents them from rising to the higher stages of culture.

In this way national autonomy counteracts the beneficial aspects of regional autonomy and nullifies it.

That is why the mixed type of autonomy which combines national-cultural autonomy and regional autonomy as proposed by *N*. is also unsuitable. This unnatural combination does not improve matters but makes them worse, because in addition to retarding the development of the belated nations it transforms regional autonomy into an arena of conflict between the nations organized in the national unions.

Thus cultural-national autonomy, which is unsuitable generally, would be a senseless, reactionary undertaking in the Caucasus.

So much for the cultural-national autonomy of *N*. and his Caucasian fellow-thinkers.

Whether the Caucasian Liquidators will take "a step forward" and follow in the footsteps of the Bund on the question of organization also, the future will show. So far, in the history of Social-Democracy federalism in organization always preceded national autonomy in programme. The Austrian Social-Democrats introduced organizational federalism as far back as 1897, and it was only two years later (1899) that they adopted national autonomy. The Bundists spoke distinctly of national autonomy for the first time in 1901, whereas organizational federalism had been practised by them since 1897.

The Caucasian Liquidators have begun from the end, from national autonomy. If they continue to follow in the footsteps of the Bund they will first have to demolish the whole existing organizational edifice, which was erected at the end of the 'nineties on the basis of internationalism.

But, easy though it was to adopt national autonomy, which is still not understood by the workers, it will be difficult to demolish an edifice which it has taken years to build and which has been raised and cherished

by the workers of all the nationalities of the Caucasus.
This Herostratian undertaking has only to be begun and
the eyes of the workers will be opened to the nationalist
character of cultural-national autonomy.

———

While the Caucasians are settling the national question in the usual manner, by means of verbal and written
discussion, the All-Russian Conference of the Liquidators has invented a most unusual method. It is a
simple and easy method. Listen to this:

> "Having heard the communication of the Caucasian delega-
> tion to the effect that . . . it is necessary to demand national-
> cultural autonomy, this conference, while expressing no opinion
> on the merits of this demand, declares that such an interpretation
> of the clause of the programme which recognizes the right of every
> nationality to self-determination does not contradict the precise
> meaning of the programme."

Thus, first of all they "express no opinion on the
merits" of the question, and then they "declare." An
original method. . . .

And what does this original conference "declare"?

That the "demand" for national-cultural autonomy
"does not contradict the precise meaning" of the programme,
which recognizes the right of nations to self-determination.

Let us examine this proposition.

The clause on self-determination speaks of the rights
of nations. According to this clause, nations have the
right not only of autonomy but also of secession. It
is a question of *political* self-determination. Whom did
the Liquidators want to fool when they endeavoured
to misinterpret this right of nations to political self-

determination, which has long been recognized by the whole of international Social-Democracy?

Or perhaps the Liquidators will try to wriggle out of the situation and defend themselves by the sophism that cultural-national autonomy "does not contradict" the rights of nations? That is to say, if all the nations in a given state agree to arrange their affairs on the basis of cultural-national autonomy, they, the given sum of nations, are fully entitled to do so and nobody may *forcibly impose* a different form of political life on them. This is both new and clever. Should it not be added that, speaking generally, a nation has the right to abolish its own constitution, replace it by a system of tyranny and revert to the old order on the grounds that the nation, and the nation alone, has the right to determine its own destiny? We repeat: in this sense, neither cultural-national autonomy nor any other kind of nationalist reaction "contradicts" *the rights of nations*.

Is that what the esteemed conference wanted to say?

No, not that. It specifically says that cultural-national autonomy "does not contradict," not the rights of nations, but *"the precise meaning" of the programme*. The point here is the programme and not the rights of nations.

And that is quite understandable. If it were some nation that addressed itself to the conference of Liquidators, the conference might have directly declared that the nation has a right to cultural-national autonomy. But it was not a nation that addressed itself to the conference, but a "delegation" of Caucasian Social-Democrats—bad Social-Democrats, it is true, but Social-Democrats nevertheless. And they inquired not about the rights of nations, but whether cultural-national autonomy contradicted *the principles of Social-Democracy*, whether it did not "contradict" *"the precise meaning" of the programme of Social-Democracy.*

Thus, *the rights of nations and "the precise meaning" of the programme of Social-Democracy* are not one and the same thing.

Evidently, there are demands which, while they do not contradict the rights of nations, may yet contradict "the precise meaning" of the programme.

For example. The programme of the Social-Democrats contains a clause on freedom of religion. According to this clause any group of persons *have the right* to profess any religion they please: Catholicism, the religion of the Orthodox Church, etc. Social-Democrats will combat all forms of religious persecution, be it of members of the Orthodox Church, Catholics or Protestants. Does this mean that Catholicism, Protestantism, etc., "do not contradict the precise meaning" of the programme? No, it does not. Social-Democrats will always protest against persecution of Catholicism or Protestantism; they will always defend the right of nations to profess any religion they please; but at the same time, on the basis of a correct understanding of the interests of the proletariat, they will carry on agitation against Catholicism, Protestantism and the religion of the Orthodox Church in order to achieve the triumph of the socialist world outlook.

And they will do so just because there is no doubt that Protestantism, Catholicism, the religion of the Orthodox Church, etc., "contradict the precise meaning" of the programme, i.e., the correctly understood interests of the proletariat.

The same must be said of self-determination. Nations have a right to arrange their affairs as they please; they have a right to preserve any of their national institutions, whether beneficial or harmful—nobody can (nobody has a right to!) *forcibly* interfere in the life of a nation. But that does not mean that Social-Democracy will not combat and agitate against the harmful institutions of nations and against the inexpedient demands of nations. On the contrary, it is the duty of Social-Democracy to conduct such agitation and to endeavour to influence the will of nations so that the nations may arrange their affairs in the way that will best correspond to the interests of the proletariat. For this reason Social-Democracy, while fighting for the right of nations to self-determination, will at the same time agitate, for instance, against the secession of the Tatars, or against cultural-national autonomy for the Caucasian nations; for both, while not contradicting the *rights* of these nations, do contradict *"the precise meaning" of the programme*, i.e., the interests of the Caucasian proletariat.

Obviously, "the rights of nations" and the "precise meaning" of the programme are on two entirely different planes. Whereas the "precise meaning" of the programme expresses the interests of the proletariat, as scientifically formulated in the programme of the latter, the rights of nations may express the interests of any class—bourgeoisie, aristocracy, clergy, etc.—depending on the strength and influence of these classes. On the one hand are the *duties* of Marxists, on the other the *rights* of nations, which consist of various classes. The rights of nations and the principles of Social-Democracy may or may not "contradict" each other, just as, say, the pyramid of Cheops may or may not contradict the famous conference of the Liquidators. They are simply not comparable.

But it follows that the esteemed conference most unpardonably muddled two entirely different things. The result obtained was not a solution of the national question but an absurdity, according to which the rights of nations and the principles of Social-Democracy "do not contradict" each other, and, consequently, every demand of a nation may be made compatible with the interests of the proletariat; consequently, no demand of a nation which is striving for self-determination will "contradict the precise meaning" of the programme!

They pay no heed to logic. . . .

It was this absurdity that gave rise to the now famous resolution of the conference of the Liquidators which declares that the demand for national-cultural autonomy "does not contradict the precise meaning" of the programme.

But it was not only the laws of logic that were violated by the conference of the Liquidators.

By sanctioning cultural-national autonomy it also violated its duty to Russian Social-Democracy. It most definitely did violate "the precise meaning" of the programme, for it is well known that the Second Congress, which adopted the programme, *emphatically repudiated* cultural-national autonomy. Here is what was said at the congress in this connection:

"*Goldblatt* (Bundist): . . . I deem it necessary that special institutions be set up to protect the freedom of cultural development of nationalities, and I therefore propose that the following words be added to § 8: '*and the creation of institutions which will guarantee them complete freedom of cultural development.*'" (This, as we know, is the Bund's definition of cultural-national autonomy.—*J. St.*)

"*Martynov* pointed out that general institutions must be so constituted as to protect particular interests also. It is impossible to create a *special* institution to guarantee freedom for cultural development of the nationalities.

"*Yegorov*: On the question of nationality we can adopt only negative proposals, i.e., we are opposed to all restrictions upon nationality. But we, as Social-Democrats, are not concerned with whether any particular nationality will develop as such. That is a spontaneous process.

"*Koltsov*: The delegates from the Bund are always offended when their nationalism is referred to. Yet the amendment proposed by the delegate from the Bund is of a purely nationalist character. We are asked to take purely offensive measures in order to support even nationalities that are dying out."

In the end "*Goldblatt's amendment was rejected by the majority, only three votes being cast for it.*"

Thus it is clear that the conference of the Liquidators did "contradict the precise meaning" of the programme. It violated the programme.

The Liquidators are now trying to justify themselves by referring to the Stockholm Congress, which they allege sanctioned cultural-national autonomy. Thus, V. Kossovsky writes:

"As we know, according to the agreement adopted by the Stockholm Congress, the Bund was allowed to preserve its national programme (pending a decision on the national question by a general Party congress). This congress recorded that national-cultural autonomy at any rate does not contradict the general Party programme."*

---

* *Nasha Zarya*, No. 9-10, 1912, p. 120.

But the efforts of the Liquidators are in vain. The Stockholm Congress never thought of sanctioning the programme of the Bund—it merely agreed to leave the question open for the time being. The brave Kossovsky did not have enough courage to tell the whole truth. But the facts speak for themselves. Here they are:

"An amendment was moved by Galin: 'The question of the national programme *is left open in view of the fact that it is not being examined* by the congress.' (*For*—50 votes, *against*—32.)

"*Voice*: What does that mean—open?

"*Chairman*: When we say that the national question is left open, it means that the Bund may maintain its decision on this question until the next congress"* (our italics.—*J. St.*).

As you see, the congress even did "not examine" the question of the national programme of the Bund—it simply left it "open," leaving the Bund itself to decide the fate of its programme until the next general congress met. In other words, the Stockholm Congress avoided the question, expressing no opinion on cultural-national autonomy one way or another.

The conference of the Liquidators, however, most definitely undertakes to give an opinion on the matter, declares cultural-national autonomy to be acceptable, and endorses it in the name of the Party programme.

The difference is only too evident.

Thus, in spite of all its artifices, the conference of the Liquidators did not advance the national question a single step.

All it could do was to squirm before the Bund and the Caucasian national-Liquidators.

---

* See *Nashe Slovo*, No. 8, 1906, p. 53.

VII

THE NATIONAL QUESTION IN RUSSIA

It remains for us to suggest a positive solution of the national question.

We take as our starting point that the question can be solved only in intimate connection with the present situation in Russia.

Russia is in a transitional period, when "normal," "constitutional" life has not yet been established and when the political crisis has not yet been settled. Days of storm and "complications" are ahead. And this gives rise to the movement, the present and the future movement, the aim of which is to achieve complete democratization.

It is in connection with this movement that the national question must be examined.

Thus the complete democratization of the country is the *basis* and condition for the solution of the national question.

When seeking a solution of the question we must take into account not only the situation at home but also the situation abroad. Russia is situated between Europe and Asia, between Austria and China. The growth of democracy in Asia is inevitable. The growth of imperialism in Europe is not fortuitous. In Europe, capital is beginning to feel cramped, and it is reaching out towards foreign countries in search of new markets, cheap labour and new fields of investment. But this leads to external complications and to war. No one can assert that the Balkan War[143] is the end and not the beginning of the complications. It is quite possible, therefore, that a combination of internal and external conditions may arise in which one or another nationality in Russia may find it necessary to raise and settle the question of its independence. And, of course, it is not for Marxists to create obstacles in such cases.

But it follows that Russian Marxists cannot dispense with the right of nations to self-determination.

Thus, *the right of self-determination is an essential element* in the solution of the national question.

Further. What must be our attitude towards nations which for one reason or another will prefer to remain within the framework of the whole?

We have seen that cultural-national autonomy is unsuitable. Firstly, it is artificial and impracticable, for it proposes artificially to draw into a single nation people whom the march of events, real events, is disuniting and dispersing to every corner of the country. Secondly, it stimulates nationalism, because it leads to the viewpoint in favour of the "demarcation" of people according to national curiae, the "organization" of nations, the "preservation" and cultivation of "national peculiarities"—all of which are entirely incompatible with Social-Democracy. It is not fortuitous that the Moravian separatists in the Reichsrat, having severed themselves from the German Social-Democratic deputies, have united with the Moravian bourgeois deputies to form a single, so to speak, Moravian "kolo." Nor is it fortuitous that the separatists of the Bund have got themselves involved in nationalism by acclaiming the "Sabbath" and "Yiddish." There are no Bundist deputies yet in the Duma, but in the Bund area there is a clerical-reactionary Jewish community, in the "controlling institutions" of which the Bund is arranging, for a beginning, a "get-together" of the Jewish workers and bourgeois.* Such is the logic of cultural-national autonomy.

Thus, *national* autonomy does not solve the problem.

What, then, is the way out?

The only correct solution is *regional* autonomy, autonomy for such crystallized units as Poland, Lithuania, the Ukraine, the Caucasus, etc.

The advantage of regional autonomy consists, first of all, in the fact that it does not deal with a fiction bereft of territory, but with a definite population inhabiting a definite territory. Next, it does not divide people according to nations, it does not strengthen national barriers; on the contrary, it breaks down these barriers and unites the population in such a manner as to open the way for division of a different kind, division according to classes. Finally, it makes it possible to utilize the natural wealth of the region and to develop its productive forces in the best possible way without awaiting the decisions of a common centre— functions which are not inherent features of cultural-national autonomy.

Thus, *regional autonomy is an essential element* in the solution of the national question.

Of course, not one of the regions constitutes a compact, homogeneous nation, for each is interspersed with national minorities. Such are the Jews in Poland, the

---

* See *Report of the Eighth Conference of the Bund*, the concluding part of the resolution on the community.

Letts in Lithuania, the Russians in the Caucasus, the Poles in the Ukraine, and so on. It may be feared, therefore, that the minorities will be oppressed by the national majorities. But there will be grounds for fear only if the old order continues to prevail in the country. Give the country complete democracy and all grounds for fear will vanish.

It is proposed to bind the dispersed minorities into a single national union. But what the minorities want is not an artificial union, but real rights in the localities they inhabit. What can such a union give them *without* complete democratization? On the other hand, what need is there for a national union *when there is* complete democratization?

What is it that particularly agitates a national minority?

A minority is discontented not because there is no national union but because it does not enjoy the right to use its native language. Permit it to use its native language and the discontent will pass of itself.

A minority is discontented not because there is no artificial union but because it does not possess its own schools. Give it its own schools and all grounds for discontent will disappear.

A minority is discontented not because there is no national union, but because it does not enjoy liberty of conscience (religious liberty), liberty of movement, etc. Give it these liberties and it will cease to be discontented.

Thus, *equal rights of nations in all forms (language, schools, etc.) is an essential element* in the solution of the national question. Consequently, a state law based on complete democratization of the country is required, prohibiting all national privileges without exception and every kind of disability or restriction on the rights of national minorities.

That, and that alone, is the real, not a paper guarantee of the rights of a minority.

One may or may not dispute the existence of a logical connection between organizational federalism and cultural-national autonomy. But one cannot dispute the fact that the latter creates an atmosphere favouring unlimited federalism, developing into complete rupture, into separatism. If the Czechs in Austria and the Bundists in Russia began with autonomy, passed to federation and ended in separatism, there can be no doubt that an important part in this was played by the nationalist atmosphere that is naturally generated by cultural-national autonomy. It is not fortuitous that national autonomy and organizational federalism go hand in hand. It is quite understandable. Both demand demarcation according to nationalities. Both presume organization according to nationalities. The similarity is beyond question. The only difference is that in one case the population as a whole is divided, while in the other it is the Social-Democratic workers who are divided.

We know where the demarcation of workers according to nationalities leads to. The disintegration of a united workers' party, the splitting of trade unions according to nationalities, aggravation of national friction, national strike-breaking, complete demoralization within the ranks of Social-Democracy—such are the results of organizational federalism. This is eloquently borne out by the history of Social-Democracy in Austria and the activities of the Bund in Russia.

The only cure for this is organization on the basis of internationalism.

To unite locally the workers of all nationalities of Russia into *single, integral* collective bodies, to unite these collective bodies into a *single* party—such is the task.

It goes without saying that a party structure of this kind does not preclude, but on the contrary presumes, wide autonomy for the *regions* within the single integral party.

The experience of the Caucasus proves the expediency of this type of organization. If the Caucasians have succeeded in overcoming the national friction between the Armenian and Tatar workers; if they have succeeded in safeguarding the population against the possibility of massacres and shooting affrays; if in Baku, that kaleidoscope of national groups, national conflicts are now no longer possible, and if it has been possible to draw the workers there into the single current of a powerful movement, then the international structure of the Caucasian Social-Democracy was not the least factor in bringing this about.

The type of organization influences not only practical work. It stamps an indelible impress on the whole mental life of the worker. The worker lives the life of his organization, which stimulates his intellectual growth and educates him. And thus, acting within his organization and continually meeting there comrades from other nationalities, and side by side with them waging a common struggle under the leadership of a common collective body, he becomes deeply imbued with the idea that workers are *primarily* members of one class family, members of the united army of socialism. And this cannot but have a tremendous educational value for large sections of the working class.

Therefore, the international type of organization serves as a school of fraternal sentiments and is a tremendous agitational factor on behalf of internationalism.

But this is not the case with an organization on the basis of nationalities. When the workers are organized according to nationality they isolate themselves within their national shells, fenced off from each other by organizational barriers. The stress is laid not on what is *common* to the workers but on what distinguishes them from each other. In this type of organization the worker is *primarily* a member of his nation: a Jew, a Pole, and so on. It is not surprising that *national* federalism in organization inculcates in the workers a spirit of national seclusion.

Therefore, the national type of organization is a school of national narrow-mindedness and stagnation.

Thus we are confronted by two *fundamentally* different types of organization: the type based on international solidarity and the type based on the organizational "demarcation" of the workers according to nationalities.

Attempts to reconcile these two types have so far been vain. The compromise rules of the Austrian Social-Democratic Party drawn up in Wimberg in 1897 were left hanging in the air. The Austrian party fell to pieces and dragged the trade unions with it. "Compromise" proved to be not only utopian, but harmful. Strasser is right when

he says that "separatism achieved its first triumph at
the Wimberg Party Congress."* The same is true in
Russia. The "compromise" with the federalism of the
Bund which took place at the Stockholm Congress ended
in a complete fiasco. The Bund violated the Stockholm
compromise. Ever since the Stockholm Congress the
Bund has been an obstacle in the way of union of the
workers locally in a *single* organization, which would
include workers of all nationalities. And the Bund
has obstinately persisted in its separatist tactics in
spite of the fact that in 1907 and in 1908
Russian Social-Democracy repeatedly demanded that
unity should at last be established from below
among the workers of all nationalities.[144] The Bund,
which began with organizational national autonomy,
in fact passed to federalism, only to end in complete
rupture, separatism. And by breaking with the Russian Social-Democratic Party it caused disharmony and
disorganization in the ranks of the latter. Let us recall
the Jagiello affair,[145] for instance.

The path of "compromise" must therefore be discarded as utopian and harmful.

One thing or the other: *either* the federalism of the
Bund, in which case the Russian Social-Democratic
Party must re-form itself on a basis of "demarcation" of
the workers according to nationalities; *or* an international
type of organization, in which case the Bund must reform itself on a basis of territorial autonomy after the
pattern of the Caucasian, Lettish and Polish Social-
Democracies, and thus make possible the direct

---

* See his *Der Arbeiter und die Nation*, 1912.

union of the Jewish workers with the workers of the other nationalities of Russia.

There is no middle course: principles triumph, they do not "compromise."

Thus, *the principle of international solidarity of the workers is an essential element* in the solution of the national question.

Vienna, January 1913

First published in *Prosveshcheniye*,[146]
Nos. 3-5, March-May 1913

Signed: *K. Stalin*

THE SITUATION
IN THE SOCIAL-DEMOCRATIC GROUP
IN THE DUMA

In *Pravda*, No. 44, a "statement" appeared from the seven Social-Democratic deputies in the Duma in which they attack the six workers' deputies.[147]

In the same issue of *Pravda* the six workers' deputies answer the seven and describe their attack as the first step towards a split.

Thus, the workers are faced with the question whether there is or is not to be a united Social-Democratic group in the Duma.

Until now the Social-Democratic group has been united, and has been strong in its unity, sufficiently strong to make the enemies of the proletariat reckon with it.

Now it may break up into two parts, to the amusement and joy of the enemies. . . .

What has happened? Why have the members of the Social-Democratic group fallen out so sharply? What induced the seven deputies to attack their comrades in the columns of a newspaper, in front of the enemies of the working class?

They raise two questions in their "statement": the question about contributing to *Luch* and *Pravda*, and the question of merging these two papers.

The seven deputies are of the opinion that it is the duty of the Social-Democratic deputies to contribute to both papers, and that the refusal of the six deputies to contribute to *Luch* is a violation of the unity of the Social-Democratic group.

But is that so? Are the seven deputies right?

Firstly, is it not strange to expect someone to contribute to a newspaper whose policy he not only does not agree with, but considers harmful? Can the orthodox Bebel, for example, be compelled to contribute to a revisionist paper, or can the revisionist Vollmar be compelled to contribute to an orthodox newspaper? In Germany they would laugh at such a demand, because there they know that united action does not preclude differences of opinion. In this country, however . . . in this country, thank God, we are not yet cultured.

Secondly, we have the direct guidance of experience in Russia, which shows that it is possible for deputies to contribute to two different papers without undermining the unity of the group. We have in mind the third group.[148] It is no secret to anyone that of the 13 members of the Social-Democratic group in the Third Duma, nine contributed *only* to *Zvezda*, two only to *Zhivoye Delo*,[149] while the remaining two refrained entirely from contributing to either newspaper. . . . For all that, however, this did not undermine the unity of the third group one iota! The group, all the time, acted as one.

Obviously, the seven deputies are on a false path in demanding that contributing to *Luch* should be obligatory. Apparently, they are still not quite clear on the question.

Further, the seven deputies demand that *Pravda* and *Luch* should be merged in one, non-factional newspaper.

But how should they be merged? Is it possible to merge them in one newspaper?

Do the seven deputies, these "ideological supporters" of *Luch*, really not know that *Luch* is the first to reject such a merger? Have they read No. 108 of *Luch*, which contains the statement that *"unity cannot be achieved by mere mechanical measures, such as the merging of the two organs, etc."*?

If they have read it, how can they talk seriously about a merger?

Secondly, are the seven deputies aware of the liquidationist leaders' attitude towards unity in general, and towards having one common organ in particular?

Listen to what P. Axelrod, the inspirer of *Luch*, says. Here is what he wrote in *Nevsky Golos*, No. 6, when a section of the St. Petersburg workers decided to publish one non-factional newspaper to offset *Zvezda* and *Zhivoye Delo*:

"The idea of a non-factional Social-Democratic organ is at the present time a utopia and, moreover, a utopia which objectively runs counter to the interests of Party-political development and the organizational unity of the proletariat under the banner of Social-Democracy. Drive nature out of the door and it will fly in through the window. . . . Can the proposed workers' organ take a neutral stand between the two opposite camps? . . . Obviously not" (see *Nevsky Golos*, No. 6).

Thus, according to Axelrod, one common newspaper is not only impossible but harmful, because it "runs counter to the interests of the political development of the proletariat."

Let us hear what the other inspirer of *Luch*, the notorious Dan, has to say.

"Great political tasks," he writes, "make inevitable a relentless war against anti-Liquidationism. . . . Anti-Liquidationism is a constant brake, constant disruption." It is necessary. . . "to exert every effort to kill it in embryo" (see *Nasha Zarya*, No. 6, 1911).

Thus, "relentless *war* against anti-Liquidationism," i.e., against *Pravda*, "*to kill* anti-Liquidationism," i.e., *Pravda*—that is what Dan proposes.

After all this, how can the seven deputies talk seriously about merging the two newspapers?

Whom do they want to merge, to unite?

One thing or the other:

Either they have not yet understood the question and have not yet managed to grasp the stand taken by *Luch*, whose supporters they claim to be—and in that case they themselves "know not what they do."

Or they are true *Luch*-ists, are ready with Dan "to kill anti-Liquidationism"; like Axelrod, do not believe that a single paper is possible, but talk *loudly* about unity in order *surreptitiously* to prepare the ground for a split in the Duma group. . . .

Be that as it may, one thing is beyond doubt: the workers are confronted with the question of maintaining the integrity of the Social-Democratic group, which is threatened with disruption.

The group is in danger!

Who can save the group, who can safeguard the integrity of the group?

The workers, and the workers alone! Nobody but the workers!

Hence, it is the duty of the class-conscious workers to raise their voices against the splitting efforts within the group, no matter from what quarter they come.

It is the duty of the class-conscious workers to call to order the seven Social-Democratic deputies who are attacking the other half of the Social-Democratic group.

The workers must intervene in the matter forthwith in order to safeguard the unity of the group.

It is impossible to remain silent now. More than that—silence now is a crime.

Pravda, No. 47,   Reprinted from the newspaper
February 26, 1913
Signed: *K. Stalin*

THE ANNIVERSARY
OF THE LENA MASSACRE[150]

Comrades!

A year has passed since 500 of our comrades were shot down on the Lena. On April 4, 1912, 500 of our brothers in the Lena goldfields were shot down for declaring a peaceful economic strike, shot down by order of the Russian tsar to please a handful of millionaires.

Gendarme Captain Treshchenko, who perpetrated this massacre in the name of the tsar and who received high awards from the government and generous rewards from the gold-mine owners, is now frequenting aristocratic bars and waiting for an appointment as a chief of a department in the Secret Service. On the spur of the moment a promise was made to provide for the families of the murdered men, but this turned out to be an insolent lie. A promise was made to introduce state insurance for the workers on the Lena, but it turned out to be a fraud. A promise was made to "investigate" the affair, but actually even the investigation made by their own envoy, Senator Manukhin, was hushed up.

"So it was, so it will be," was the Minister-butcher Makarov's retort from the floor of the Duma. And he proved to be right: the tsar and his mininsters were, and will be, liars, perjurers, shedders of blood, a camarilla which carries out the will of a handful of brutal land-lords and millionaires.

On January 9, 1905, faith in the old, pre-revolution autocracy was killed by the shooting in the Winter Palace Square in St. Petersburg.

On April 4, 1912, faith in the present, "renovated," post-revolution autocracy was killed by the shooting on the distant Lena.

All those who believed that we were already living under a constitutional system, all those who believed that the old atrocities were no longer possible, became convinced that this was not so, that the tsarist gang was still lording it over the great Russian people, that the Nicholas Romanov monarchy was still demanding for its altar the sacrifice of hundreds and thousands of Russian workers and peasants, that the whips and bullets of the tsar's hirelings—of the Treshchenkos who were displaying their prowess against unarmed Russian citizens—were still swishing and whistling all over Russia.

The shooting on the Lena opened a new page in our history. The cup of patience was filled to overflowing. The sluice gates of popular indignation were burst open. The river of popular anger began to flood. The words of that tsar's flunkey Makarov, "So it was, so it will be," poured oil on the flames. Their effect was the same as that produced in 1905 by the order of that other blood-hound of the tsar, Trepov: "Spare no bullets!" The labour movement began to surge and foam like a stormy sea. The Russian workers retaliated to the Lena shooting by a united protest strike in which nearly half a million joined. And they held aloft our old red banner on which the working class once again inscribed the three chief demands of the Russian Revolution:

An eight-hour day—for the workers.

Confiscation of all landlords' and tsar's land—for the peasants.

A democratic republic—for the whole people!

A year of struggle lies behind us. Looking back we can say with gratification: a beginning has been made, the year has not passed in vain.

The Lena strike merged with the May Day strike. The glorious May Day of 1912 inscribed a golden page in the history of our labour movement. Since that time the struggle has not waned for a moment. Political strikes are spreading and growing. In answer to the shooting of the 16 sailors in Sevastopol, 150,000 workers came out in a revolutionary strike, thereby proclaiming the alliance between the revolutionary proletariat and the revolutionary armed forces. By means of a strike, the St. Petersburg proletariat expressed their protest against the trickery with the elections to the Duma from the workers' curiae. On the day of the opening of the Fourth Duma,[151] on the day the Social-Democratic group moved an interpellation on the insurance question, the workers of St. Petersburg organized one-day strikes and demonstrations. And lastly, on January 9, 1913, as many as 200,000 Russian workers went on strike in honour of the memory of the fallen fighters, calling on all democratic Russia to launch a fresh struggle.

Such is the main result of 1912.

Comrades! The first anniversary of the Lena massacre is drawing near. We must make our voices heard on that day in one way or another. It is our duty to do so.

We must show that we honour the memory of our murdered comrades. We must show that we have not forgotten that bloody April 4, just as we have not forgotten Bloody Sunday, January 9.

We must mark the Lena anniversary everywhere by meetings, demonstrations, collections of money, and so forth.

And let the whole of working-class Russia on that day join in one mighty shout:

Down With the Romanov Monarchy!
Long Live the New Revolution!
Long Live the Democratic Republic!
Glory to the Fallen Fighters!

The Central Committee of the R.S.D.L.P.

Reprint and Distribute!
Prepare to Celebrate the First of May!

Written in January-February
1913

Reprinted from a hectographed
copy of the leaflet

NOTES

¹ K. Kautsky's pamphlet was translated into Georgian and published in Tiflis in March 1907. No. 7 of the Bolshevik newspaper *Dro*, of March 18, 1907, announced the publication of K. Kautsky's pamphlet in the Georgian language with a preface by Koba (J. V. Stalin). p. *1*

² Cadets—the abbreviated title of the Constitutional-Democratic Party—the principal party of the liberal-monarchist bourgeoisie, formed in October 1905 (see J. V. Stalin, *Works*, Vol. 1, p. 405, Note 52). p. *5*

³ *First Symposium*—a Menshevik symposium, published in St. Petersburg in 1906. **p.** *6*

⁴ *Nashe Delo* (*Our Cause*)—a weekly Menshevik journal published in Moscow from September 24 to November 25, 1906. p. *7*

⁵ *Tovarishch* (*Comrade*)—a daily newspaper published in St. Petersburg from March 1906 till December 1907. Although not officially the organ of any party, it was actually the organ of the Left-wing Cadets. Mensheviks also contributed to the newspaper. p. *7*

⁶ *Otkliki* (*Echoes*)—Menshevik symposia published in St. Petersburg in 1906-07. Three volumes were issued. p. *9*

⁷ *Mir Bozhy* (*God's World*)—a monthly magazine of a liberal trend, began publication in St. Petersburg in 1892. In the

'90's of the nineteenth century it published articles by the
"legal Marxists." During the 1905 revolution, Mensheviks
contributed to the magazine. From 1906 to 1918 it was published under the name of *Sovremenny Mir* (*The Contemporary
World*).

p. *9*

8 *Golos Truda* (*The Voice of Labour*)—a Menshevik newspaper
published in St. Petersburg from June 21 to July 7, 1906.

p. *11*

9 Trudoviks or Group of Toil—a group of petty-bourgeois democrats formed in April 1906, consisting of the peasant deputies in the First State Duma (see J. V. Stalin, *Works*,
Vol. 1, p. 266, Note 77).

Popular Socialists—a petty-bourgeois organization which
split off from the Right wing of the Socialist-Revolutionary Party in 1906. Their political demands did not go beyond
a constitutional monarchy. Lenin called them "Social-Cadets"
and "Socialist-Revolutionary Mensheviks."   p. *14*

10 This refers to the Social-Democratic conference held in St.
Petersburg on January 6, 1907, to discuss the tactics to be
pursued in the elections to the Second State Duma. The conference was attended by 40 Bolsheviks and 31 Mensheviks.
The Central Committee of the R.S.D.L.P., on which the Mensheviks were in the majority, proposed that the conference
should divide up into a city and gubernia conference. The
Mensheviks counted on gaining a larger number of votes in
this way. The conference rejected this proposal as being
contrary to the Party Rules. In protest against this
the Menshevik delegates left the meeting. The remaining
delegates resolved to continue the conference. After hearing
a report by V. I. Lenin, the conference expressed itself against
concluding election agreements with the Cadets on the ground
that such agreements would not only be impermissible in principle, but also positively harmful politically. It adopted a resolution "to bring up forthwith the extremely important question for St. Petersburg of agreements with the revolutionary

democracy." The Menshevik representatives of the Central Committee who were present at the conference declared that the decisions of the conference were not binding on the St. Petersburg Social-Democratic organization, and the Mensheviks who left the conference advocated in the press the conclusion of a bloc with the Cadets. p. *16*

[11] *Rech (Speech)*—a daily newspaper, the central organ of the Cadet Party, published in St. Petersburg from February 1906 to October 26, 1917. p. *17*

[12] *Chveni Tskhovreba (Our Life)*—a Georgian daily Bolshevik newspaper published legally in Tiflis under the direction of J. V. Stalin; it began publication on February 18, 1907. In all, thirteen numbers were issued. It was suppressed on March 6, 1907, for its "extremist trend." p. *20*

[13] *Na Ocheredi (On the Order of the Day)*—a Menshevik weekly published in St. Petersburg from December 1906 to March 1907. Four issues in all were published. p. *21*

[14] *Dro (Time)*—a Georgian daily Bolshevik newspaper, published in Tiflis after the suppression of *Chveni Tskhovreba* from March 11 to April 15, 1907, under the direction of J. V. Stalin. M. Tskhakaya and M. Davitashvili were members of the editorial staff. In all, 31 numbers were issued. p. *22*

[15] See Karl Marx and Frederick Engels, *Selected Works*, Eng. ed., Vol. I, Moscow 1951, pp. 64, 65.
Neue Rheinische Zeitung was published in Cologne from June 1, 1848 to May 19, 1849, and was directed by K. Marx and F. Engels. p. *24*

[16] Gurko—Deputy-Minister of the Interior; Lidval—a big speculator and swindler who in 1906 received from Gurko a contract to supply grain to the famine-stricken areas. The complicity of a high official of the tsarist government in Lidval's speculations led to a sensational trial which was called the

"Lidvaliad." Gurko suffered no other consequences than removal from his post. p. 25

[17] The Octobrists, or the Union of October Seventeenth—a counter-revolutionary party of the big commercial and industrial bourgeoisie and the big landowners was formed in November 1905. It fully supported the Stolypin regime, the home and foreign policy of tsarism. p. 25

[18] *Parus* (*The Sail*)—a daily newspaper, organ of the Cadets, published in Moscow in 1907. p. 25

[19] *Segodnya* (*Today*)—a gutter-type bourgeois evening newspaper published in St. Petersburg in 1906-08. p. 26

[20] *Slovo* (*The Word*)—a daily newspaper which began publication in St. Petersburg in December 1904. From October 1905 to July 1906 it was the organ of the Octobrist Party. p. 26

[21] G. P. Telia was born in 1880 and died in Sukhum on March 19, 1907. He was buried on March 25 in the village of Chagani, Kutais Uyezd. p. 28

[22] This refers to the First of May demonstration of the Tiflis workers which took place on April 22, 1901, under the direct leadership of J. V. Stalin. The demonstration was held in the Soldatsky market place, in the central part of Tiflis, and about 2,000 persons took part in it. During the demonstration a clash occurred with the police and troops. Fourteen workers were injured and over 50 were arrested. Reporting the Tiflis demonstration, Lenin's *Iskra* stated: "The events that occurred on Sunday April 22 (Old Style) in Tiflis are of historical significance for the whole of the Caucasus: on that day the open revolutionary movement commenced in the Caucasus" (*Iskra*, No. 6, July 1901). p. 29

[23] On February 23, 1903, in conformity with the decision adopted by the Tiflis Committee of the R.S.D.L.P., a demonstration of Tiflis workers was held. About 6,000 persons took part in

the demonstration, which ended in a collision with troops; 150 persons were arrested.   p. *29*

24 *Proletariatis Brdzola (The Proletarian Struggle)*—an illegal Georgian newspaper, the organ of the Caucasian Union of the R.S.D.L.P. (see J. V. Stalin, *Works*, Vol. 1, p. 398, Note 21).   ·   p. *31*

25 *Akhali Tskhovreba (New Life)*—a Georgian daily Bolshevik newspaper published in Tiflis from June 20 to July 14, 1906. Twenty issues appeared. The paper was directed by J. V. Stalin. M. Davitashvili, G. Telia, G. Kikodze and others were regular contributors.   p. *31*

26 The Fifth Congress of the R.S.D.L.P. was held in London from April 30 to May 19, 1907. On all the main questions the congress adopted Bolshevik resolutions. J. V. Stalin was present at the congress as the delegate from the Tiflis organization. He summed up the proceedings of the congress in his article "The London Congress of the R.S.D.L.P. (Notes of a Delegate)," (see pp. 47-80 of this volume).   p. *33*

27 The Bund—The General Jewish Workers' Union of Poland, Lithuania, and Russia—was formed in October 1897 (see J. V. Stalin, *Works*, Vol. 1, p. 394, Note 7).   p. *33*

28 Spilka—the Ukrainian Social-Democratic League, which stood close to the Mensheviks, was formed at the end of 1904 as a result of a break away from the petty-bourgeois nationalist Revolutionary Ukrainian Party (RUP). Ceased to exist during the Stolypin reaction.   p. *33*

29 *Lakhvari (The Spear)*—a Georgian daily Menshevik newspaper published in Tiflis from April to June 1907.   p. *36*

30 *Skhivi (The Ray)*—a daily newspaper published by the Georgian Mensheviks in Tiflis from December 1905 to January 1906.   p. *40*

31 The Second State Duma was dispersed by the tsarist government on June 3, 1907. The Social-Democratic group in the Duma, consisting of 65 deputies, was falsely charged with armed conspiracy. Most of the Social-Democratic deputies were sentenced to penal servitude and permanent exile.   p. *42*

32 The article "The London Congress of the R.S.D.L.P. (Notes of a Delegate)" was not finished. Its completion was prevented by the intensified police shadowing of J. V. Stalin in the latter half of 1907 and his subsequent arrest.   p. *47*

33 A. Vergezhsky—the nom de plume of A. V. Tyrkova; she was a contributor to the Cadet newspaper *Rech*.   p. *47*

34 E. D. Kuskova—one of the authors of the programme of the Economists known as the "Credo." In 1906-07 she was a contributor to semi-Cadet and semi-Menshevik newspapers and journals.   p. *47*

35 G. A. Alexinsky—a member of the Bolshevik section of the Social-Democratic group in the Second State Duma. After the London Congress of the R.S.D.L.P. he advocated the tactics of boycotting the Third State Duma. Subsequently, he left the Bolshevik Party. After the October Socialist Revolution he became a White émigré.   p. *52*

36 The question of the Stuttgart International Socialist Congress (the Seventh Congress of the Second International) was originally included in the agenda of the London Congress of the R.S.D.L.P. but was subsequently withdrawn by the congress. The Stuttgart Congress took place in August 5-11 (18-24), 1907. The Bolsheviks were represented by V. I. Lenin, A. V. Lunacharsky, M. M. Litvinov and others.   p. *55*

37 Ryadovoi ("rank-and-filer")—the pseudonym of A. A. Malinovsky, better known as Bogdanov. (He also used the pseudonym of Maximov.) Joined the Bolsheviks in 1903, but

left the Bolshevik Party after the London Congress of the R.S.D.L.P. (see Note 80 in this volume). Died in 1928. p. *55*

[38] Concerning the split in the St. Petersburg organization, see J. V. Stalin's article "The Election Campaign in St. Petersburg and the Mensheviks" (see pp. 14-20 of this volume).

p. *56*

[39] Draft appeal on the land question "In the Name of the State Duma" that was drawn up by the Cadets and published on July 5, 1906, in answer to the government's announcement of June 20, 1906, concerning peasant land ownership. The Cadets urged the peasants to take no action until the Duma had finally drafted the land law. The Central Committee of the R.S.D.L.P., which was controlled by the Mensheviks, instructed the Social-Democratic group in the Duma to support the Cadets' appeal. The group, however, voted against it. p. *57*

[40] Narodovtsy (National-Democrats)—the counter-revolutionary nationalist party of the Polish bourgeoisie formed in 1897. During the revolution of 1905-07 it became the principal party of the Polish counter-revolution, the party of the Polish Black Hundreds. p. *60*

[41] This refers to the speeches delivered at the Fifth (London) Congress of the R.S.D.L.P. by the Menshevik deputies in the Second State Duma A. L. Japaridze and I. G. Tsereteli (see *Minutes of the Fifth Congress of the R.S.D.L.P.*, 1935, Russ. ed., pp. 250 and 354-355). p. *60*

[42] Guesdists—the supporters of Jules Guesde, the Left-wing Marxist trend in the ranks of the French Socialists. In 1901 the Guesdists founded the Socialist Party of France. They fought the opportunists in the French labour movement and opposed the policy of concluding agreements with the bourgeoisie and of Socialists entering bourgeois governments. On the outbreak of the world imperialist war Guesde took a national-defence stand and entered the bourgeois government. A

section of the Guesdists who remained true to revolutionary Marxism subsequently joined the Communist Party of France.

p. *66*

43 This refers to an article by Yuri Pereyaslavsky (G. Khrustalyov).

Bakinsky Dyen (The Baku Day)—a daily liberal newspaper published from June 1907 to January 1908. p. *70*

44 Y. Larin, also L. A. Rin, the pseudonyms of M. A. Lourier—a Menshevik Liquidator who in 1907 advocated the convocation of a "broad labour congress." In 1917 Y. Larin joined the Bolshevik Party.

El (I. I. Luzin)—a Menshevik Liquidator. p. *71*

45 This refers to the pamphlet *The All-Russian Labour Congress and the "Bolsheviks"* published in Georgian in Tiflis in 1907. "Brodyaga" ("Tramp")—the nom de plume of the Menshevik Georgy Eradze. "Shura," the pseudonym of the Menshevik Pyshkina, wife of Eradze. p. *71*

46 Cherevanin's article on the Labour Congress was published in the Menshevik symposium *The Political Situation and Tactical Problems*, Moscow 1906. p. *74*

47 Lindov—the pseudonym of G. D. Leiteisen. p. *76*

48 In the autumn of 1907 the Baku Committee, under the direction of Comrade Stalin, conducted the election campaign for the Third State Duma. The meeting of voters' delegates representing the Baku workers held on September 22 elected Bolsheviks as electors who were finally to choose the workers' deputy for the Duma. The "Mandate," which was drawn up by J. V. Stalin, was adopted at this meeting and printed in leaflet form at the printing plant of the Balakhany District Committee of the R.S.D.L.P. p. *81*

49 This article was written in connection with the proposed convocation of a conference of the oil owners with representatives of the Baku workers. The tactics of boycotting the conference, which the Bolsheviks pursued at that time, met with wide support among the masses of the workers. From October 10 to November 1, 1907, meetings of workers were held in the oil fields and works in Baku to discuss the question of the conference. Two-thirds of the workers attending these meetings expressed themselves against participating in the conference. The Mensheviks, who advocated participation in the conference at all costs, sustained defeat.   p. *84*

[50] Oil workers—the workers employed in boring oil wells and bailing oil. Mechanics—the workers employed in the machine shops, electric power stations and other auxiliary plants serving the oil wells.   p. *86*

[51] "Beshkesh" (gift)—the term applied to the system, widely practised by the Baku oil owners, of giving the workers small sops in the form of bonuses with the object of keeping them out of the political struggle and of splitting the labour movement. The amounts of these bonuses varied and were fixed entirely at the discretion of the employer. The Bolsheviks strongly opposed the inclusion of bonuses in strike demands and fought for increases in basic wage rates.   p. *87*

[52] Kochegar (stoker)—the pseudonym of I. Shitikov (Samartsev)—the official editor and publisher of the newspaper *Gudok*.   p. *88*

[53] *Neftyanoye Delo (Oil Affairs)*—the organ of the oil owners, published by the Council of the Congress of Oil Owners in Baku in 1899-1920.

The Council of the Congress, the organization of the oil owners, was elected at congresses of oil owners from among the representatives of the biggest firms. It was the function of the Council to wage an organized struggle against the working class, to protect the interests of the oil owners in dealings with the government, to ensure high profits for the oil owners, etc.   p. *90*

[54] Dashnaktsakans, or Dashnaks—members of the Armenian bourgeois nationalist party known as the Dashnaktsutyun.

In fighting for the interests of the Armenian bourgeoisie, the
Dashnaks stirred up national strife among the working people
of Transcaucasia.   p. *91*

55 In November 1907 the Baku Bolsheviks headed by J. V. Stalin
issued the slogan: "A conference with guarantees, or no conference at all." The terms on which the workers agreed to
participate in the conference were the following: active participation in the conference campaign by the trade unions, the
wide discussion of demands by the workers, freedom to convene
the future Delegate Council, the date of the conference to be
chosen by the workers. An extensive campaign was instituted
in the Baku oil fields and works for the election of the Delegate
Council which was finally to adopt the terms on which the
workers were to participate in the conference and elect representatives to the organization commission which was to convene the conference. These delegates were elected at open
meetings. The majority of the workers voted for the line proposed by the Bolsheviks. The Dashnaks and Socialist-Revolutionaries, who advocated a boycott of the conference, and
the Mensheviks, who were in favour of a conference without
any guarantees, found no support among the masses. p. *100*

56 *Gudok* (*The Siren*)—a legal Bolshevik weekly newspaper, the
organ of the Baku oil industry workers' union. No. 1 of *Gudok*
was issued on August 12, 1907. The paper published a number
of leading articles written by J. V. Stalin which are included
in the present volume. Frequent contributors to the paper
were S. Shaumyan, A. Japaridze, S. Spandaryan, and others.
No. 34, the last issue to be published under Bolshevik editor-
ship, appeared on June 1, 1908. After that *Gudok* passed into
Menshevik hands. The Bolsheviks began to issue in Baku
a new legal trade union newspaper called *Bakinsky Rabo-
chy* (*The Baku Worker*), the first number of which came out
on September 6, 1908.   p. *101*

57 As many as 1,500 workers took part in a strike at the Mirzoyev
oil fields in Baku. The strike began on February 14, 1908, and
lasted 73 days.   p. *102*

[58] The election of the workers' delegates was concluded in the beginning of February 1908, but the convocation of the Delegate Council was postponed by order of Vorontsov-Dashkov, the Viceroy of the Caucasus. The first meeting of the Council took place on March 30, 1908, and the ensuing ones on April 6, 10, 26 and 29. Subsequently, G. K. Ordjonikidze wrote concerning the proceedings of the Council as follows: "While dark reaction was rampant all over Russia, in Baku a real workers' parliament was in session. In this parliament all the demands of the Baku workers were openly formulated and our speakers expounded our whole minimum programme." In the Council 199 delegates voted for the Bolshevik proposal for a conference with guarantees, and 124 votes were cast for the proposal to boycott the conference. The supporters of a boycott—the Socialist-Revolutionaries and Dashnaks—left the meeting. The proposal to present the Mandate as an ultimatum was adopted by 113 votes against 54.   p. *110*

[59] *Promyslovy Vestnik (Oil-Field News)*—a legal Menshevik newspaper, the organ of the mechanics' union, published in Baku two or three times a week in November and December 1907 and from March to July 1908.   p. *112*

[60] K—za (P. Kara-Murza)—a member of the Cadet Party, editor of *Neftyanoye Delo*, the organ of the Baku oil owners. p. *117*

[61] "Kochi"—robber, a hired assassin.   p. *120*

[62] Khanlar Safaraliyev—a Bolshevik working man and talented organizer of the Azerbaijan workers. After a successful strike at the Naphtha oil fields he, on the night of September 19, 1907, was mortally wounded by an assassin hired by the oil owners and died several days later. In response to the appeal of the Bibi-Eibat District Committee of the R.S.D.L.P., the workers declared a general two-day strike and demanded that the Naphtha Producers' Association remove from the oil field Khanlar's murderer—the foreman driller Jafar, and also the manager Abuzarbek. Khanlar's funeral developed

into a mighty protest demonstration in which 20,000 workers participated. J. V. Stalin delivered a speech at Khanlar's graveside. *p. 125*

[63] J. V. Stalin wrote this review of the press in the summer of 1908 in the Baku jail, where he was detained from March 25 to November 9, 1908, when he was deported to Solvychegodsk. *p. 132*

[64] *Napertskali (The Spark)*—a daily newspaper published by the Georgian Mensheviks in Tiflis from May to July 1908. *p. 132*

[65] *Azri (Thought)*—a Menshevik Georgian newspaper published in Tiflis from January 29 to March 2, 1908. *p. 132*

[66] In 1904 the brothers Shendrikov (Lev, Ilya and Gleb) formed in Baku a Zubatov, i.e., police-controlled, organization known as the Organization of the Balakhany and Bibi-Eibat Workers, subsequently renamed the Baku Workers' Union. The Shendrikovs conducted a campaign of slander against the Bolsheviks. By advancing narrow craft economic slogans they disorganized the strike movement, tried to disrupt the preparations for an armed insurrection, agitated for the formation of "conciliation boards," co-operatives, etc. They were subsidized by the oil owners and the tsarist authorities. The Mensheviks officially recognized the Zubatov organization of the Shendrikovs as a party organization. The Baku Bolsheviks exposed the Shendrikovs as hirelings of the tsarist secret police and utterly defeated them.

The journal *Pravoye Delo (The Just Cause)* was published by the Shendrikovs in St. Petersburg. No. 1 appeared in November 1907, and No. 2-3 in May 1908. Groshev and Kalinin, who are mentioned later on, were Mensheviks who supported the Shendrikovs. *p. 135*

[67] A. Gukasov—one of the biggest oil owners in Baku and the leading member of the oil owners' Council of the Congress. *p. 136*

[68] The meeting of the organizing committee which was responsible for the arrangements to convene the conference with the oil owners was held on May 13, 1908. Fourteen oil owners and 15 workers were present. On that same day the newspapers published an announcement that representatives of trade unions would not be permitted to go on the committee. The workers' delegation that appeared at the meeting refused to allow the proceedings to start unless representatives of the trade unions took part. Using this refusal as a pretext, chairman of the committee Junkovsky (a member of the Caucasian Viceroy's Council) closed the meeting. p. *138*

[69] "Land and freedom," "By struggle you will achieve your rights"—the slogans of the Socialist-Revolutionary Party.

p. *140*

[70] The general strike commenced on July 1, 1903, in Baku, on July 14 in Tiflis and on July 17 in Batum. The strike affected the whole of Transcaucasia and spread to South Russia (Odessa, Kiev, Yekaterinoslav and other places). p. *141*

[71] The Baku general strike began on December 13, 1904, with strikes at the oil fields of Rothschild's, Nobel's and Mirzoyev's in the Balakhany and Bibi-Eibat oil districts. From December 14 to 18 it spread to most of the enterprises in Baku. The strike was led by J. V. Stalin. The leaflets issued by the Baku Committee during the first days of the strike contained political slogans and also the following economic demands—an eight-hour day, higher wages, abolition of fines, etc. During the strike numerous meetings of workers were held. The strike ended in a victory for the workers and the conclusion of a collective agreement between the workers and the oil owners, the first of its kind to be concluded in the history of the Russian labour movement. "This strike was like a clap of thunder heralding a great revolutionary storm" (see *History of the C.P.S.U.(B.), Short Course*, Moscow 1952, p. 94). The importance of the December strike in Baku is dealt with in detail in the present volume. See "The December Strike and the December Agreement," pp. 174-78. p. *141*

[72] *Baku*—a bourgeois newspaper published with brief inter-
ruptions from 1902 to 1918. The newspaper expressed the
interests mainly of the Armenian oil and commercial bourgeoisie. p. *147*

[73] This refers to an article entitled "The Workers' Commission
in Baku" published in No. 4 of the Georgian Menshevik newspaper *Khomli* of July 17, 1908. p. *148*

[74] L. A. Rin's (Y. Larin's) pamphlet "The Conference With the
Oil Owners" was published by the mechanics' union in 1907.
p. *148*

[75] *Proletary* (*The Proletarian*)—an illegal newspaper founded by
the Bolsheviks after the Fourth ("Unity") Congress of the Party.
It appeared from August 21 (September 3), 1906 to November 28
(December 11), 1909. Altogether 50 numbers were issued—
the first 20 in Finland, and the rest in Geneva and Paris.
Actually *Proletary* was the central organ of the Bolsheviks
and was edited by V. I. Lenin. During the Stolypin reaction
the paper played a leading role in preserving and strengthening
the Bolshevik organizations. p. *151*

[76] *Golos Sotsial-Demokrata* (*The Voice of the Social-Democrat*)—
the organ of the Menshevik Liquidators, published abroad
from February 1908 to December 1911. The editorial board
consisted of G. V. Plekhanov, P. B. Axelrod, Y. O. Martov,
F. I. Dan and A. S. Martynov. In view of the paper's pro-
nouncedly liquidationist trend, Plekhanov ceased contributing to it in December 1908 and subsequently formally
resigned from the editorial board. In spite of the decision
adopted by the Plenum of the Central Committee of the
R.S.D.L.P. in January 1910 that the paper should cease
publication, the Mensheviks continued to issue it, openly
advocating Liquidationism in its columns. p. *151*

[77] *Sotsial-Demokrat* (*The Social-Democrat*)—the Central Organ
of the R.S.D.L.P., published from February 1908 to January
1917. The first issue was published in Russia, but after that

the paper was published abroad, first in Paris and then in Geneva. In conformity with the decision of the Central Committee of the R.S.D.L.P., the editorial board of the Central Organ was constituted of representatives of the Bolsheviks, Mensheviks and Polish Social-Democrats. The paper published leading articles by V. I. Lenin. On the editorial board of the paper Lenin fought for a consistent Bolshevik line. A section of the editorial board (Kamenev and Zinoviev) took up a conciliatory attitude towards the Liquidators and tried to thwart Lenin's policy. The Mensheviks Martov and Dan sabotaged the work of the editorial board of the Central Organ and at the same time openly defended Liquidationism in the columns of *Golos Sotsial-Demokrata*. Lenin's uncompromising struggle against the Liquidators led to the resignation of Martov and Dan from the editorial board of *Sotsial-Demokrat* in June 1911. Beginning with December 1911 the paper was edited by V. I. Lenin. It published a number of articles by J. V. Stalin which are reproduced in the present volume. The *Sotsial-Demokrat* systematically published information on the work of the local Party organizations in Russia, including those in Transcaucasia. p. *151*

[78] The Third Conference of the R.S.D.L.P. (the "Second All-Russian Conference") was held on July 21-23, 1907, and the Fourth Conference of the R.S.D.L.P. (the "Third All-Russian Conference") was held on November 5-12, 1907. p. *159*

[79] This was the heading of a section of the *Bakinsky Proletary*. p. *169*

[80] The enlarged editorial board of *Proletary* was in fact the Bolshevik centre, elected at a meeting of the Bolshevik section of the Fifth (London) Congress of the R.S.D.L.P. held in 1907. The meeting of the enlarged editorial board was held in Paris on June 8-17 (21-30), 1909, under the direction of V. I. Lenin. The meeting condemned Otzovism and Ultimatumism as "Liquidationism inside out." It described the "party" school set up by the Otzovists in Capri as "the centre of a group that is breaking away from the Bolsheviks." A. Bogdanov

(supported by V. Shantser) refused to submit to the decisions of the enlarged editorial board of *Proletary* and was expelled from the Bolshevik organization.   p. *170*

81 The resolution of the Baku Committee was published in *Proletary*, No. 49, on October 3 (16), 1909, with the following editorial note: "We have not said anything different from what the Baku comrades have said about the Otzovists, Ultimatumists and God-builders. The Baku comrades themselves 'protest against the conduct of Comrade Maximov who declared that he would not submit to the decisions of the editorial board.' But if Comrade Maximov had submitted to the decisions of the organ of the Bolsheviks and had not launched a whole campaign of disruption against the Bolshevik group, there would have been no 'break-away.' 'The refusal to submit' is in itself, of course, a 'break-away.' We have discussed the question of our alleged 'splitting' policy at great length in the present issue in the article 'A Talk With St. Petersburg Bolsheviks' concerning a resolution of a similar nature which they had sent us, and which we received before the Baku resolution." The article "A Talk With St. Petersburg Bolsheviks" was written by V. I. Lenin (see V. I. Lenin, *Works*, 4th Russ. ed., Vol. 16, pp. 49-59).   p. *172*

82 "Amshara" (fellow countryman)—the common appellation given the Iranian unskilled labourers who came to work in Baku.   p. *175*

83 The "Letters From the Caucasus" were written in November-December 1909 and were intended for publication in *Proletary* or *Sotsial-Demokrat*. As *Proletary* had ceased publication by that time the "Letters" were sent to the Central Organ of the R.S.D.L.P., *Sotsial-Demokrat*. Owing to the fact that the second letter contained sharp criticism of Liquidationism, the Menshevik section of the editorial board of *Sotsial-Demokrat* refused to allow it to be published in the columns of the Central Organ and it was therefore published in *Diskussionny Listok* (*Discussion Sheet*), a supplement to *Sotsial-Demokrat*.   p. *179*

84 The regulations of June 12, 1890, concerning the Zemstvo administrative bodies,were introduced by the tsarist government in place of the regulations of 1864. The new regulations, which introduced electorates according to social estates in place of the former property qualification for election to the Zemstvo, gave the nobility an absolute majority in most of the Uyezd Zemstvo Assemblies and made the Zemstvo more dependent upon the central government. p. *183*

85 *Bakinsky Proletary (The Baku Proletarian)*—an illegal Bolshevik newspaper published in Baku from June 20, 1907 to August 27, 1909. Seven issues appeared. The first came out as the organ of the Balakhany District of the Baku organization of the R.S.D.L.P., the second as the organ of the Balakhany and Cherny Gorod districts of the Baku organization of the R.S.D.L.P., while the third and subsequent issues came out as the organ of the Baku Committee of the R.S.D.L.P. The paper was edited by J. V. Stalin, who wrote a number of leading articles for it which are reproduced in the present volume. Among the contributors were S. Shaumyan, A. Japaridze and S. Spandaryan. After the appearance of the fifth issue, publication was suspended and was resumed on August 1, 1909, when J. V. Stalin returned to Baku after his escape from exile in Solvychegodsk. No. 7, the last issue, came out on August 27, 1909. The editorial board of *Bakinsky Proletary* was closely connected with *Proletary* and *Sotsial-Demokrat*. p. *186*

86 *Trud (Labour)*—the name of the united consumers' co-operative society organized in the beginning of 1908 by the workers of the city of Baku and the Baku oil districts and having about 1,200 members. It opened branches in the Balakhany, Bibi-Eibat, Zavokzalny and Cherny Gorod districts. In 1909 the co-operative society published a weekly journal called *Trudovoi Golos (The Voice of Labour)*. The Bolsheviks took an active part in the work of this co-operative society. p. *191*

87 The aim of the clubs "Znanie—Sila" ("Knowledge Is Power") and "Nauka"("Science") was to promote self-education among the oil

industry workers.They organized general educational and technical classes, circles and lectures. They obtained their funds from
membership dues and also from receipts from lectures and theatri-
cal performances. The "Knowledge Is Power" club, which served
the oil-field districts, was directed by Bolsheviks; the "Science"
club was directed by Mensheviks.   *p. 191*

[88] The temperance congress was opened in St. Petersburg on
December 28, 1909, and lasted several days. Five hundred
and ten delegates attended. The workers' group numbered
43 delegates, of whom two represented the Baku workers.
Some of the workers' delegates were arrested by the police
immediately after the congress closed.   *p. 192*

[89] *Dasatskisi (The Beginning)*—a Georgian legal Menshevik newspaper published in Tiflis from March 4 to 30, 1908.   *p. 194*

[90] An, N. and Kostrov—pseudonyms of Noah Jordania, the leader
of the Georgian Liquidator Mensheviks.   *p. 194*

[91] G. V. Plekhanov uttered these words in a speech he delivered at
the International Socialist Congress in Paris in 1889.

                                                           p. 198

[92] This refers to the agrarian law (ukase) issued by the tsarist
Minister Stolypin on November 9, 1906, granting the peasants
the right to leave the village communities and to set up individual homesteads.   *p. 202*

[93] This refers to the plenum of the Central Committee
of the R.S.D.L.P. that was held in Paris on January 2-23
(January 15-February 5), 1910. The plenum adopted a resolution on the necessity of "abolishing all more or less
organized groups and of transforming them into trends that
will not disrupt the unity of Party activities." On the insistence
of V. I. Lenin, the plenum condemned Liquidationism and
Otzovism, although the terms "Liquidationism" and "Otzovism"
were not used in the resolution. The predominance of conciliatory elements at the plenum rendered possible the adoption
of a number of anti-Leninist decisions. In spite of V. I. Lenin's

protests, several Liquidator Mensheviks were elected to the central bodies of the Party. After this plenum the Liquidators intensified their struggle against the Party.   p. *217*

94 This refers to the decision to reorganize ("reform ") the central bodies of the Party, i.e., the Central Committee, the editorial board of the Central Organ, the Bureau of the Central Committee Abroad, and the Collegium of the Central Committee in Russia. This decision was adopted by the plenum of the Central Committee of the R.S.D.L.P. held in January 1910 (see *Resolutions and Decisions of C.P.S.U.(B.) Congresses, Conferences and Central Committee Plenums*, Part I, 6th Russ. ed., 1940, pp. 157, 158).   p. *217*

95 J. V. Stalin's term of exile was to expire at the end of June 1911.   p. *218*

96 *Mysl (Thought)*—a legal Bolshevik monthly magazine of philosophical and social-economic questions, published in Moscow from December 1910 to April 1911.Five numbers were issued.The magazine was founded by V. I. Lenin, and he was its actual director. Nos. 1-4 contained articles by him. Among the contributors were V. V. Vorovsky, M. S. Olminsky and I. I. Skvortsov-Stepanov. In addition to Bolsheviks, Plekhanov and other pro-Party Mensheviks contributed to the magazine. p. *218*

97 *Rabochaya Gazeta (The Workers' Newspaper)*—a popular Bolshevik newspaper published in Paris from October 30 (November 12), 1910 to July 30 (August 12), 1912. It was organized and directed by V. I. Lenin. The Prague Conference of the Party held in January 1912 noted the services rendered by *Rabochaya Gazeta* in defending the Party and the Party principle and recognized it as the official organ of the Central Committee of the Party.   p. *218*

98 *Zvezda (The Star)*—a legal Bolshevik newspaper published in St. Petersburg from December 16, 1910 to April 22, 1912, first as a weekly and later two or three times a week. Its activities were directed by V. I. Lenin, who regularly sent articles

for it from abroad. Regular contributors to the paper were
V. M. Molotov, M. S. Olminsky, N. G. Poletayev, N. N. Baturin, K. S. Yeremeyev, and others. Contributions were also
received from Maxim Gorky. In the spring of 1912, when
J. V. Stalin was in St. Petersburg, the paper came out under
his direction, and he wrote a number of articles for it which
are reproduced in the present volume. The circulation of individual issues of the paper reached 50,000 to 60,000. *Zvezda*
paved the way for the publication of the Bolshevik daily *Pravda*.
On April 22, 1912, the tsarist government suppressed *Zvezda*.
It was succeeded by *Nevskaya Zvezda (The Neva Star)*, which
continued publication until October 1912. p. *218*

99 The leaflet headed "For the Party!" was written by J. V. Stalin
at the beginning of March 1912 and was widely distributed
all over the country together with the leaflet entitled "The
Election Platform of the R.S.D.L.P." written by V. I. Lenin.
No. 26 of *Sotsial-Demokrat* published a communication from
the Bureau of the Central Committee stating: "The Central
Committee has published in Russia the leaflets: 1) 'For the
Party!' (6,000); 2) 'The Election Platform' (10,000). These
leaflets have been delivered to 18 centres, including a number
of the largest ones. . . . The Central Committee's leaflets were
eagerly welcomed everywhere, the only complaint being that
there were so few of them." On March 29, 1912, G. K. Ordjonikidze wrote from Kiev that both leaflets "created a very
good impression, and readers went into raptures over them."
Somewhat later N. K. Krupskaya wrote on V. I. Lenin's
instructions: "We have received your two letters (about local
affairs and the plans in view) and the two leaflets: 'For the
Party!' and the 'Platform.' We heartily welcome them."
  p. *219*

100 The leaflet referred to the Sixth All-Russian Party Conference
that was held in Prague on January 5-17 (18-30), 1912. This
conference united the Bolshevik organizations and registered
the independent existence of the Bolshevik Party. By a decision of the conference the Mensheviks were expelled from the
Party and the formal unity of the Bolsheviks and Mensheviks

within one party was ended forever. The Prague Conference inaugurated a Party of a new type (see *History of the C.P.S.U.(B.), Short Course*, Moscow 1952, pp. 217-25).

p. *219*

101 The leaflet "Long Live the First of May!" was written by J. V. Stalin in Moscow, at the beginning of April 1912. It was printed clandestinely at a legal printing plant in Tiflis and all the copies were subsequently sent to St. Petersburg.

p. *225*

102 Clause 87 of the Fundamental Law of the State authorized the Council of Ministers to submit Bills directly to the tsar for his signature when the State Duma was not in session. This enabled Stolypin to issue a number of important laws, on the agrarian question in particular, without the consent of the Duma.   p. *233*

103 *Zaprosy Zhizni (Requirements of Life)*—a magazine published in St. Petersburg in 1909-12. In the summer of 1912 V. I. Lenin wrote to Maxim Gorky: "Incidentally, it is a queer magazine—Liquidationist-Trudovik-Vekhist" (see V. I. Lenin, *Works*, 4th Russ. ed., Vol. 35, p. 30).

p. *236*

104 Peaceful Renovators—the Party of Peaceful Renovation, which represented the big commercial and industrial bourgeoisie and the big landlords; was formed in 1906. Lenin called it "the Party of Peaceful Depredation."   p. *236*

105 *Delo Zhizni (Life's Cause)*—a legal liquidationist Menshevik magazine published in St. Petersburg from January 22 to October 31, 1911.   p. *238*

106 *Nasha Zarya (Our Dawn)*—a legal monthly magazine, the organ of the liquidationist Mensheviks, published in St. Petersburg from 1910 to 1914.   p. *238*

107 The Progressives—a liberal monarchist group of the Russian bourgeoisie standing between the Octobrists and the Cadets.

The leaders of this group were the Moscow industrialists Ryabushinsky, Konovalov, and others.   p. *245*

[108] The elections to the Fourth State Duma took place in the autumn of 1912, but the Bolsheviks, headed by V. I. Lenin and J. V. Stalin, began to prepare for the election campaign as early as the spring of that year. The Bolshevik Party came out independently in the elections with the slogans of a democratic republic, an eight-hour day and confiscation of the land of the landlords. In March 1912 V. I. Lenin wrote "The Election Platform of the R.S.D.L.P.," which was published in leaflet form and distributed in a number of the biggest towns of Russia. The Bolshevik election campaign was conducted under the direct guidance of J. V. Stalin. His arrest on April 22, 1912, temporarily interrupted this work. He returned to St. Petersburg after escaping from his place of exile in Narym in September 1912, when the election campaign was at its height.   p. *246*

[109] *Zemshchina*—a Black-Hundred newspaper, the organ of the deputies of the extreme right in the State Duma; published in St. Petersburg from 1909 to 1917.   p. *251*

[110] *Novoye Vremya* (*New Times*)—organ of the reactionary nobility and bureaucratic circles; published in St. Petersburg from 1868 to October 1917. In 1905 it became one of the organs of the Black Hundreds.   p. *252*

[111] *Golos Moskvy* (*The Voice of Moscow*)—a daily newspaper, organ of the Octobrist Party, published in Moscow from December 1906 to 1915, edited and published by A. I. Guchkov.
                                                       p. *252*

[112] *Pravda* (*Truth*)—a daily Bolshevik workers' newspaper published in St. Petersburg from April 22, 1912 to July 8, 1914. It was founded on the instructions of V. I. Lenin on the initiative of J. V. Stalin. As a member of the Central Committee of the Party, J. V. Stalin directed the drafting of *Pravda's*

platform and took part in making up the first issue. On April 22, the day on which the first issue appeared, J. V. Stalin was arrested. He was able to resume his activities on *Pravda* only in the autumn of 1912, after his escape from his place of exile in Narym. From October 1912 to February 1913 a number of leading articles written by J. V. Stalin appeared in *Pravda*. These are reproduced in the present volume. Members of the editorial board and constant contributors to the paper were V. M. Molotov, M. S. Olminsky, N. N. Baturin, Y. M. Sverdlov, Maxim Gorky, K. N. Samoilova, and others. In the course of two and a half years the tsarist government suppressed *Pravda* eight times, but thanks to the support of the workers it came out again under different names (*Rabochaya Pravda* (*Workers' Truth*), *Severnaya Pravda* (*Northern Truth*), *Pravda Truda* (*Labour's Truth*), *Za Pravdu* (*For the Truth*), etc.). (For the importance of *Pravda* and its role see *History of the C.P.S.U.(B.)*, *Short Course*, Eng. ed., Moscow 1952, pp. 231-39.)   p. *255*

[113] "Mandate of the St. Petersburg Workers to Their Labour Deputy" was written at the beginning of October 1912. It was unanimously adopted at meetings of workers in the largest plants in St. Petersburg and at the assembly of the workers' voters' delegates held on October 17, 1912. J. V. Stalin directed the discussion of the "Mandate" at impromptu meetings in the factories. V. I. Lenin attached exceptional importance to the "Mandate." On sending it to the printers for publication in *Sotsial-Demokrat* he wrote on the margin: "*Return* without fail!! Keep clean. *Highly important* to preserve this document." The "Mandate" was published in *Sotsial-Demokrat*, No. 28-29, November 5 (18), 1912. In a letter to the editorial board of *Pravda* Lenin wrote: "You must publish this 'Mandate' to the St. Petersburg Deputy without fail in a prominent place in large type" (see V. I. Lenin, *Works*, 4th Russ. ed., Vol. 35, p. 38).   p. *257*

[114] The term "interpretation" appeared in connection with the "ruling" Senate's interpretation of the electoral laws in a

sense favourable for the government. In "interpreting" the laws the authorities arbitrarily annulled elections.   p. *257*

115 The first election of electors in the workers' curia of the St. Petersburg Gubernia took place at the gubernia assembly of voters' delegates on October 5, 1912. In spite of the fact that 21 of the largest plants in St. Petersburg had been deprived of the right to vote, among the six electors elected by the assembly there were four Bolsheviks. As a result of the pressure of the masses, the right to vote of the workers in the "interpreted" plants was restored. On October 14, 1912, new elections of voters' delegates took place at these plants, and on October 17 the second assembly was held of voters' delegates from the workers' curia of the St. Petersburg Gubernia. At this assembly a second election of electors took place, and five candidates polled an absolute majority—two Bolsheviks and three Mensheviks. Next day a supplementary poll was taken to elect a sixth elector, and a Bolshevik was elected.

The course of the election struggle is described in detail in J. V. Stalin's correspondence to the *Sotsial-Demokrat* entitled "The Elections in St. Petersburg," pp. 279-94 of this volume.   p. *260*

116 *Luch* (*The Ray*)—a legal daily newspaper published in St. Petersburg by the Menshevik Liquidators from September 1912 to July 1913. In the columns of the *Luch* the Liquidators openly attacked the underground Party. The newspaper was run with the aid of funds obtained mainly from the bourgeoisie.
          p. *260*

117 This refers to the Obukhov Works.   p. *263*

118 The leaflet "To All the Working Men and Working Women of Russia!" concerning the eighth anniversary of "Bloody Sunday," January 9, 1905, was written by J. V. Stalin in December 1912. Urging the necessity of issuing such a leaflet, V. I. Lenin wrote from Cracow to J. V. Stalin in St. Petersburg on November 23 (December 6), 1912, as follows: "Dear friend, in connection with January 9, it is extremely important to

think the matter over and prepare for it beforehand. A leaflet must be ready in advance calling for meetings, a one-day strike and demonstrations (these must be arranged on the spot, it is easier to judge on the spot). . . . The slogans proclaimed in the leaflet must be the three main revolutionary slogans (a republic, the eight-hour day and the confiscation of the land of the landlords) with special emphasis on the tercentenary of the 'shameful' Romanov dynasty. If you are not fully and absolutely certain of being able to have such a leaflet done in St. Petersburg it will have to be done in good time here and sent on" (see V. I. Lenin, *Works*, 4th Russ. ed., Vol. 18, p. 401).   p. *273*

[119] In August-October 1912 among the political prisoners confined in the Kutomar and Algachi hard-labour prisons (Nerchinsk penal servitude area in the Trans-Baikal) mass hunger strikes and suicides took place in protest against the brutality of the prison administration. This called forth workers' protest strikes and student meetings in St. Petersburg, Moscow and Warsaw.   p. *273*

[120] In October 1912, 142 sailors of the Black Sea Fleet were tried before a naval court-martial in Sevastopol on the charge of organizing a mutiny in the fleet. Seventeen of the accused were sentenced to death, 106 were sentenced to penal servitude, and 19 were acquitted. In Moscow, St. Petersburg, Kharkov, Nikolayev, Riga and other towns, mass strikes and demonstrations were held in protest against these sentences.
                                                                 p. *274*

[121] At the end of 1911 new documents appeared in the press exposing the government's frame-up against the Social-Democratic deputies in the Second Duma. It transpired that the evidence brought against them had been entirely fabricated by the secret police in St. Petersburg. In the middle of November 1911, the Social-Democratic group in the Third Duma moved an interpellation calling for a revision of the case of the Social-Democratic deputies in the Second Duma. The Duma

rejected the interpellation. As a result mass meetings of many thousands took place in St. Petersburg, Riga, Warsaw and other towns, at which resolutions were passed demanding the release of the convicted deputies. p. *275*

[122] J. V. Stalin was the Central Committee's representative during the election campaign in St. Petersburg. The Executive Commission of the St. Petersburg Committee was a small committee of members of the St. Petersburg Committee appointed to direct current work. p. *280*

[123] The Liquidators left out of the election platform which they issued in September 1912 the main political demands of the minimum programme of the R.S.D.L.P. Instead of the demand for a democratic republic they inserted the demand for universal suffrage "in the election of the State Duma and local government bodies," and instead of the demand for the confiscation of the land of the landlords they inserted the demand for "a revision of the agrarian legislation of the Third Duma." p. *283*

[124] This refers to the so-called "August" conference of the Liquidators which was held in Vienna in August 1912 as a counterstroke to the Prague Conference of the Bolsheviks. p. *286*

[125] The Bolshevik "X" was N. G. Poletayev; the Liquidator "Y" was probably E. Mayevsky (V. A. Gutovsky).

The St. Petersburg Liquidators "Ab. . . and L. . ." mentioned lower down were V. M. Abrosimov and V. Levitsky (V. O. Zederbaum). p. *288*

[126] *Nevsky Golos (The Voice of the Neva)*—a legal weekly newspaper published by the Menshevik Liquidators in St. Petersburg May-August 1912. p. *290*

[127] See "Letters From the Caucasus," pp. 194-97 in this volume. p. *297*

128 In No. 9 of *Dnevnik Sotsial-Demokrata* (*A Social-Democrat's Diary*) G. V. Plekhanov criticized the statements made by the Georgian Menshevik Liquidator S. Jibladze in *Golos Sotsial-Demokrata*.   p. *297*

129 Pan-Islamism—a reactionary religious and political ideology which arose in Turkey in the latter half of the nineteenth century among the landlords, the bourgeoisie and the clergy and later spread among the propertied classes of other Moslem peoples. It advocated the union into a single whole of all peoples professing the Moslem religion. With the aid of Pan-Islamism the ruling classes among the Moslem peoples tried to strengthen their positions and to strangle the revolutionary movement among the working people of the Orient. p. *298*

130 *Marxism and the National Question* was written at the end of 1912 and the beginning of 1913 in Vienna. It first appeared in the magazine *Prosveshcheniye* (*Enlightenment*), Nos. 3-5, 1913, under the title "The National Question and Social-Democracy" and was signed K. Stalin. In 1914 it was published by the Priboy Publishers, St. Petersburg, as a separate pamphlet entitled *The National Question and Marxism*. By order of the Minister of the Interior the pamphlet was withdrawn from all public libraries and reading rooms. In 1920 the article was republished by the People's Commissariat for Nationalities in a *Collection of Articles* by J. V. Stalin on the national question (State Publishing House, Tula). In 1934 the article was included in the book: J. Stalin, *Marxism and the National and Colonial Question. A Collection of Articles and Speeches*. Lenin, in his article "The National Programme of the R.S.D.L.P.," referring to the reasons which were lending prominence to the national question at that period, wrote: "This state of affairs, and the principles of the national programme of Social-Democracy, have already been dealt with recently in theoretical Marxist literature (prime place must here be given to Stalin's article)." In February 1913, Lenin wrote to Maxim Gorky: "We have a wonderful Georgian here who has sat down to write a big article for *Prosveshcheniye* after collecting *all* the

Austrian and other material." Learning that it was proposed
to print the article with the reservation that it was for
discussion only, Lenin vigorously objected, and wrote:
"Of course, we are absolutely against this. It is a *very
good* article. The question is a burning issue, and we shall
not yield one jot of principle to the Bundist scum." (Archives
of the Marx-Engels-Lenin Institute.) Soon after J. V. Stalin's
arrest, in March 1913, Lenin wrote to the editors of *Sotsial-
Demokrat*: ". . . Arrests among us are very heavy. Koba has
been taken. . . . Koba managed to write a long article (for
three issues of *Prosveshcheniye*) on the national question. Good!
We must fight for the truth and against separatists and opportunists of the Bund and among the Liquidators." (Archives of
the Marx-Engels-Lenin Institute.)   p. *300*

[131] *Zionism*—a reactionary nationalist trend of the Jewish bourgeoisie, which had followers among the intellectuals and the
more backward sections of the Jewish workers. The Zionists
endeavoured to isolate the Jewish working-class masses from
the general struggle of the proletariat.   p. *301*

[132] The Brünn Parteitag, or Congress, of the Austrian Social-
Democratic Party was held on September 24-29, 1899. The
resolution on the national question adopted by this congress
is quoted by J. V. Stalin in the next chapter of this work
(see p. 333).   p. *326*

[133] "Thank God we have no parliament here"—the words uttered
by V. Kokovtsev, tsarist Minister of Finance (later Prime
Minister), in the State Duma on April 24, 1908.   p. *329*

[134] See Chapter II of the *Manifesto of the Communist Party* by Karl
Marx and Frederick Engels (Karl Marx and Frederick Engels,
Selected Works, Eng. ed., Vol. I, Moscow 1951, p. 49).
                                                      p. *341*

[135] The Vienna Congress (or *Wimberg* Congress—after the name
of the hotel in which it met) of the Austrian Social-Democratic
Party was held June 6-12, 1897.   p. *343*

[136] The reference is to an article by Karl Marx entitled "Zur Judenfrage" ("The Jewish Question"), published in 1844 in the *Deutsch-Französische Jahrbücher*. (See Marx/Engels, *Gesamtausgabe*, Erste Abteilung, Band 1, Halbband 1.) *p. 344*

[137] The Eighth Conference of the Bund was held in September 1910 in Lvov. *p. 350*

[138] In an article entitled "Another Splitters' Conference," published in the newspaper *Za Partiyu*, October 2 (15), 1912, G. V. Plekhanov condemned the "August" Conference of the Liquidators and described the stand of the Bundists and Caucasian Social-Democrats as an adaptation of socialism to nationalism. Kossovsky, leader of the Bundists, criticized Plekhanov in a letter to the Liquidators' magazine *Nasha Zarya*. *p. 354*

[139] The Seventh Congress of the Bund was held in Lvov at the end of August and beginning of September 1906. *p. 355*

[140] *Iskra* (*The Spark*)—the first all-Russian illegal Marxist newspaper founded by V. I. Lenin in 1900 (see J. V. Stalin, *Works*, Vol. 1, p. 400, Note 26). *p. 357*

[141] *Karl Vaněk*—a Czech Social-Democrat who took an openly chauvinist and separatist stand. *p. 358*

[142] *Chveni Tskhovreba* (*Our Life*)—a daily newspaper published by the Georgian Mensheviks in Kutais from July 1 to 22, 1912. *p. 360*

[143] The reference is to the first Balkan War, which broke out in October 1912 between Bulgaria, Serbia, Greece and Montenegro on the one hand, and Turkey on the other. *p. 373*

[144] See the resolutions of the Fourth (the "Third All-Russian") Conference of the R.S.D.L.P. held November 5-12, 1907, and of the Fifth (the "All-Russian 1908") Conference of the R.S.D.L.P. held December 21-27, 1908 (January 3-9, 1909).

(See *Resolutions and Decisions of C.P.S.U.(B.) Congresses, Conferences and Central Committee Plenums*, Vol. 1, 6th Russ. ed., 1940, pp. 118, 131.)   p. *380*

[145] E. J. Jagiello—a member of the Polish Socialist Party (P.P.S.) was elected to the Fourth State Duma for Warsaw as a result of a bloc formed by the Bund, the Polish Socialist Party and the bourgeois nationalists against the Polish Social-Democrats. By a vote of the seven Menshevik Liquidators against the six Bolsheviks, the Social-Democratic group in the Duma adopted a resolution that Jagiello be accepted as a member of the group.
                                                                                          p. *380*

[146] *Prosveshcheniye (Enlightenment)*—a Bolshevik monthly published legally in St. Petersburg, the first issue appearing in December 1911. It was directed by Lenin through regular correspondence with the members of the editorial board in Russia (M. A. Savelyev, M. S. Olminsky, A. I. Elizarova). When J. V. Stalin was in St. Petersburg he took an active part in the work of the journal. *Prosveshcheniye* was closely connected with *Pravda*. In June 1914, on the eve of the First World War, it was suppressed by the government. One double number appeared in the autumn of 1917.   p. *381*

[147] In December 1912 the workers' deputies in the Fourth Duma agreed to allow their names to be included in the list of contributors to *Luch*. At the same time they continued to contribute to *Pravda*. Actually, they did not contribute to *Luch*. Later, on the instructions of the Central Committee they announced that they withdrew their names from the list of contributors to *Luch*. This gave rise to a fierce controversy between the Bolshevik six and the Menshevik seven, the two sections of the Social-Democratic group in the Duma.   p. *382*

[148] This refers to the Social-Democratic group in the Third State Duma.   p. *383*

[149] *Zhivoye Delo (The Living Cause)*—a legal weekly newspaper published by the Menshevik Liquidators in St. Petersburg from January to April 1912.   p. *383*

[150] The leaflet "The Anniversary of the Lena Massacre" was written by J. V. Stalin in Cracow in January-February 1913. It was copied by hand by N. K. Krupskaya, was duplicated on a hectograph and sent to Russia, where it was distributed in St. Petersburg, Kiev, Moghilev, Tiflis and other towns.

p. *387*

[151] The Fourth State Duma was opened on November 15, 1912.

p. *389*

BIOGRAPHICAL CHRONICLE

(*1907 to March 1917*)

1907

January 1

No. 1 of the newspaper *Mnatobi* (*The Torch*), directed by J. V. Stalin, appears.

No. 8 of the newspaper *Akhali Droyeba* (*New Times*) publishes the continuation of J. V. Stalin's work *Anarchism or Socialism?*

February 10

J. V. Stalin writes the preface to the Georgian edition of K. Kautsky's pamphlet *The Driving Forces and Prospects of the Russian Revolution*.

February 18

No. 1 of the newspaper *Chveni Tskhovreba* (*Our Life*), directed by J. V. Stalin, appears, containing his article "The Election Campaign in St. Petersburg and the Mensheviks."

February 21-28

Nos. 3, 5, 8 and 9 of *Chveni Tskhovreba* publish the continuation of J. V. Stalin's work *Anarchism or Socialism?*

March 11

No. 1 of the newspaper *Dro* (*Time*), directed by J. V. Stalin, appears.

March 13

No. 2 of *Dro* publishes J. V. Stalin's article "The Autocracy of the Cadets or the Sovereignty of the People?"

March 17	No. 6 of *Dro* publishes J. V. Stalin's leading article "The Proletariat Is Fighting, the Bourgeoisie Is Concluding an Alliance With the Government."
March 22	No. 10 of *Dro* publishes J. V. Stalin's article "Comrade G. Telia. In Memoriam."
March 28 and 30	*Dro* publishes the decisions of the worker Bolsheviks in Tiflis to elect J. V. Stalin as a delegate to the Fifth Congress of the R.S.D.L.P.
April 4-6 and 10	Nos. 21-23 and 26 of *Dro* publish the continuation of J.V. Stalin's work *Anarchism or Socialism?*
April 8	No. 25 of *Dro* publishes J. V. Stalin's leading article "The Advanced Proletariat and the Fifth Party Congress."
April 10	No. 26 of *Dro* publishes J. V. Stalin's article "Muddle. . ."
April 13	No. 29 of *Dro* publishes J. V. Stalin's article "Our Caucasian Clowns."
April 30- May 19	J. V. Stalin takes part in the proceedings of the Fifth ("London") Congress of the R.S.D.L.P. as the delegate of the Tiflis organization.
First half of June	On returning from the Fifth ("London") Congress of the R.S.D.L.P., J. V. Stalin visits Baku and Tiflis and delivers reports on the congress at meetings of the Social-Democratic organizations of Baku, Tiflis and a number of districts in Western Georgia. J. V. Stalin leads the struggle of the Bolsheviks against

the Mensheviks, Socialist-Revolutionaries and others.

June 20

No. 1 of the underground Bolshevik newspaper *Bakinsky Proletary* (*The Baku Proletarian*), edited by J. V. Stalin, appears, containing the leading article written by him: "The Dispersion of the Duma and the Tasks of the Proletariat," and also his article "The London Congress of the Russian Social-Democratic Labour Party (Notes of a Delegate)."

Summer-Autumn

J. V. Stalin speaks at discussion meetings organized in the districts of Baku in which he exposes the policy of the Mensheviks and the Socialist-Revolutionaries.

J. V. Stalin directs the campaign to boycott the conference with the oil owners.

July 10

No. 2 of *Bakinsky Proletary* publishes the continuation of J. V. Stalin's article "The London Congress of the Russian Social-Democratic Labour Party (Notes of a Delegate)."

End of July

The Baku Bolsheviks, headed by J. V. Stalin, hold a Party conference of the oil districts, which declares in favour of organizing a general strike.

August 12

Appearance of No. 1 of the newspaper *Gudok* —the legal Bolshevik organ of the Baku oil industry workers' union, formed on the initiative of J. V. Stalin.

August 24

At a delegate meeting of five district Social-Democratic organizations and of the Moslem Social-Democratic group "Gummet," J. V. Stalin is elected a member of the organizing committee set up to convene a city Party conference.

September-
October

J. V. Stalin directs the campaign during the Third State Duma elections.

The "Mandate" to the Social-Democratic deputies in the Third State Duma, written by J. V. Stalin, is adopted at a meeting of delegates of the workers' curia in Baku held on September 22.

September 29

J. V. Stalin delivers a speech at the grave of Khanlar Safaraliyev, a working man Bolshevik who was killed by the hired agents of the capitalists.

No. 4 of *Gudok* publishes J. V. Stalin's article "Boycott the Conference!"

October 25

At a Baku city conference of Bolsheviks, J. V. Stalin is elected a member of the Baku Committee of the R.S.D.L.P.

First half of
November

A meeting of the Baku Committee of the R.S.D.L.P., which J. V. Stalin attended, is held in the premises of the Sabunchi Hospital.

November 22

The Baku Committee of the R.S.D.L.P., directed by J. V. Stalin, conducts a one-day strike to protest against the prosecution of the Social-Democratic group in the Second State Duma.

End of November J. V. Stalin arrives in Tiflis on Party business.

November 1907-
March 1908

J. V. Stalin directs the campaign for the participation of the Baku workers in a conference with the oil owners on the condition that the rights of the workers are guaranteed.

1908

January 13	No. 14 of *Gudok* publishes J. V. Stalin's leading article "Before the Elections."
January-February	The Baku Bolsheviks, directed by J. V. Stalin, organize a series of big strikes.
February 3	No. 17 of *Gudok* publishes J. V. Stalin's leading article "More About a Conference With Guarantees."
February	The Baku Committee of the R.S.D.L.P., directed by J. V. Stalin, organizes a "Self-Defence Staff" in connection with the growing frequency of assaults by Black Hundreds.
March 2	No. 21 of *Gudok* publishes J. V. Stalin's article "What Do Our Recent Strikes Tell Us?"
March 9	No. 22 of *Gudok* publishes J. V. Stalin's leading article "The Change in the Oil Owners' Tactics."
March 16	No. 23 of *Gudok* publishes J. V. Stalin's leading article "We Must Prepare!"
March 25	J. V. Stalin, under the alias Gaioz Nizharadze, is arrested and confined in the Bailov prison in Baku.
March 25-November 9	While in prison J. V. Stalin establishes and maintains contact with the Baku Bolshevik organization, directs the Baku Committee of the R.S.D.L.P. and writes articles for the *Bakinsky Proletary* and *Gudok*. He also conducts propaganda among the political pris-

oners, holds debates with the Socialist-Revolutionaries and Mensheviks and organizes the study of Marxist literature by the political prisoners.

March 30

No. 25 of *Gudok* publishes J. V. Stalin's leading article "Economic Terrorism and the Labour Movement."

*April 21-
May 18*

Nos. 28, 30 and 32 of *Gudok* publish J. V. Stalin's article "The Oil Owners on Economic Terrorism."

July 20

No. 5 of *Bakinsky Proletary* publishes J. V. Stalin's articles "Flunkey 'Socialists'" and "Hypocritical Zubatovites."

The same issue of the newspaper publishes as a supplement J. V. Stalin's article "The Conference and the Workers."

November 9

J. V. Stalin is deported to the Vologda Gubernia for two years to remain under open police surveillance.

1909

January

J. V. Stalin arrives in Vologda under escort and is confined in the Vologda prison.

January 27

J. V. Stalin's place of exile is decided: Solvychegodsk, Vologda Gubernia.

February 8

On the way to his place of exile under escort J. V. Stalin falls sick with relapsing fever and is taken from the Vyatka prison to the Vyatka Gubernia Zemstvo Hospital.

February 20   J. V. Stalin is transferred from the hospital to the Vyatka prison.

February 27   J. V. Stalin arrives in Solvychegodsk.

June 24   J. V. Stalin escapes from Solvychegodsk.

Beginning of July   While on his way J. V. Stalin stays several days in St. Petersburg.

First half of July   J. V. Stalin secretly arrives in Baku and directs the work of restoring and consolidating the Bolshevik organizations in Baku and Transcaucasia.

August 1   After a year's suspension, *Bakinsky Proletary* resumes publication with No. 6, which contains J. V. Stalin's leading article "The Party Crisis and Our Tasks."

August 2   The Baku Committee of the R.S.D.L.P., directed by J. V. Stalin, adopts a resolution on the state of affairs on the editorial board of *Proletary* supporting "the stand taken by the majority of the editorial board represented by Comrade Lenin."

August 27   No. 7 of *Bakinsky Proletary* publishes the conclusion of J. V. Stalin's article "The Party Crisis and Our Tasks," and also the article "The Forthcoming General Strike."

First half of September   J. V. Stalin leaves Baku for Tiflis, where he organizes and directs the struggle of the Tiflis Bolshevik organization against the Menshevik Liquidators.

End of September   J. V. Stalin takes measures to re-establish the underground printing plant of the Baku Committee.

October 19- beginning of November	J. V. Stalin arrives in Tiflis and makes preparations for the convocation of the Tiflis City Party Conference and for the publication of the Bolshevik newspaper *Tiflissky Proletary*.
Not later than November 12	J. V. Stalin returns to Baku from Tiflis.
December 13	The Baku Committee of the R.S.D.L.P. issues a leaflet written by J. V. Stalin, "The December Strike and the December Agreement" (on the occasion of the fifth anniversary of the Baku strike of 1904).
November- December	J. V. Stalin writes "Letters From the Caucasus" for the Central Organ of the Party.

1910

Beginning with 1910, J. V. Stalin is a representative of the Central Committee of the Party ("agent of the C.C.").

―――

January 5	No. 1 of the newspaper *Tiflissky Proletary*, founded with the direct participation of J.V. Stalin, appears.
January 22	The Baku Committee of the R.S.D.L.P. adopts a resolution drafted by J. V. Stalin urging the necessity of convening a general Party conference, of transferring the practical centre for directing the activities of the Party to Russia and of publishing an all-Russian leading newspaper.
March 23	J. V. Stalin is arrested under the alias Zakhar Grigoryan Melikyants.

J. V. Stalin's leaflet "August Bebel, Leader of the German Workers," appears.

March 26

J. V. Stalin is confined in the Bailov Prison in Baku.

September 7

While in prison J. V. Stalin receives the order of the Viceroy of the Caucasus dated August 27 prohibiting him from residing in the Caucasus for five years.

September 23

J. V. Stalin is taken under escort to Solvychegodsk.

October 29

J. V. Stalin arrives in Solvychegodsk.

November 1910-June 1911

J. V. Stalin establishes contact with V. I. Lenin. He organizes meetings of exiles at which papers are read and current political questions are discussed.

December 31

J. V. Stalin writes a letter to the Central Committee of the Party ("A Letter to the Central Committee of the Party from Exile in Solvychegodsk").

1911

March-June

The police make repeated searches in J. V. Stalin's lodgings (at the house of M. P. Kuzakova) in Solvychegodsk

June 1

At a conference of members of the Central Committee of the R.S.D.L.P., held in Paris, J. V. Stalin is appointed in his absence an alternate member of the Organizing Committee for convening the Party conference.

June 23-26

J. V. Stalin in Solvychegodsk is kept under close arrest for three days for organizing a meeting of exiled Social-Democrats.

June 27	J. V. Stalin is released from open police surveillance in view of the expiration of his period of exile. Being prohibited from residing in the Caucasus, in the capitals and industrial centres, he chooses Vologda as his place of residence as it is on the way to St. Petersburg.
July 6	J. V. Stalin, furnished with a transit permit, leaves Solvychegodsk for Vologda.
July 16	J. V. Stalin arrives in Vologda.
July-September	In Vologda J. V. Stalin is kept under secret police surveillance.
July	J. V. Stalin writes a letter to the editorial board of *Rabochaya Gazeta* (*Workers' Newspaper*), directed by Lenin, informing it of his intention to work in St. Petersburg or in Moscow.
September 6	J. V. Stalin secretly leaves Vologda for St. Petersburg.
September 7	J. V. Stalin arrives in St. Petersburg and registers with the passport of P. A. Chizhikov.
September 7-9	J. V. Stalin meets the Bolsheviks S. Todria and S. Alliluyev and establishes contact with the St. Petersburg Party organization.
September 9	J. V. Stalin is arrested and confined in the St. Petersburg House of Preliminary Detention.
December 14	J. V. Stalin is deported to Vologda for three years, to remain under open police surveillance.
December 25	J. V. Stalin arrives in Vologda.

1912

*Between January
5(18) and 17(30)*
At the Sixth ("Prague") General Party Conference, J. V. Stalin is in his absence elected
a member of the Central Committee of the
Bolshevik Party.

The conference sets up a practical centre known
as the Russian Bureau of the Central Committee
to direct revolutionary activities in Russia
and places J. V. Stalin in charge of this centre.

*Middle of
February*
On the instructions of V. I. Lenin, G. K. Ordjonikidze, a member of the Russian Bureau of
the Central Committee, goes to see J. V. Stalin
in Vologda to inform him of the decisions of
the Prague Conference.

February 29
J. V. Stalin escapes from exile in Vologda.

*Beginning of
March*
J. V. Stalin writes the leaflet "For the Party!"
which is published in the name of the Central
Committee of the R.S.D.L.P. and is widely
distributed in Russia.

*First half of
March*
J. V. Stalin visits Baku and Tiflis to organize
the work of the Transcaucasian Bolshevik
organizations in carrying out the decisions of
the Prague Conference. He writes Circular
Letter No. 1 of the Central Committee of the
R.S.D.L.P. to the Party organizations an-
nouncing the definite formation of the Central
Committee.

March 29
J. V. Stalin conducts a conference of the Party
workers of the Bolshevik district organiza-

tions in Baku. The conference endorses the decisions of the Prague Conference.

March 30   J. V. Stalin writes a report on the conference in Baku for the *Sotsial-Demokrat.*

April 1   J. V. Stalin leaves Baku for St. Petersburg.

Beginning of   On the way to St. Petersburg J. V. Stalin
April   stops in Moscow and meets G. K. Ordjonikidze.

J. V. Stalin writes the leaflet "Long Live the First of May!"

J. V. Stalin sends to Tiflis a copy of the resolution adopted by a group of Moscow Party workers welcoming the decisions of the Prague Conference and the newly-formed Central Committee.

On behalf of the Central Committee of the R.S.D.L.P., J. V. Stalin writes to Clara Zetkin requesting her to transfer the Party funds held by her to the Central Committee for the purpose of conducting the Fourth State Duma election campaign.

April 10   J. V. Stalin secretly arrives in St. Petersburg.

April 10-22   J. V. Stalin edits the Bolshevik workers' newspaper *Zvezda* in which the following articles of his are published: "A New Period" (leading article), "Life Triumphs!", "They Are Working Well. . . .", "The Ice Has Broken! . . ." (leading article), "How They Are Preparing for the Elections," "Deductions" (leading article), and others.

Middle of April   J. V. Stalin makes arrangements with the members of the Social-Democratic group in the Third State Duma N. G. Poletayev and I. P. Pokrovsky, as well as with the Bolshevik journalists M. S. Olminsky and N. N. Baturin, for the publication of the newspaper *Pravda* and for the drafting of its programme, and together with them makes up the first number of that newspaper.

April 22   No. 1 of the workers' daily newspaper *Pravda* appears containing J.V.Stalin's article "Our Aims."

J. V. Stalin is arrested and confined in the preliminary detention prison in St. Petersburg.

July 2   J. V. Stalin is deported under escort from St. Petersburg to the Narym territory, to be kept under open police surveillance for three years.

July 18   J. V. Stalin, accompanied by a prison warder, leaves Tomsk on the steamer *Kolpashevets* for his place of exile in Narym.

September 1   J. V. Stalin escapes from exile in Narym.

September 12   J. V. Stalin arrives in St. Petersburg.

September-October   J. V. Stalin directs the Fourth State Duma election campaign and organizes the struggle against the Menshevik Liquidators.

J. V. Stalin edits *Pravda*.

October 4   A meeting of the Executive Commission of the St. Petersburg Committee is held under J. V. Stalin's direction at which a decision is adopted to call a one-day strike in protest against the annulment of the election of voters' delegates at the biggest plants in St. Petersburg (Putilov's and others).

Beginning of October	J. V. Stalin conducts a secret Party conference at which the tactics to be adopted in the struggle against the Liquidators is discussed and the workers' candidate for the Fourth State Duma is nominated.
	J. V. Stalin writes "Mandate of the St. Petersburg Workers to Their Labour Deputy."
Middle of October	J. V. Stalin sends "Mandate of the St. Petersburg Workers" to V. I. Lenin on the editorial board of *Sotsial-Demokrat*, in which paper it was published in the issue No. 28-29 of November 5 (18), 1912.
October 17	The "Mandate" written by J. V. Stalin is adopted at the assembly of voters' delegates of the workers' curia in the St. Petersburg Gubernia.
October 19	No. 147 of *Pravda* publishes the leading article by J. V. Stalin "The Will of the Voters' Delegates."
October 21 (November 3)	On the instructions of V. I. Lenin, N. K. Krupskaya writes to *Pravda* and the members of the Social-Democratic group in the Duma stating that it is extremely important for J. V. Stalin to visit Cracow.
October 24	No. 151 of *Pravda* publishes J. V. Stalin's article "The Results of the Elections in the Workers' Curia of St. Petersburg."
October 25	No. 152 of *Pravda* publishes J. V. Stalin's article "Today Is Election Day."

End of October	J. V. Stalin visits Moscow for a short period and establishes contact with the newly-elected working men Bolshevik deputies of the Fourth State Duma.
October 29	J. V. Stalin returns to St. Petersburg from Moscow.
Before November 10	J. V. Stalin secretly arrives in Cracow to visit V. I. Lenin.
November 11(24)	V. I. Lenin sends the "Mandate" he had received from J. V. Stalin to *Pravda* with instructions to publish it "in a prominent place in large type."
First half of November	J. V. Stalin takes part in a meeting of the members of the Central Committee of the R.S.D.L.P. in Cracow.
End of November- beginning of December	Returning to St. Petersburg from Cracow, J. V. Stalin directs the activities of the Social-Democratic group in the Fourth State Duma.
November 23 (December 6)	V. I. Lenin writes to J. V. Stalin on preparations for the anniversary of January 9 and on the need for leaflets to be published in connection with it.
First half of December	On the instructions of V. I. Lenin, N. K. Krupskaya writes to J. V. Stalin urging him to come to Cracow for a meeting of the members of the Central Committee of the R.S.D.L.P. and the six Bolshevik deputies in the Fourth Duma.
End of December	J. V. Stalin secretly leaves for Cracow.

December 28, 1912   J. V. Stalin takes part in the "Feb-
(January 10, 1913)- ruary" conference of the Central Committee
January 1 (14), 1913 of the R.S.D.L.P. with Party workers and
the Bolshevik members of the Social-Democrat-
ic group in the Duma, held under the direction
of V. I. Lenin. At this conference V. I. Lenin
and J. V. Stalin propose measures for improving the work of the editorial board of *Pravda*

End of December   The leaflet written by J. V. Stalin "To All the
1912-beginning   Working Men and Working Women of Russia!"
of January 1913   is issued.

1913

January 12   No. 30 of *Sotsial-Demokrat* publishes
J. V. Stalin's articles "The Elections in St.
Petersburg (A Letter From St. Petersburg)"
and "On the Road to Nationalism (A Letter
From the Caucasus)."

Latter half of   J. V. Stalin arrives in Vienna from Cracow.
January   In Vienna he arranges for the printing in
Paris of the "Announcement" written by
V. I. Lenin concerning the "February" con-
ference and of the resolutions adopted by
that conference.

January   J. V. Stalin writes the work *The National
Question and Social-Democracy* which is published in Nos. 3-5 of the magazine *Prosveshcheniye* in March-May 1913.

January-February J. V. Stalin writes the leaflet "The Anniversary of the Lena Massacre."

Middle of February J. V. Stalin returns to St. Petersburg from
abroad. Together with Y. M. Sverdlov he

proceeds to reorganize the editorial board of *Pravda* in conformity with V. I. Lenin's instructions.

February 23

J. V. Stalin is arrested in the hall of the Kalashnikov Exchange at a concert arranged by the St. Petersburg Bolshevik organization and is taken to prison.

February 26

No. 47 of *Pravda* publishes the article by J. V. Stalin "The Situation in the Social-Democratic Group in the Duma."

July 2

J. V. Stalin is deported under escort to the Turukhansk region to remain under open police surveillance for four years.

July 11

J. V. Stalin arrives in Krasnoyarsk.

July 15

J. V. Stalin leaves Krasnoyarsk for Turukhansk.

August 10

J. V. Stalin arrives in Turukhansk and from there is sent to his place of exile, the hamlet of Kostino.

1914

First half of March

J. V. Stalin is transferred to the hamlet of Kureika, north of the Arctic Circle, and is placed under closer police surveillance.

1915

February 27

J. V. Stalin writes a letter to V. I. Lenin from the village of Monastyrskoye, where he had gone to visit a fellow-exile S. Spandaryan.

In this letter J. V. Stalin criticizes the defencist line of Plekhanov and of international Social-Democracy, which had taken an opportunist stand.

Summer

J. V. Stalin takes part in a meeting held in the village of Monastyrskoye of the exiled members of the Russian Bureau of the Central Committee of the R.S.D.L.P. and of the Bolshevik group in the Fourth State Duma. At this meeting the question of the trial of the Bolshevik deputies is discussed.

November 10

J. V. Stalin writes to V. I. Lenin and N. K. Krupskaya from his place of exile in Turukhansk.

1916

February 5

J. V. Stalin writes a letter to the Party Centre abroad concerning his work on articles on the national question.

February 25

In a letter to the Bolshevik centre abroad, sent through Inessa Armand, J. V. Stalin inquires about his article "Cultural-National Autonomy," which he had sent abroad.

March 12

J. V. Stalin, in conjunction with S. Spandaryan and other exiles, writes a letter to the journal *Voprosy Strakhovaniya (Insurance Questions)*.

December 14

In connection with the drafting of summarily exiled persons into the army J. V. Stalin is sent under escort to Krasnoyarsk.

1917

Beginning of February	The Drafting Commission in Krasnoyarsk exempts J. V. Stalin from military service.
February 20	J. V. Stalin leaves Krasnoyarsk for Achinsk, where he had received permission to reside until the expiration of his period of exile.
March 8	J. V. Stalin with a group of exiles leaves Achinsk for Petrograd.

Printed in the Union of Soviet Socialist Republics